OPTIMISM

Success in the Media Against All Odds
A Memoir

BATT JOHNSON

Print ISBN: 979-8-35092-194-6
eBook ISBN: 979-8-35092-195-3

About the Author

B att Johnson is part of American broadcast history. His performance as the husband with "ring around the collar" in a national network Wisk television commercial, was said to be the highest rated in the 135-year history of Lever Brothers.

He has a unique, and compelling life story of successfully mastering the art of traveling a road seldom traveled.

He is a trailblazer, one of the top broadcasters in Rock 'n Roll, Jazz, Smooth Jazz, Country, Urban, and Big Band formats.

Radio & Records Magazine once ranked him at number 9, the only African American on that top-10 list for the entire U.S.

He has performed in television commercials, news, TV home shopping hosting, plays, films, videos, modeling, hand modeling, and cartoon voices.

As a professor he taught at New York University, Cornell University, the New York Institute of Technology, Mercy College and the Weist-Barron School of Television. As a media trainer, he worked with doctors, lawyers, business executives, politicians, the U.S. Air Force, the U.S. Tennis Association, and some of the Stars, All-Stars, and a Hall of Famer of the NBA.

Batt Johnson's fascinating adventures in over 20 countries, performing on French and African radio, and living in South Korea, are all captivating stories. He also became a proficient Argentine tango dancer, author, and instructor, sometimes dancing until nine in the morning in Buenos Aires, Argentina.

Introduction

I wrote this book during a very dark period in American history. I was angry, I was frustrated, and I was frightened. Donald J. Trump was President of the United States during this time, COVID-19 was running rampant, and countless millions were dying world-wide. Some were friends. We were on lockdown. I spent up to four days at a time in my apartment, leaving only to go to the grocery store. Sometimes, when I was feeling brave, I would go for a short walk to get additional exercise.

This was the time for me to dig deep within myself to see what is really there, what kind of person I am, and what kind of person I want to be when the Pandemic of 2020 is over. I dug deep and I found positivity and optimism.

Optimism is at the heart of my belief system. I always trust that the outcome of my choices will turn out favorably. The term optimism itself comes from the Latin word *optimum*, which means *best*.

When I am involved with a project or an event, I always put forth my best effort to create the best possible environment for a successful outcome for all.

It is so incredibly easy to look at the American social landscape and blame others for one's lack of advancement.

Sure, it is easier for some who were born with a certain genetic makeup to prevail. But few things can surpass hard work, stubbornness, self-love and raw desire.

If I love something, I LOVE it and nothing and no one can keep me from it. I am an individual. I am my own man.

As a competitive person, it feels so good to win. I attempt to stack the deck in my favor and do all I can to ensure that verdict.

The desire to win is not a selfish act. You can win and give away your proceeds, which I often do. Giving is another way to ensure the glistening of your heart.

Keep it moving, keep it positive, keep it optimistic. You will get your fair share, don't worry. IF you have given, you will be given *to*.

The love of my career, working as a radio & television broadcaster, and an actor in film and television commercials, has caused me to realize that I had a slightly different outlook on life.

My outlook was slightly more positive, which allowed me to withstand much of the negativity that surrounded me because of the color of my skin.

I was optimistic and determined to be successful. I attempted to allow common sense to be my main guiding force in this life. Something I did not realize at the time is that all of the answers were within me. All I had to do was find them, and then use them for the greater good.

Dreams DO come true. Conscious dreams are no more than "focusing in" on a desired goal or achievement, thinking about it, and seeing yourself accomplishing it in your mind, over and over again. The mind automatically makes choices based on your innermost desires and continuous thoughts and input into your brain. All you have to do is get out of your own way.

Optimism can be used as a tool, a weapon, a tactic, or a technique. I chose to use it as a propellant to get me to my next station in life, and help anyone along the way who needs it.

I believe that I have been given certain gifts and abilities. I have chosen to share my gifts. Teaching and writing are avenues that allow me to do so.

My thinking is not like that of *The Little Train That Could* when he said, "I think I can, I think I can!" Those were words I would never say. My words are more like, "I am going to___!"

Not, I *think* I can, or I *want* to, or I *hope* to. When my mind is made up, I just DO it, whatever the "IT" is.

Your attitude about what you do makes the difference between a champion and someone who was just in the room. When your sights are set on a specific goal, you unconsciously *and* consciously move in the direction of your goal.

If you want to achieve a certain goal, you must put in the mental work that goes into achieving that goal, even before the actual work of that goal begins. Most people have a limited belief system. It is like a thousand-pound weight on your shoulders and you don't even know it is there.

I believe that you are what you think, and you will become what you wish. If you spend time thinking about what could happen if you make a mistake or, make a wrong choice, and even worse, what will happen if you are not perfect. Guess what? You are going to make a mistake and you will *never* be perfect.

If you change your thinking, you can change your life, but to do this you must be committed to your goal. Within the traditional mode of thought, I do not fit. But I am committed to allowing my unique individuality to be my ignited torch.

Each time a professional athlete enters a sports arena, court, or field, he or she must possess the proper attitude. The wrong attitude could become their most fearless opponent.

Athletes have a strong survival instinct, a killer's instinct, an-eat-or-be-eaten mentality. They wear their pride on their sleeves.

They protect their athletic crowns and prowess like a mother bear protects her cubs. They have a winning mentality. If you want to win, you have to play like you mean it.

My attitude when I walked into the auditioning room to compete for an acting job was, "*I own this room and everything in it. This job is mine to have.*" I didn't care how many "stars" were in the room. You can adopt this attitude for any situation.

I did not enter with an attitude of "I am God's gift to acting." Do not mistake my confidence for cockiness. I only use this as a way to solidify my confidence.

I once auditioned for a movie when I had laryngitis and could hardly speak, but I auditioned anyway. I got a callback, then I got the job…ahead of individuals with much better credits. My attitude and belief system are what gave me the courage to audition while sick.

I auditioned with no fear because I know that it is up to *me* to control the performing environment. You must seize the initiative and own the stage. When you show self-confidence, the audience can feel it, in turn, you can feel them. This simple give and take will help you become a better performer, a better business person . . . a better you.

Take time every day to feed your very powerful subconscious mind images of self-confidence and success because you are what you think, and you will become what you focus on.

Keep in touch with your optimism. It will become your best friend.

TABLE OF CONTENTS

PART 1

The Events That Shaped Me

PART II

The Form That Became Me

PART 1

The Events That Shaped Me

CHAPTER 1

News Born-News Bound

EXTRA! EXTRA!

Get today's news right here!

Get today's news!

Don't push, don't shove!
There is plenty for everyone!

HEADLINE

FIRST NEGRO BABY BORN in St. PETERS HOSPITAL in OLYMPIA, WASHINGTON

Get your copy HERE!!

Hurry! Hurry, before we sell out!

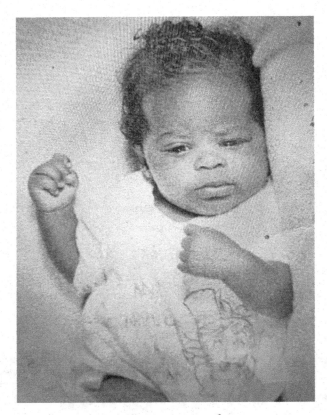

Yes, I was born snapping my fingers.

I was born Richard Johnson. My birth certificate says Negro. My family lived on a farm in Thurston County, Olympia Washington, in the Great North West of the United States of America. I was the first African American baby born in St. Peters Hospital.

It happened on a Monday morning, February 3rd at 3:05.

I wonder if the nurses and doctors were running around the hospital shouting, "What is it? What is it? We have never seen anything like it before here. What is it? I'm afraaaaaid! Is it going to bite me?"

Relax, people. It is not as if *Godzilla* suddenly appeared from the womb of a pregnant African American woman. He is just a newborn, a baby, a child, a person, a human. Of course, he is going to look like his mother.

I find it extremely interesting that the common, everyday process of childbirth, more specifically *my* birth, was such an issue, such a spectacle, something that was news worthy. Thank you for the attention. This sheds a certain light on our reaction when we are within the immediate sphere of those who do not look like us.

No, I was not born with a silver spoon in my mouth, but I was born in the media with a newspaper article written about me. I often wonder if this had anything to do with me eventually going into show business. Looking back, I have been performing since I was two years old.

Did that newspaper article lead me to becoming a professional radio broadcaster, actor and being on stage hosting concerts with Janis Joplin, Queen Latifah, the Beach Boys, the Miracles, Dizzy Gillespie, Cheech & Chong, Crosby Stills, Nash & Young, Kool & the Gang, Chicago Transit Authority, Black Sabbath, and many others?

Yes, Black Sabbath, that is a whole other story that I will tell you later.

I never thought that I would travel to over twenty countries, become an actor, and perform in international television commercials, movies, corporate films for some of the biggest companies in the world, international infomercials, and audition for Woody Allen, Norman Lear, Penny Marshall and others.

One day, as I was sitting next to Mr. Lear in the Joyce Theatre in New York, observing a run-through of a new play called *American Passion* that was to go to Broadway. I was thinking, "I can't be-LIEVE I'm sitting next to NORMAN LEAR. This could be my ticket to Broadway.

One of the lead actors, Roscoe, was experiencing health issues and I was to replace him in the show. I was fantasizing about Norman Lear writing another "All in the Family" type television sitcom. Only *this* one would be called "All About Batt." Dream aborted, dream denied, the show closed, next!

CHAPTER 2

Batt Who?

I wrote my previous books to show you what I think. I wrote this book to show you who I am, for it is not about the shade or tone of my skin but the color of my behavior that is important.

My last book, *Tango Intoxication* was fourteen years of off-and-on writing. Wrote some, put it on the shelf. Wrote some, put it on the shelf.

This book was very different. I wrote something every day, sometimes twice or three times a day. It was during the pandemic. I was on lockdown and I had the time.

But it was fun, it was exciting, some of it was even interesting. Any creator will tell you they always have doubts as to the likeability quotient of their project.

While reading this book you may think that I hate white people or that I hate black people, or that I hate both. Neither is even close to being accurate.

I do not like using the word, "white" when referring to people, because it further legitimizes the black/white dichotomy and the great American lie and divide. "White" people aren't white and "black" people aren't black. Much more on this later.

This is a very delicate balance for me. I am in love with the red, I am in love with the yellow, black, white, and brown. I am in love with people and the possibilities they possess.

I am a multi-cultural, multi-national, multi-racial, multi-peopled, sensitive person. I often say that there is a thin line between that which makes me want to laugh and that which makes me want to cry. I enjoy both sides of that line, for we all need a good laugh and a good cry on occasion.

This book is a purging of my thoughts and experiences over many years, as they relate to race in this country as I have experienced it, particularly as a person of high melanin content in a world of little, as I was growing up as an American media professional.

I will attempt to take you where I have been in a far less painful fashion than what I experienced. I am not writing this to anger anyone but I am certain it will have that impact on some.

For some of those around me, there was often an issue with the shade, tint, tone, and color of my skin. I never saw anything wrong with my skin. My eyes work perfectly well, I don't understand why I don't see what others see when they look at me. Why is my skin color so darn important?

I was inspired to write this book by the international protests against police brutality, the continuous murdering of African American people by the police, and the dehumanized maltreatment of African American people.

When I saw the protests in other countries I thought, "this is a big deal." When I saw the gargantuan size of the protests in Germany, of all places, is when I knew I had to say something.

The murders of George Floyd in Minneapolis, Minnesota who was choked and suffocated to death by a policeman's knee on his neck for nine minutes and twenty-nine seconds; Jacob Blake in Kenosha, Wisconsin who was shot seven times in the back by police; Breonna Taylor in Louisville,

Kentucky, murdered in her own home late at night; Raychard Brooks in Atlanta, Georgia, who was shot in the back three times as he ran from police for sleeping in his car in a fast food parking lot; Daunte Wright in Minneapolis, Minnesota who was stopped for a minor traffic infraction and shot by a female officer who said she thought she was pulling out her taser and not her gun; the 1991 beating of Rodney King by the LAPD; the racist, incompetent and deranged 45th President of the United States, and the COVID-19 Coronavirus; this confluence of events had a very moving, emotional, and profound impact on me and forced me to write my story.

COVID-19 is the worst public health crisis in over one hundred and two years…all of that in the summer of 2020. Whew! I am tired just writing about it.

In 1977, thirty-one-year-old, Haitian born Abner Louima was arrested outside of a Brooklyn, New York night club. He was taken to the 70th Precinct where he withstood a horrible, horrible beating by four cops, Charles Schwarz, Thomas Wiese, Thomas Bruder and Justin Volpe. Volpe performed of one of the most depraved, inhumane, cripplingly demonic acts ever. He was accused and found guilty of shoving a broom stick up the rectum of Louima, who had to undergo three major surgeries. Abner Louima was awarded $8.75 million in a civil police brutality lawsuit against the City of New York.

On February 4, 1999, four undercover New York City police officers took time off from their daily shift, for a little target practice in the street as they pumped a staggering *forty-one* bullets into the body, and even the foot of unarmed African immigrant, Amadou Diallo. All of this was because he pulled out his cell phone to make a phone call…and they didn't go to jail!

One does not have to be a genius to directly connect the murders of unarmed African Americans in the last four-hundred and one years, to an over 58% increase in firearm sales in the first six months of 2020 to African American men *and* women.

The first gun control legislation was written in 1640 banning African Americans from owning guns, slaves or not. Something is happening in this country and it does not look good.

I do not have any outrageous experiences of shootings, lynch mobs, stabbings, gang violence, gun violence, and the Ku Klux Klan in my life story. My story is not one of international fame and glory, but rather one of courage, confidence, forgiveness, determination and the giving of love.

It took courage to get back up and continue my voyage after being knocked down several times for no reason other than the melanin content I am walking around with. If I can offer anyone anything with my life story, I want to offer courage and inspiration to all who may seek it.

When I enrolled into the Bill Wade School of Radio & Television Broadcasting when I got out of the U.S. Army on June 28, 1968, I was hoping to get a job in broadcasting. I had no idea it was going to happen or be a more than forty-year-long career, from 1968 to 2008. Acting in plays, films, television, TV commercials, movies, radio, modeling, hand modeling, and becoming a university adjunct professor, was never a thought.

For me, acting was something "other" people did, not me. I guess I was too young to know that the people in the movies and television shows that I watched did not look like me. I did not know that those opportunities were not available to me. I had no idea.

But I kind of knew something was up when an African American was going to be on the Ed Sullivan show or the Tonight show starring Johnny Carson. My mother would always gather us to watch this special event. When I was a child I wanted to *be* Johnny Carson. I wanted to *be* Steve Allen.

Steve Allen is an American icon. In 1954 he leapt into national stardom by being the co-creator and the first host of an original television format. The show was called "The Tonight Show." This was the very first late-night television variety/entertainment/talk show. *All* of the late-night shows of today, were modeled after *this* groundbreaking phenomenon.

When I was working at WQEW radio in New York, Steve Allen came by the radio station for an interview with my boss. I knew he was going to be there, so I went in early. When the interview was over, I walked into the studio and introduced myself.

I said, "Mr. Allen, my name is Batt Johnson and I work on the air here. When I was a child I used to watch your show on television, wanting to do that work so badly. It is an absolute *thrill* to meet you…a *thrill*." I then dropped to my knees and raised both hands in the air and back to the floor, to the air and to the floor, as I chanted *I'm not worthy! I'm not worthy! I'm not worthy!*

Steve said to my boss, who was standing right there, "Gee, when is this guy going to finish? I could have written another song by now." This happened to be on my birthday. I don't remember if I mentioned it being my birthday to him but he wrote me a nice letter, dated February 3, my birthday.

STEVE ALLEN
15201 BURBANK BOULEVARD
SUITE B
VAN NUYS, CALIFORNIA 91411
(818) 988-3830

Third
February
1998

Mr. Batt Johnson
~~----~~-E
New York, NY 10025

Dear Batt,

It was a pleasure meeting you recently when I was at the station.

I'm by no means certain that I deserved all your compliments but they do fall pleasantly on the ear.

Knowing of your interest in Golden Age-style music I trust you'll enjoy the enclosures.

All good wishes.

Cordially,

Steve Allen

SA/jh

Enc.: Tom Kubis' "Keep Swingin'" CD, Ann Jillian's "In The Middle Of Love", "Words & Music By…" CD and "75th Birthday Celebration" CD.

A letter to me from my childhood hero, Steve Allen

My mom would gather us and place us in front of the TV. It was a big deal. "Ooohh, the Jackson5 are going to be on TV tonight! The Supremes are going to be on The Steve Allen Show tonight!"

At the time, I didn't know it, but that was my training ground when I was a child. I was on a steady, daily diet of watching such classic American black and white television shows as: Have Gun Will Travel, The Honeymooners, Leave It to Beaver, Topper, The Twilight Zone, The Alfred Hitchcock Hour, Ozzie & Harriet, Amos & Andy (notice this is the only black show listed here. There were no other black shows on at this time.), The Lone Ranger, Topper, Gun Smoke, The Rifleman, Sea Hunt, I Love Lucy, Father Knows Best, The Millionaire, Maverick and the spinoff, Sugarfoot, Rawhide, Perry Mason, Sky King, Voyage to the Bottom of the Sea, The Andy Griffith Show, The Cisco Kid, McHale's Navy, Bat Masterson, The Beverly Hillbillies, Dragnet, The Dick Van Dyke Show, The Untouchables, My Three Sons, The Phil Silvers Show, F-Troop, The Fugitive, Wagon Train, Casper, Wanted Dead or Alive, and Highway Patrol, to name a few.

No wonder I am the way I am. Now it all makes sense. In fact, a scene for the Highway Patrol TV series, starring Broderick Crawford, was shot at my dad's gas station because it looked like Tijuana, Mexico. No, I did not meet Broderick Crawford, but I think my fire was about to be fueled for the business.

Once I decided what I wanted, I forged ahead and I didn't look back. You can do the same, but it takes courage, discipline, and desire. As African Americans, we are not a monolith. We are many things with many talents and skills. We are not all thugs and hoodlums, singers or athletes. But whatever we are, whatever we do, we bring a special touch of uniqueness to the project, on this you can rely.

I had two sisters who were seven and eight years older than I. I lost my oldest sister a few years ago. She always had health problems of varying sorts. That is how I became a resident of San Diego, California. The weather in Washington was too cold, damp and rainy for her, so our family doctor recommended a drier, warmer climate. We had relatives in San Diego, so, south we went. I am so happy and proud to have been raised in San Diego.

The Johnson children on the beach in San Diego, California. My oldest sister, Gloria (L), me the youngest (M), my sister Connie (R), the middle child.

San Diego has the greatest weather in all of America. Someone once said the most boring job ever, is that of a weather forecaster in San Diego. Groundhog's day weather, same every day, every day. Clear, blue skies with a high of 78. The news is next. Clear, blue skies with a high of 78. The news is next. Clear, blue skies with a high of 78. The news is next. Clear...

MY BIRTH CERTIFICATE SAYS "NEGRO"

When I hear people, particularly the media, speak in such false, absolute terms when speaking of certain groups of people, I find it abhorrent, repugnant, and ignorant. Frankly, I have a problem with the terms, "black people," "white people," and "brown people." We never hear the term "yellow people" anymore. Perhaps that is because so many Caucasian men have married Asian woman, especially after the Viet Nam War. The term "people of color" is less offensive to me but that too makes little to no sense. The question arises, who are the people of color? Aren't ALL people, people of color? Even those with albinism have color.

If there is a group of people who are "people of color," there must be a group of people who don't have any color. Should we be saying, "people of color and the color challenged"? Or "people of color and those without"? Or "people of no color"? Or The colorless? Or the people in need of color. Poor souls, they have no color. It is off to the tanning bed and the beach. They could also buy some tan spray and stay home. Why? Aren't you satisfied with what God gave you?

Why would you want to alter the color you have been given? Go to the beach to get a tan to look more like the people you hate? Hhmm, there is something here that doesn't make sense.

White people are not white. Do you know what the color white looks like? If you see a white person you should call 911 immediately because that person is about to die of extremely low blood pressure at any moment.

When I hear the term, "black and brown people," I wince because the blacks ARE brown. Someone got it *all* wrong.

I was thinking about this the other day. "IF" you believe white people are white, take a really close look at a "white" businessman in a white shirt, suit and tie. The collar of his white shirt will be next to his neck. If you think the collar of the shirt and the neck of the man are the same color, you should go back to pre-school and learn your colors because you have been misled somewhere along your developmental path.

The people we call white, aren't white, they are pink or as my dear friend, Gayle Madeira, who is not African American, would say, they're orange, we're all orange.

Don't laugh, this is not a joke, she is a professional, award-winning artist. She knows her colors. She knows what she is talking about. More on this later.

So, to me, that represents a lie calling African American people black, and Caucasian people white. Black people aren't black, another lie, they are brown. Asians aren't yellow, another lie. Native Americans are not red. Latins, are brown, well, most are.

A lie could be described as an assertion that is believed to be false, typically used with the purpose of deceiving someone, as in an intentionally false statement. Or it could be an unintentionally false statement. Only the truth is the truth, everything else has a different name. I call it a "lie."

We are brainwashed. This is easily achieved when people are not paying attention, or don't care. Very often when we hear the same lie over and over again, those who are not thinking for themselves begin to believe those lies.

In my heart of hearts, I reject the terms black people and white people. I use it in this book because I want you to read and digest my content and not wonder why I use terms like Caucasian, people of African descent, people of color, pink people, people of no color, and the colorless.

In our American culture, when you hear the term "race or racism" we automatically think that a black person is involved. Why? Think about it. Why do we automatically think that a black person is involved when we hear the word race or racism? Why does the news media always refer to a "black man" being shot by a white policeman and not "a man was shot by the police today"? A black man. A black man. A black man.

They constantly use those terms to further separate and demonize us, the black man, the descendant of slaves. The important issue is not about slavery but more about shining a light on the brutality of the individuals who created slavery in America. Blaming the victim does not make any sense or make anything better.

NEGRO! NEGRO! NEGRO!

I was in a taxi coming from a private tango lesson with the great Julio Balmaceda (RIP) at his studio in the Boedo neighborhood in Buenos Aires, Argentina. As usual, the taxi driver asked me where I was from. I said, "New York," then I asked him where was he from. He said, Poland. That surprised me.

He then said, "You, you New York. Frank Sinatra, Louie Armstrong!" and broke out into song, "It's up to you New York, Neeewww Yooorrk." I started singing like Louie Armstrong, which both surprised and delighted him. He laughed pretty loudly about that. He said he loved Louie Armstrong.

As we approached a stop sign, we noticed some homeless young people sleeping on the sidewalk, on and in cardboard boxes.

The taxi driver started shouting, "NEGRO!" "NEGRO!" "NEGRO!" I thought, "Did he learn that word in Poland or here in Argentina?" I know Argentina has a horribly racist past but why is he yelling at me? I thought we had a friendship. Heck, we were just singing Sinatra together, I even broke out my Louie for him.

If he didn't want me in his taxi, why did he pick me up in the first place? Actually, he was looking at and pointing at those kids sleeping on the street who were Argentinian.

I was really confused.

As he pulled away from the traffic signal, he quickly swiveled his head around and apologized to me. He said, "Oh, no, no, I no talk you. That's say when young people no work. They hurt Argentina."

Thank you for the apology. I was about to jump out of the taxi in the middle of, who knows where, Buenos Aires, and walk home. I was thinking I can't even go to the other end of the earth without being called a name. What the heck is this?

I was happy I misunderstood! Am I too sensitive?

CHAPTER 3

Black Crime! Black on Black Crime!

Here we go again! I woke up this morning, turned on the television and saw, yet another news story about a young black man shooting another young black man in the streets. Why does this keep happening? Do these young people have no hope and see no light in their future? Many have become gang members, drug dealers, thieves, robbers, pushing themselves further and further to a bottom. Why not? If the president of the "United States" is a criminal and has, thus far, gotten away with all of his criminality, this must be the way to go. Heck, if he can do it and get away with it, it must be Ok. No? NO!

No one likes hearing negative things about their group of people. If you don't like hearing negative things, don't commit negative acts. It is simple… or is it? No. If one is lucky enough to have come from a good family, that is the best start. But I think it takes a certain mentality to brush off and cast aside all of the negativity you hear about your group of people every day, over years. When one hears it for so long, it is not difficult to understand why many believe what they hear…and see.

The African American community has to step it up. We HAVE to stop defending criminals, reprobates, lawbreakers and miscreants simply because they are black. If you are a thug and are bringing the quality of our skin down, you must go.

You cannot ask, politely ask, or even demand that the police stop killing individuals of African descent until individuals of African descent stop killing individuals of African descent.

American psychiatrist and author, Dr. Frances Cress Welsing once said, "We're the only people on this entire planet who have been taught to sing and praise our demeanment.

'I'm a bitch. I'm a hoe. I'm a gangster. I'm a thug. I'm a dog.' If you can train people to demean and degrade themselves, you can oppress them forever. You can even program them to kill themselves and they won't even understand what happened."

There is an old proverb that says, "There is nothing like the love and enveloping arms of a mother." There is another that says, "A young boy's best guide is the wit, wisdom, and teaching hand of his father, the person he will most likely grow to emulate." Author James Baldwin once said, "Children have never been very good at listening to their elders, but they have never failed to imitate them."

One of the books I wrote is called, *The Wit and Wisdom of African American Men*. It is an easy to read, compilation and handy reference guide to insightful, spiritually, and intellectually developed, and inspired thought from some of our most admired African American male thinkers, leaders, heroes, and humorists.

Musician Stevie Wonder displayed his *Wit* when he said, "Before I ride with a drunk, I'll drive myself." Boxing Champion and entrepreneur George Foreman said, "My kid's idea of a hard life is to live in a house with only one phone." Actor-comedian Damon Wayans said, "I grew up so poor that plenty of nights I had sleep for dinner."

You will read the *Wisdom* of some of the brightest and most insightful African American men of the Twentieth Century.

Harvard University Professor Henry Louis Gates, Jr. said, "Black males have long intrigued the Western imagination, whether as gods and kings in much of classical antiquity, or devils and sambos since the high Middle Ages."

Dr. Martin Luther King, Jr. said, "We must develop and maintain the capacity to forgive. He who is devoid of the power to forgive is devoid of the power to love."

Activist Dick Gregory said, "When it comes to food for thought, some of us are on a hunger strike." Educator Booker T. Washington, "Excellence is to do a common thing in an uncommon way." Colin Powell said, "Let racism be a problem to someone else...Let it drag *them* down. Don't use it as an excuse for your own shortcomings."

Actor Denzel Washington adds, "A person completely wrapped up in himself makes a small package." Malcolm X, said, "Education is our passport to the future, for tomorrow belongs to the people who prepare for it today."

Once while I was interviewing actor and filmmaker, Spike Lee, he said, "You know, the first thing we have to do is keep these young brothers from killing each other."

How do we do that? By inspiring, feeding their minds a message of hope and by celebrating our positive role models. I believe that we are what we think. What we *do* is the direct result of what we have been *thinking* and feeding our subconscious mind.

South African Activist and Anglican Archbishop, Desmond Tutu said, "When your dreams turn to dust, vacuum." I say, "If you're going to dream, dream big, in very explicit detail and in *color*." Richard Pryor once said, "Try to make the world laugh, it already has enough to cry about."

While I was filming a Kodak national network television commercial with Bill Cosby (Before he got into trouble), he said to me, "The problem with some of these young black men and boys today is that they would rather be hip and cool instead of smart."

Shooting a Kodak television commercial with Bill Cosby before he got into trouble.

If some of the great African American minds of our past wanted to be hip and cool instead of smart . . .

- Daniel Hale Williams (1856–1931) would have never been in a position to perform the world's first open-heart surgery.

- Garrett A. Morgan (1877–1963) could not have invented the traffic light.

- Dr. Charles R. Drew (1904–1950) would have never founded the world's first blood bank.

These are significant achievements that had an impact on the *world* for generations.

In spite of the fact that Reverend Jesse Jackson ran for President of the United States in 1984 and 1988, and Colin Powell was considering it, and Barak Obama did it in 2008 *and* 2012, the image of the African American male is more tainted than ever before. Fortunately for our entire society, and the world, there are forces at work to remedy that blighted image.

We have to stop behaving in anti-social ways, ways that do not reflect the fact that it is *we* who are superior, superior in many ways. We have to stop committing crimes that cause us to be the largest population in most jails and prisons across North America. I realize that these may be considered controversial words to some but there is power in our pigment, "Pigmentational Power" that many who possess it, are not using it.

You may not completely understand or agree with my position. But, if no crime is committed, no penalty is due. That is…unless you happen to run into a bigot with a gun, or a badge, or both. I hope your redneck radar engages before it is too late.

Granted, there are many factors working against us and not all are able to rise above their given situation. We all channel our Africanity through various conduits.

Some academic research has shown that the lack of quality education opportunities, poverty, exposure to harmful chemicals like lead paint, bad neighborhoods, government-controlled redlining of neighborhoods, and other factors, all contribute to the high crime rates in many African American communities. There are far too many guns on American streets and too many with the wrong mentality to use them.

Celebrated comedian Richard Pryor once said, "They call me angry, an angry black man, angry. But since I got me some money, I ain't angry no more." I ask, is that the answer?

We call each other "brother" but we sometimes treat each other like "the other" or like an enemy. Why? Why do we constantly hurt each other? When we do that, we are saying to the greater society, "Yep, you're right. We are not worthy, we are savages, we are not together, we are not ready."

Once, while hanging out in the dressing room of a jazz club in New York, a very famous African American bass player, Percy Heath, who has been famous since the 1950s, whom I knew fairly well, approached me and said the following. Oh, one last point. He said this because he saw me come into the club with two Caucasian men and a Caucasian woman.

He said, "Batt, you need to be re-born. I like you a lot but you need to be 're-niggahfied!' You hang out with too many white people." I said, "But white people are people too." He said, "naaww they ain't, Batt. Naaww they ain't."

A dear friend, who is not African American, once said to me, "Batt, if a Greek, an Italian, an African, a Swede, and a Jew are walking down the street together, where do you think your eye will go first? Who sticks out? Only the dark-skinned African sticks out. Why? Because he or she is the one who looks the most different.

This is something we were taught in first grade. We used to get mimeographed sheets of paper that smelled like a chemical with light purple text and drawings on them. For instance, they would have a drawing of a taxi, taxi, taxi, apple, taxi. Circle the one that is different? Cow, cow, cow, house, cow. Circle the one that is different? Is that part of our education or indoctrination?

So, my take on this is, as possessors of a dark brown to light brown skin tone in this country, we must cherish it, protect it, and covet it, for in this society, it is one of the things that make us different and special in so many ways, even though we constantly hear rhetoric to the contrary.

We are special. Our color is the thing one sees first. I often wonder, "Why is my skin tone so important to others?" It is like my shoe size, number of even numbers in my social security number or what I had for dinner last Thursday. Who CARES?!! What is WRONG with people?

Yes, African Americans are a powerful and important people. A people so powerful that an entire nation was willing to lethally do battle for them, kill for them, spill blood, and lose loved ones for them, for four long years. Can you imagine being willing to kill people who look like you to keep control of people who don't look like you, and that you hate? If the Southern portion of the United States hated peoples of African descent so much, why were they killing people who looked like themselves to keep the Africans they hated so much? Money! In the United States, money is always the answer. Always!

The American Civil War was fought from April 12, 1861 to May 9, 1865 between the Union (the North) and the Confederacy (the South) in the United States. The reason for the war was over free African labor, or slavery, and the expansion of it into territories acquired from the Louisiana Purchase (1803), and the Mexican-American War (1846–1848).

Although some would disagree, police are people too.

If you have a moment, I suggest viewing comedian Chris Rock's video, "How NOT to Get Your Ass Kicked by the Police." You can see it on YouTube. https://www.youtube.com/watch?v=OevMc-K8XHY

There is always the aspect of access. How can the black man get a job to feed himself and his family if the greater, money holding white American community won't hire him? How can he advance when he has often gone to inferior schools? They are inferior schools because the superior teachers are afraid to go into those communities for fear of bodily harm or worse, death. This is real.

At some point all individual groups will have to come together, talk and come about a reasonable, equitable solution. Parents have to raise their children better, governments have to do better, and individual people must do better with each other.

The massive national and international protests of the summer of 2020 were all about police brutality and equality. If there is anything the holders of that power don't want to hear about or give up, it is their power.

Laws must change, laws must be enforced. Laws must develop teeth. Our laws should NOT be negotiable. Right is right, red is red, water is water. The gradations in the law is what softens and removes the teeth in the law, in my "unschooled non-legal opinion." Any idiot can see. The legal system is not just or equitable, especially for the poor.

Themis is the Greek Goddess of divine justice, the symbol of law and equality in our country. She has the scales representing justice in one hand and a sword representing authority and power in the other. She is also blind-folded to symbolize the saying, "justice is blind."

Actually, she blindfolded herself because she cannot bear to witness the continuous miscarriage of justice by those in power against those without. How can, all be equal "in the eyes of the law" when those enforcing the law come from a biased system that favors *them*?

CHAPTER 4

The United States Army

"WE CAN SERVE YOU, BUT WE CAN'T SERVE HIM"

On June 28, 1966, I was drafted into the United States Army during the Vietnam War troop build-up. I feel they stole some important years of my developing life by forcing me from my home, friends and extended family to teach me how to kill people.

Being drafted felt like a legal kidnapping. I didn't want to go into the Army, and I didn't want to dodge the draft by going to Mexico or Canada. If they caught me, I would have been sent straight to jail or worse, prison. That was not an option for me.

I went willingly into the Army, unlike the 45th president of the United States, who dodged the draft with a lie about having bone spurs (a small, pointed outgrowth of bone, usually caused by inflammation, such as from osteoarthritis or tendonitis).

I was a student at San Diego City College and working at a Jack in the Box, a fast food drive-thru restaurant chain. My mother called me one day while I was at work. She said, "That thing is here." I said, "What thing mom?" "It's your draft notice." I thought, oh man, they *GOT* me!

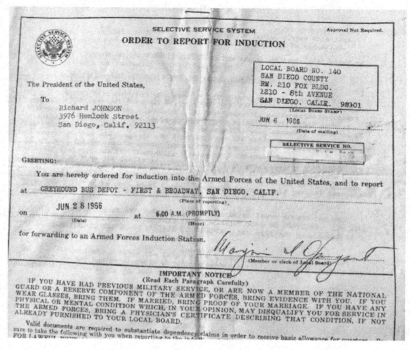

When I received this draft notice, my initial thought, was heck, they GOT me!

I said "Don't, worry mom, everything will be okay." I went home and I saw the notice and I thought, ooh, nooo! Yep, the name is correct. Yep, right address. Yep, the social security number is correct. Yep, they got the right guy.

I have always felt like I'm divinely guided, and sheltered from evil by angels surrounding me, protecting me and nothing bad could ever happen to me in my life. I don't have to worry about a thing, ever. Maybe that's a part of my attitude about myself in this life.

It is not a question of whether the glass is half empty or half full because the glass is always half empty *and* half full. The upper half is empty, while the lower half is full.

Guys were trying everything to get out of the draft. Many guys were claiming to have bone spurs. One guy said, if you put a bar of soap under your armpits, it will raise your blood pressure and they won't take you. I thought,

I have asthma, maybe they won't take me because of that, but the doctor said that was a long time ago and I outgrew it.

Draft day came. I went to the bus station in downtown San Diego to be sent to the Los Angeles Induction Center to be processed. The bus arrived in LA. We got off the bus and a marine in his dress uniform with red hair cut in a flat top, freckles come out. He walked up to us and started yelling and cursing at us in his thick, Alabama, Mississippi, Georgia accent.

"OKAY, ALL YOU BOYS, YOU LITTLE SISSIES, GET YOUR ASSES IN LINE. LINE UP! LINE UP! ALL YOU LITTLE FREAKS LINE UP, GODDAMN IT, HURRY THE FUCK UP, WE AIN'T GOT ALL GODDAMN DAY!!! THIS AIN'T NO FUCKIN' PICNIC!!!

I was thinking, "We're civilians, why is he yelling and cursing at us?"

Then he said, "OKAY, I'M GONNA TAKE ALL YOU LITTLE WORMS FROM HERE DOWN TO HERE. YOU GO WITH THAT SERGEANT OVER THERE!

They took a group of guys, and sent them to OJT (on the job training), in the jungles of Vietnam. Another group of guys were sent to Hawaii for jungle warfare training. I missed Vietnam by only three guys. There were two other guys in front of me. I was the third guy.

Instead of Vietnam, I was sent to Fort Bliss, Texas in Western Texas for basic training. This is when they teach you how to survive, how to kill people, how to throw a hand grenade, how to shoot a rifle, how to fight with hand-to-hand, close combat training, how to kill someone with a bayonet, you know, fun stuff like that.

They put us on the night infiltration course, gave us nuclear training, ssurvival, evasion and escape training, overseas orientation, and immunizations. I think this is about time to get scared. But I wasn't.

They made me climb a rope, scale a wall, crawl under low hanging barbed wire in the mud without getting my rifle wet, go into a building filled with tear gas, sit for a few minutes, then take my protective mask off. The door was locked so we could not get out until the drill sergeant let us out.

The chamber had a concentration, although a controlled concentration, of CS gas, or orto-chlorobenzylidene-malononitrile. Just looking at that name makes my body hurt. Tear gas also happens to be the active ingredient in Mace.

Can you imagine twenty or thirty young men coughing, sneezing, crying, water and other fluids running out of their nose and mouth, convulsing and throwing up? When they finally let us out of the tear gas chamber, we were back in the one hundred-twelve-degree dry heat under the West Texas desert sky. Romantic. These are just some of the things we painfully endured in preparation for defending this country.

Private Johnson in basic training

One of the sergeant's favorite methods of waking us up on many mornings was to throw a big, galvanized iron trash can down the middle of the barracks floor as they yelled and screamed at the top of their lungs, every curse word and insult they could think of.

GET YOUR LITTLE SISSY ASSES OUT OF THOSE FUCKIN' BUNKS! YOU GODDAMN MAGGOTS! YOU FUCKIN' CALIFORNIA BABIES. THERE AIN'T NOTHIN' BUT TWO THINGS IN CALIFORNIA, QUEERS AND STEERS AND I DON'T SEE NO FUCKIN' HORNS ON YOU!

GET THE FUCK UP! COME ON, LET'S GO, LET'S GO, LET'S GO, LET'S GO, YOU FUCKIN' LITTLE GIRLS!!!! I GOT A SIX-MONTH OLD AT HOME THE FUCK TOUGHER THAN YOU!!!! COME ON!!!! LET'S GO!!

They would yell at us all day, every day, but they would never touch us, hit or slap us. They were not allowed to. There were many times when we wanted to punch them.

Some days we had to go on these twelve-mile forced marches, as they were called. A forced march is not like a sunny Sunday stroll in the park with your loved one on the way to a picnic. We were not walking or marching. We were basically running and jogging with big, heavy combat boots on. Don't forget, this is West Texas in June, hot as hell.

We were dressed in full combat gear with at least a forty-five-pound pack on our backs complete with a sleeping tent, steel combat helmet or steel pot as it is called. There is another helmet under that which is made of fiberglass. At the bottom of the pack we had our entrenching tool (shovel) for digging holes for the tent stakes and holes to create a latrine (bathroom).

U.S. Army basic combat training, never a dull moment.

We had a rifle, dummy ammunition, a water canteen, and lots of other gear and clothing. These forced marches often led to going on bivouac (this means camping in the open air but we had our tents.) where we would camp in the hot desert for two-or-three days eating c-rations, which I think are now called MREs (meals ready to eat).

We had inspections on a regular basis, both scheduled and unscheduled. They were terrifying. We would line up in formation and the drill sergeant would slooowly walk by each and every one of us, inspecting our *everything*.

Once a fly landed on one of my fellow soldier's lapel just as they were inspecting him. The sergeant said, "Troop!!! What's that goddamn fly doing on your lapel, didn't you shower today, you dirty maggot?" "Yes, SIR, I did!"

"Get down and give me twenty-five." These are pushups, with his rifle on top of his hands on the hot, one hundred-twelve plus degree Texas summer asphalt. It was HOT! When you looked at the ground in the distance you could see waves of heat coming off the sand or the asphalt. Every time he came down doing the pushups he had to kiss his rifle. This was their way of getting us to make friends with our weapon because this is the thing that could save our lives. All of this just because a fly landed on his shirt.

If you make a mistake and call your rifle or your weapon, your gun, you're really asking for it. Then you have to stand at attention, in the hot sun, holding your weapon with one hand stretched out away from your body. The other hand is used to point at your crouch and your weapon alternately, as you recite, as many times as they tell you, the famous U.S. Army ditty that goes like this.

This is my weapon (pointing at the rifle), this is my gun (pointing at your crouch).

This is for shooting (pointing at the rifle), and this is for fun (pointing at your crouch).

This is my weapon, this is my gun.

This is for shooting, and this is for fun.

This is my weapon, this is my gun.

This is for shooting, and this is for fun.

I told this story to a friend. He said, "That's from the movie *An Officer & a Gentleman*. I said, "you're so young, you don't know anything, do you? Where do you think they got it?"

After the inspection outdoors, we went indoors so they could inspect our rooms and our gear. Each bed had a footlocker at the bottom of the bed. This contained our toiletries, a certain amount of dress and combat socks, spit shined shoes and boots, highly polished brass belt buckle and other shined brass for our Army dress shirts and dress jackets, and other items.

Every item had a specific location and angle. Everything must be perfectly placed. They would also inspect how well our bed was made and it had to be tight enough for a quarter to bounce off of it.

Just minutes before the inspection I noticed a pair of dirty socks stuck in one of my boots. Oh, nooooo! What the heck am I going to do? I can't go down to the laundry room and wash them. The sergeants and the officers were on their way up to our second-floor barracks. Now, what do I do? I'm screwed!

So, I took the dirty socks and hid them, or so I thought, inside the sleeve of my dress jacket that was facing the inside of my locker so they couldn't see the bulge.

They came to my foot locker and inspected everything. I was shaking like a leaf, which surprised me because I thought I was tough.

It looked like everything passed inspection. Then they went to my standing locker and the DI (drill instructor) said, "JOHNSON!!" What the hell is THIS?!" I said, "d, d, dir, dirty socks, SIR!" "What the fuck are they doing inside your jacket sleeve, troop?" "I, I, I, I," "Spit it out, soldier.!!! You what?"

"GET DOWN ON THAT GODDAMN FLOOR AND GIVE ME THE DYING COCKROACH…_NOW_, PRIVATE!!!!"

The dying cockroach is when you have to lie on your back, feet together, arms extended over your head with your palms facing up with hands and feet one inch off the floor until they say you can put them down.

Gee, that is painful! All of these "exercises" are not designed as punishment, though they were. They were designed to make you tough and strong so you can survive the rigors of war and be able to go back home and see your girlfriend and your mother again.

Immediately after basic training in Western Texas, I was sent to Advanced Individual Training (AIT) in Eastern Texas at Fort Wolters in Mineral Wells, Texas. During World War II, it was called Camp Wolters and it served as a German POW camp. AIT is where you are tested and evaluated as to what your job would be during your stay as a soldier.

I tried everything to not become an infantryman, a ground pounder, carry a rifle and a heavy backpack dodging booby traps looking for Viet Cong enemies to kill in the jungle.

So, I took a Spanish test and I took a typing test. The guy interviewing me said, "What do you want to do in the military?" I said, "I don't know, I've never been in the military before! How could I know? I love cars, maybe I can work in the motor pool."

He said, "No, you're too intelligent for that. Why don't you take this test and see where you score?" So, I took the Spanish test. It was basic and I did okay, I think. Then I took the typing test at a different location.

I arrived at the new location, the sergeant gave me some paper and a small booklet and said, "Sit over there at typewriter number seven and type this." Okay, I sat, I put the paper in the typewriter.

Mr. Super Confident, here. I'm going to knock this out of the park. I was really confident because I took typing in the eighth grade and I was the fastest male typist in that class.

I knew that I could nail this. So, Mr. Super Confident put the paper in the typewriter and the sergeant says "You ready?" "Yes, I'm ready." "Okay, go!"

I start typing, brrrrrrrrapapapap!! Paaaapppppap!!! Pow! Pow! Pow! Bam! Bam! My fingers were flying. They were at war with those keys. Smoke was coming out of that typewriter. Sparks were flying, the table was shaking. The windows were rattling.

I finished and took the paper out of the machine. I walked up to him, and handed him the paper. He looked at the paper. He looked at me, he looked at the paper. He looked at me. He handed the paper back to me and said, "I think you might want to do this over again." I looked at the paper and I saw %!^&, &##&*@ @&*(()*&^HFJr45, 5%%&!!eo. #39 [qoioweiq0.

I had my fingers on the wrong position on the keyboard! The wrong set of keys. I thought, I'm dead, they're going to send me to Vietnam! It's over for me! I'm going to the jungles.

He let me do it again. I did well. I scored high. I got sent to Korea and I worked at the Eighth Army Headquarters in an office called StratCom, Strategic Communications, as an administrative specialist (71L-20).

I had a Confidential, Secret, and Top-Secret security clearance. This allowed me to read these levels of messages that came into South Korea. My job was to read the message, determine its content and send it to the proper agency. Korea was really a lot of fun.

Things got a little dicey when many wounded soldiers who, were fighting in Vietnam, were sent to Korea on their way back to the U.S. from hospitals in Japan.

I can't tell you how many soldiers told me stories about being brainwashed into thinking the Vietnamese were animals and they felt NOTHING while in the jungles raping the women and young girls, then shooting them in the head, then shooting their babies. All true stories!

The Army does not just teach you how to protect yourself when someone is trying to kill you. It also teaches you how to kill other people. I heard many stories of fragging in Vietnam. This is when there is a charge on an enemy position and a soldier deliberately shoots another fellow soldier or superior officer in the back. Sometimes they use a hand grenade. Fragging was popularized in Vietnam but it occurred in all American wars but to a lesser degree.

One night while in AIT, I wanted to see, test, experience Texas, plus blow off some steam from training. At the time, they wanted me to learn how to kill people who looked like my best friend, his family and many other dear, dear friends who happened to be Asian.

Ronnie Murakami, who happens to be Japanese, was one of my best friends immediately after high school. He was one year ahead of me and lived around the corner from another good friend, Paul Valdez, a Mexican kid. I lived in a different neighborhood a couple of miles away.

When I went to Ronnie's or Paul's house, their mother would always welcome me, feed me and give me mother kind of love.

It always started with a hug at the front door. Then…food! Good mother-made Mexican food. It was the same when I went to Rick Ejima's house. Good ole mother-made Japanese food.

Ronnie and I used to do so many things together; rock concerts, pool shooting, surfing in Pacific Beach and La Jolla, California, going to Tijuana, Baja California (Mexico) to get a pitcher of green beer for a dollar and a shot of tequila for a quarter and watch the strippers.

We were just kids trying to learn about the world, innocent stuff, you understand. You only had to be eighteen years old to go to the bars in Mexico at that time.

Ronnie's dad always knew when we had been drinking because Ronnie's face would turn a bright, fire engine red. We called it the "dead fish." We called it that because Mr. Murakami, with his beautiful, thick Japanese accent, couldn't say "red face."

It sounded like he was saying "dead fish." That became our secret code for "let's go out drinking." Let's go get a dead fish. Batt didn't get a dead fish but boy, could he ever drink a lot of beer.

Often, after a drink or two, Ronnie would get a "dead fish" and would want to go find Willie Wong and beat him up. Willie was Chinese, Ronnie was Japanese, and that was my first exposure to inner Asian racism. We never found Willie Wong when Ronnie was drinking and he never beat him up, and I will never forget that.

I used to go fishing in the Pacific Ocean in Mexico with Ronnie and his dad. Of course, Mr. Murakami would drive and Matthew Ozaki and I were in the back seat and Ron in the front passenger seat. It was probably two or three in the morning. We had to go early when the fish were hungry and biting.

We were going a little south of Rosarito Beach, which is ten miles south of Tijuana. While driving through a tiny village with dirt roads and about ten houses to the whole community, there were no stop lights or stop signs.

Ronnie's dad, Mr. Murakami was driving about 15 miles an hour in a twenty-five mile an hour area. Out of the blue we hear a siren but could hardly see the flashing red lights of a Mexican police car behind us because of all the dust our car was kicking up.

They pulled us over and asked for I.D. I wonder what the cop was thinking, "Well, well, well, look what I have here. Three Japanese and a black boy. I'm going to get paid tonight."

We all showed our I.D. The policeman asked Mr. Murakami why he was driving so fast. He said, "I was only going 15 miles per hour". The policeman said, "No, you were driving too fast. You all have to go to jail." WHAAAT? Jail?

So, Mr. Murakami reached into his wallet that was on his lap and pulled out some bills (I don't know how many or how much) and handed it to the crooked, corrupt cop.

Then he let us go. All the while in my head I was hearing the song by the Kingston Trio called, "The Tijuana Jail". *"Just send our mail to the Tijuana jail. Ain't got no friends to go our bail."*

I couldn't go to jail, especially a Mexican jail. What would my parents say, what would they do? They always said that if I ever got into any kind of trouble, I'd have to stay there to teach me a lesson. Besides, I had an important exam to take on Monday for my First Class F.C.C. (Federal Communications Commission) broadcasting license.

I HAD to be there. Thank you, Mr. Murakami for paying that cop off. Whew! The same thing happens in America, but in a different form. What happens when you put a badge on a redneck?

"WE CAN SERVE YOU, BUT WE CAN'T SERVE HIM"

So, back to Mineral Wells, Texas. I wanted to go out and hang and see the town at night. I asked my friend, Jim Gerrard, an Irish kid from Costa Mesa, California, to come with me. We became instant friends when we met a month before. Probably because we were both drafted, both from Southern California and used to surf.

We went to a small restaurant for dinner, then we wanted to see if we could get a drink. We were only nineteen years old and we knew that what we were attempting to do was illegal. But we were just boys who were recently forced into the U. S. Army draft, and we were looking to discover the world. We wandered around "downtown" Mineral Wells, Texas, and found a bar/restaurant. We walked in, and sat at the bar.

The bartender came over to us, looked at us and said to me, "We can serve you, but we can't serve him." Meaning they could serve me, the African American in the redneck bar, but could not serve my Caucasian friend.

Gerrard and I both knew what that meant. The redneck bartender was trying to play reverse psychology on us. He knew that I was not going to sit there and have a drink and not have Gerrard have a drink too. Gerrard said, "What are you talking about?" The bartender repeated it. Then I said, "I want to see the manager."

I thought, "now we're getting someplace". The manager, an older lady, came out from the kitchen. Her neck was redder than the bartender's. She said (in a super thick Texas accent), "What seems to be the problem here?" Gerrard said, "The bartender said that he could serve my friend but couldn't serve me. Can you tell me what this is all about?" As she started to mumble some Texas, non-English mumbo southern jumbo, I had a feeling where this was going, and it wasn't good.

I didn't want to get into the first bar brawl of my life, so I grabbed my friend, Gerrard by the arm and said, "Let's get out of here." That was my first experience with in-your-face racism.

I was shocked and pretty darn angry. I thought I was in a movie. That kind of thing never happened in San Diego. So, to all of my American Caucasian friends, of which there are many, you should feel shame and embarrassment as to how this country was created, and what values still exist from the Civil War, the war that was fought for slavery, and the African American, who worked from sun up, to sun down for free.

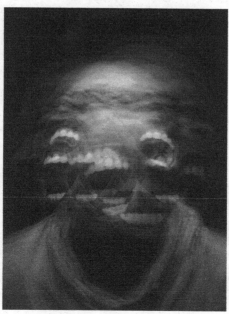

When I thought about that moment, many years later, I became really, really angry!

Here I am in the middle of nowhere, redneck, hot as hell, Texas, going through all of this rigorous, physical and mental torture, being yelled at, climbing walls, being thrown into a tear gas chamber, crawling under low hanging barbed wire in the mud with a rifle, in one-hundred ten, one-hundred-twelve degree heat and hotter, for the United States of America, and they won't serve me a damn beer, *on* United States soil *with* my United States Army uniform on, because of the degree of choclaticity of my skin. This is obviously very wrong and no one is doing anything about it. Why?

When individuals like Dr. Martin Luther King, Jr; the Reverend Al Sharpton, and attorney Benjamin L. Crump speak up for the rights of African American peoples, they are called opportunists and trouble makers. Can you not see that they are simply attempting to gain the legal equality, much-deserved respect and honor the peoples of African descent have earned?

I felt like the Harlem Hellfighters of WWI and WWII. War heroes who had their own American people turn their backs on them when they returned home. They were the 369th Infantry Regiment, formerly known as the 15th (Colored) New York National Guard Regiment. It consisted of about 380,000 African Americans, the first African American infantry unit to fight in WWI.

They spent more time in combat than any other American unit. The German enemy named them such because they were, well, *hell fighters.*

They were later given to the French as menial laborers. They thought the African Americans were not brave enough to fight. The French later changed their minds when they saw them fight. Also, the French loved them because they brought jazz to their country. The Germans respected them more than the racist, segregationist American counterparts at home.

Facing in-your-face racism for the first time was an interesting event for me, but at least they weren't launching bombs and shooting at me, *if* one could look at that as a silver lining.

What is interesting is that I'm the same color they try to achieve every summer when they lie out in the sun. What hypocrites. And people are asking why black people are upset. Hahahah. Where would America be if we didn't do all of that free labor from 1619–1863? Is that 244 years?

About two weeks after this bar event, Gerrard told me about a dream he had. He said, "I went to a store. I purchased a pack of gum. It cost fifty cents. I give the store clerk a ten-dollar bill. He gave me no change. He said I don't get any change because I am black. Johnson, I felt such anger and confusion. I think I better understand how you must feel every, damn, day."

When I came back home from the Army, my Japanese brothers were there, waiting for me. They all called me as soon as I got home. Ronnie Murakami and Matthew Ozaki had previous engagements my first Saturday night back home, so Rick Ejima picked me up at my parent's house on Ocean View Boulevard in San Diego, to take me to my first concert, The Doors (Jim Morrison).

I was thinking, concert so, you have to dress up, right? When I left America a concert meant upscale, tuxedos, suits, upscale, high class. I was not high class but I could relate to those who were. I wore my green, triple gold buckled, suede shoes, green bell-bottomed pants made of fine fabric, beautiful silk shirt and a scarf around my neck with a gold ring clasp. I was sharrrrp! Or so, I thought. I think this is early July, 1968.

When we arrived, parked the car and started walking toward the venue. I noticed people dressed in ripped jeans, tie died t-shirts, ripped shirts. Everyone was in jeans, with long hair and smelled like patchouli oil.

Holy shit! Am I ever over-dressed! Geez, America has changed. America has REALLY changed. When I saw major league, big time, A-list actors come on the "Tonight Show" starring Johnny Carson wearing jeans, is when I realized I had arrived in a vastly different America than the one I left.

I have always been in a constant state of impressing my skin, my multi-national consciousness, my love, my humanity, upon anyone who is capable of receiving it and even to those who are not.

I spent my life placing myself before individuals who do not look like me. Because he or she does or does not look like me, has no bearing on me as to how I view, interpret or interact with these individuals. They need to know us. Those who are not African American, need to know more about the African American individual in America.

They do not have the courage to act upon what they see that they know is wrong, nor do they possess the insight to know that we have a basic problem in this country when it comes to race and *they* are at the epicenter of the problem.

I was always the black guy who would often sit at the Mexican table, the white table, the Asian table, or the Samoan table (Samoa is a group of islands in Polynesia). I would not just sit at the black table during lunch when I was in elementary, junior high and high school.

I don't know if it was to make a statement about race in America or because I simply find people interesting and I wanted to get to know them and I wanted them to get to know me, us. You cannot get to know people when they are on one side of the room and you are on the other.

You think that because you don't necessarily look like me, that you are different from me. You're NOT!

Believe me, I understand the difficulty in admitting the countless wrongs that have been committed over centuries in the land called the United States of America and with that, I understand that no country, no culture, no individual is willing to give up their power.

I don't think that is what the Black Lives Matter movement is about. It is about equal rights, equal justice under the law and the erasure of police brutality from our system.

It seems as though I have always had a mental issue with race and with those who place high importance on it. These individuals do not see the big picture, the actual picture. They only see *their* picture when it is advantageous for *them*.

CHAPTER 5

The Un-United United States

The United States is a hostile country to individuals of African descent. Can you imagine being told to "Go back to where you came from!" when you have Native American blood flowing through your veins. As a "white" person, can you imagine being told, "Go back to Europe where you came from?!"

We call our country the United States of America but the United States is not united. Hawaii is out in the middle of the Pacific Ocean some 2,471 miles away, not connected, not united. Alaska is way north at the Arctic Circle, not connected, not united, about 2,288 miles from the main U.S. border.

If we are united why do the Jews live over there, white Christians and Protestants live here, Asians live there, African Americans live here, and Latins live over there? Is that united?

If we were united why do we have so many different religions? We should be one nation, one people, one religion. Oh, wait a minute. We do have one religion, it is called money.

We cannot make this a true, united country if we continue to be separate. I cannot help make this world, this country, a better place by only being among those who look like me. If we are united, we are united, yellow, black, red, white, brown.

It was 1939 in Alexandria, Virginia when Samuel Wilbert Tucker, a civil rights lawyer and an ex-military man who served in the 366th Infantry in World War II, and became a major. He went to a local public library with a friend, retired Army Sgt. George Wilson to get library cards.

The two gentlemen were refused cards by an assistant librarian who told them that the library board's policy was "not to issue cards to colored persons" according to historian J. Douglas Smith, author of *Managing White Supremacy: Race, Politics, and Citizenship in Jim Crow Virginia*. This is yet another thorn in the Un-United United States thorny past and present.

During the insurrection and storming of the Capitol Building in Washington, D.C. on January 6, 2021, how many people of African descent did you see? I counted one.

Don't you see it? This group over here is only spending time with people who look like them, and that group over there is only spending time with people who look like them, and that group over there is only spending time with people who look like them.

That looks more like isolationism than anything. We are *not* united. So, let's start with that. The name of this country is a lie.

Don't you see the lie? We are not united within the United States of America. Perhaps, "The States of America" would be a more descriptive explanation of who we are. We are more the States of America than we are the "United" States of America.

Why did it take sixty-five years for an American President to visit the original people and land of the country they stole? In July 1999, William Jefferson Clinton, the 42nd President of the United States, was the first sitting President to visit a Native American Reservation since Franklin Delano Roosevelt on June 18, 1934.

Much of the Caucasian culture of America does not respect those who do not look like them. This is seldom spoken. They slaughtered millions of Native Americans and stole their land and never apologized for it or admitted it was wrong. Because you stole it, does not mean that you own it.

Much like the way they stole the culture of the African, who they forced to come to the land of the Native American. The unwritten laws and bi-laws of the creation of America come from the idea of: "He who is the most brutal, savage, and barbaric, gains and maintains the most power through fear and murder."

They want to sweep their ill deeds under the rug and conveniently forget what they have done. But with this comes much guilt. I understand why they want to forget what they have done, but is this the behavior of superior beings?

If I broke into your home, murdered your father, raped and killed your sister and mother, then started living in your home and farming your land, am I a savage? Am I a beast? Because you stole it, does not mean you own it.

I went to a mixed-race high school, by mixed race I mean many Mexicans, Filipinos, Samoans, Japanese, some Chinese, some East Indians, Guamanians, some Native Americans, African Americans and Caucasians. I am so lucky to have that kind of social background and exposure.

I think that deep down inside, African people believe *we* are the superior ones. I remember when I was in high school, if a Caucasian beat you in an individual, one-on-on sport, you would have hell to pay. Your African American teammates would laugh at you, ridicule you, call you weak, call you a sissy, call you a punk, call you a chump, call you a wimp, among other things between catching their breath from the hearty laughter they were having at your expense.

I say this to display the view that much of black America has always had, which is one of viewing our melanin challenged brethren as inferior. Just look at how they treat their fellow human beings.

When the subject of race comes up between black and white individuals, there will always be a "white" person who says, "Oh, I'm not racist. Some of my best friends are black."

My question is: When was the last time they had a black person in their home, at their dinner table?

Comedian Chris Rock once said, "If anyone is superior, it's black people. Just look. We had many inventions that changed the world, we create the best music, we are, unequivocally the best in sports; football, baseball, track & field, basketball, hockey . . . well, as soon as they figure out how to warm up the ice, we're gonna take *that* shit over, too!"

In an interview on James Lipton's amazing television show, The Actors Studio, Chris said, "Babe Ruth was not that good of a baseball player because he never played against any black players." Wow, now that you put it that way . . .

I think I too would be jealous of a people who defy the aging process, especially if I were considered the "Master Race," the "White Supreme." It seems to me that the lack of melanin leads to early aging and general weakness. Why do black people in their sixties look like they are thirty-five? Another reason for the greater "white" society to hate us. If that makes sense.

I think there is such a thing as "black envy." I have heard many Caucasian women say they wish they had a body or a gluteus maximus like black women. I think that most Caucasians wish they could dance like their African American brethren. Why do they spend so much annually on sun tanning lotions and tanning beds? Because our brown skin is beautiful, that is why.

While interviewing renowned jazz bassist, Percy Heath for the jazz book I was writing at the time, he said to me, "You know, the music of Mozart and Beethoven is white music. Anything before and after that is black or black influenced music.

I used to belong to the Palestra Health Club, part of the University of Pennsylvania's private club in midtown New York to which my ex-wife, Lisa was on the board of directors. One day while running on the treadmill, I was watching VH-1 Television, a station I used to work on as a host.

Famed English blues and rock guitarist, Eric Clapton was being interviewed. I don't remember the question but Eric said, "As a band, every day, we do all we can to sound like the American black man."

If you know about the history of rock 'n roll, you know that it is basically music created from the blues which was created by African Americans. You may also know that only musicians from England or Europe will admit to the fact that rock 'n roll and blues are African American creations.

In all of my forty plus years in radio and the music industry, I have NEVER heard an American musician admit that. Why? Their guilt for all of their thievery and, because it is simply not part of the "white" American culture to give the black culture credit for our contributions. They will never admit that because they don't know that, or their *guilt* will not allow them to verbally express it.

I remember the "British Invasion" when countless rock groups came to America from England. I was always fascinated as to how and why, when being interviewed, they spoke like Englishmen, but when they sang, they sounded like a backwoods black Mississippi, cotton-picking, blues singer. Why? How did that happen? Because they were trying to sound "black" and "authentic," that's why.

While viewing your favorite television program, or any random program, you will be hard pressed to view ANY commercial break that does not have some African American influenced music contained within. Almost impossible!

What we have brought to this country musically, still to this day, is not recognized to the degree to which it has earned. Why? Because it is black.

I believe the European American culture hates us because they fear us.

They fear our strength, they fear our power, they fear our ability, they fear our insight, our forward thought. I think that is why the "one-drop" rule is so powerful.

The "one-drop" rule is, if you have one drop of black blood, you are considered black. How can *one* drop supersede all of the other drops? That blood must be *extremely* powerful. The average adult human body has five to six quarts of blood in it, and ONE DROP of African blood is stronger, or is the deciding factor as to what you are called. Think about it! What is interesting, is that we ALL have one drop of black blood.

Jane Elliott is an internationally recognized, Caucasian American diversity educator and human rights activist. She won the National Mental Health Association Award for Excellence in Education.

She is also known for her "Blue eyes/Brown eyes" exercise. This is an exercise that shows "white" people how discrimination actually feels. She created this in 1968, the day after Dr. Martin Luther King Jr. was assassinated.

In one of her talks, she said the following: We all came from the same black women, three-hundred-thousand to five-hundred-thousand years ago. The human race began with black women.

My cousins, and you, black women, are all my cousins. Make no mistake about this, we are all thirtieth to fiftieth cousins because we all have the same black great, great, great, great, great, great, great grandmother. So, get over the idea that you are white. There is only one race, the human race.

I find this to be very powerful because she is a "white" woman saying things that MOST "white" people could not say and do NOT want to hear… even when it is the truth.

In these times I often hear the term, "these are tough conversations to have." Why are conversations about the truth so difficult? Because no one wants to hear the truth, perhaps.

THE ONE-DROP RULE

Have you ever heard of the one-drop rule?

I thought the "one-drop rule" was just a saying in the African American community that only we knew. Upon further research, I discovered that it is a real, "legal" thing.

The one-drop rule was an actual law on the books in some southern states of the U.S. in the 20th Century but it never became a Federal law. It was part of the concept of "invisible blackness." When there were children of a mixed union, the child would be assigned to the group with the lower status.

But many mixed-race individuals were often accepted into the majority population if they looked "white" enough.

There are many, many prominent individuals in our society who are biracial. Either they identify as black or the society labels them black. I don't think it really matters what one identifies as. What really matters is what you ACTUALLY are.

If you have an Irish father and a Japanese mother but you identify as Japanese, you are still half Irish and half Japanese. How difficult is that to understand?

Babe Ruth set a new league record in baseball with his 60th home run in the 1927 season. Roger Maris broke that record in 1961. New York Yankee, Aaron Judge broke that record with his 62nd home run on Tuesday, October 4th 2022. He is biracial.

Rock star Lenny Kravitz, singer and keyboard player Alicia Keys, football stars Colin Kaepernick and Patrick Mahomes, baseball legend Derick Jeter, NBA stars Austin Rivers, Blake Griffin, Clay Thompson, Jason Kidd, singing sensation Mariah Carey, and even President Barak Obama, are all biracial.

Why do they say that Mr. Obama is the first black President of the United States of America? Why? (The African American community also said that about Bill Clinton. They said it because Clinton had many close friends who happened to be black and he feels very comfortable in a roomful of black men).

President Obama's father is from Africa and his mother is a blonde, white American whose lineage is English, Scottish, Welsh, Irish, German and Swiss. In fact, "Wild Bill" Hickok, a folk hero of the American Old West is Barack Obama's mother's 6th cousin, five times removed. That's pretty American.

We do not acknowledge his mother or her lineage AT ALL.

In the eyes of our cruelly racist society, Obama's mother is a non-entity. She is the one who nourished him in utero, gave him life, emotionally fed him, and protected that life before he was born.

But we do not give her any credit while addressing his lineage. We say he is black. I don't, I say he is a mulatto or biracial. Remember, it takes two.

That says a lot about how backward we are as a people when it comes to race in the United States. That should be an example.

Barak Obama's father did not have a child by himself, a medical and historical miracle, an immaculate male conception, a man having a child without the involvement of a biological female? Shocking!

In Brazil, Puerto Rico, Uruguay, Argentina, Cuba, South Africa, all countries that have or had a significant black population, have or had laws, written or unwritten about blackness. Why? Is it because of the power the black skin possesses? Yes.

The one-drop rule did not only apply to African Americans. During World War II, Colonel Karl Bendetsen stated that anyone who has "one drop of Japanese blood" was liable for forced internment in camps. This offends me to no end because of my upbringing with many Japanese people.

JIM CROW LAWS

I often heard about the Jim Crow laws while growing up. These were laws created by the "white" society giving them legal permission to mistreat, with impunity, an entire group of people, for no reason.

We don't punish individuals for obeying the law, but sometimes when you are of African descent, it doesn't matter. We had laws on the books to protect the law makers.

A separate drinking fountain in the United States.

The legal principle of "separate but equal," was racial segregation extended to public facilities and transportation, including the coaches of interstate trains and buses.

Facilities for African Americans were consistently inferior compared to facilities for white Americans; sometimes, there were no facilities for the black community at all.

The local Jim Crow laws (1877–1954) that institutionalized economic, social, and educational disadvantages for African Americans in the South, is the main reason my father picked up the family and moved us north.

Jim Crow was the name of a blackface character in a minstrel show around 1828. The original name was Jump Jim Crow.

My dad felt very strongly about his children NOT being raised in the South, although my mother, father and two sisters were all born in Texas. They moved from Texas to Gary, Indiana.

When they left Indiana, they moved to Olympia, Washington, which is where I was born. The thought of his children growing up like he did, where he didn't have access to the same public transportation, restrooms, restaurants, and even the same drinking fountains as the rest of the population, made him very angry and he did not want his children to experience that.

Because of these laws of the past and continually lingering racist attitudes of today, is one reason many African Americans do not vote. They do not trust the government. Looking at our history, you can see why.

It is the lawmakers who created constant barriers for the advancement or even a regular, "normal" life for the African American in America.

All Jim Crow laws were overruled by the Civil Rights Act of 1964 and the Voting Rights Act of 1965. Some of the laws have changed but the attitudes remain within many, to this day.

The non-African has fear of those with African blood. That is why the pink man gets so upset when he sees a chocolate man walking down the street with a pink woman. The man didn't choke her, smother her, strangle her, put a knife to her throat to force her to be with him, or the inverse. They are in the relationship TOGETHER! She chose *him*. He chose *her*. End of story. Grow up!

In the year 2020 I heard a guy on a television talk show say, "As a white American I am proud of the fact that my ancestors were great kidnappers and killers. We can travel, steal, kill, rape better than anyone in the whole world. We can also force people to work for us for free, thereby maximizing our profits. Profits is why we, as conquerors, came to this new land, and profits is why we will stay."

Profits is why we, as conquerors, came to this new land, and profits is why we will stay?"

This statement coming from an average midwestern citizen of the United States on a published television broadcast, meant to me, that he was all-in, and totally committed.

I could not believe what I was hearing. Much of this kind of thinking has always existed in America but was rarely spoken until Donald Trump became President in 2016. The worst thing to happen in this country in my lifetime.

I think and I know, that a lot of the disobedience and rejection of the safety precaution of wearing masks and observing social distancing protocols during the horribly destructive COVID-19 Coronavirus Pandemic of 2020, came from arrogance, ignorance, insecurity and a false sense of superiority. Much of which was perpetuated by the president at the time.

African Americans have an immeasurably robust sense of pride, and deep down inside, most do not trust the government or any other entity of authority. As you look throughout history, you will better understand why. Here are a few historical facts that lead to this governmental mistrust.

THE TUSKEGEE EXPERIMENT

From 1932 to 1972, the United States Public Health Service conducted an experiment called the Tuskegee Syphilis Study in conjunction with the Tuskegee Institute, a historically black college in Alabama. These African American men were told they would receive free health care from the Federal Government if they participated.

The Government wanted to see the effects of untreated syphilis on the human body. They enrolled six hundred poor, African American share-croppers. The men were told that the "study" would only last six months, but lasted *forty-years*. In the end, only seventy-four men lived, forty of their wives had been infected and nineteen of their children were born with congenital syphilis. By 1947, a cure, penicillin, was widely available but none of the men or their families were told of it, or were treated with it.

On May 16, 1997, President Bill Clinton formally apologized to the victims on behalf of the United States, saying it was shameful and racist. He said, "What was done cannot be undone, but we can end the silence. We can stop turning our heads away. We can look at you in the eye, and finally say, on behalf of the American people, what the United States government did was shameful and I am sorry."

This is just one of the many hidden atrocities inflicted upon peoples of African descent in America. These stories are why many African Americans and other minorities did not get flu shots and would not take the Covid-19 coronavirus vaccine during the pandemic of 2020–2022.

OTHER INHUMANE EXPERIMENTAL CRUELTIES ON THE BLACK COMMUNITY

A man by the name of J. Marion Sims, who is still referred to as "the father of gynecology," performed surgical experiments on African female slaves between 1845 and 1849, even when anesthesia was available, he used none.

One of these women was operated on as many as thirty times, eventually died from infections.

In San Quentin Prison, from 1913 to 1951, chief surgeon, Dr. Leo Stanley, performed testicular experiments on prisoners. He would often remove the testicles of executed prisoners and implant them into living prisoners. Sometimes using the testicles of rams, goats, and boars. Dr. Stanley believed he was helping society by preventing the "unfit" from reproducing.

There were also human radiation experiments on the human bodies of the poor, the black, the powerless, and the sick by the U.S. military, the Atomic Energy Commission and other governmental agencies.

These are just some of the reasons there is a lack of trust in the government by the African American and other minority communities in America.

I believe that with this lack of governmental trust comes a desire to maintain a culture that is truly "black," thereby maintaining a distance from the "white" society. Black walk, black talk, black dress, black dance, black music, black names for the children, black creativity in general, all as a means of remaining separate, independent, and *free.*

When the greater society decides to adopt (steal) some of these African Americanisms…poof! The African American community creates something new… again.

LITTLE KNOWN AFRICAN AMERICAN AND CHINESE CONTRIBUTIONS TO THE U.S. RAILROAD SYSTEM

In many cases in American history, the achievements and accomplishments of non-Caucasian individuals are not recognized or celebrated when it comes to the building of this country.

In 1863 there was a massive labor force of Chinese workers hired to help construct the First Transcontinental Railroad, connecting the Eastern United States with the West.

Obviously, this gave great rise to the rapid population and economic growth of this part of the country. Horses, oxen and covered wagons that took months, or even years to cross the great plains, rivers and the Sierra Nevada and Rocky Mountains were no longer useful because of the railroad.

Tunnels had to be dug, in which the workers slept on cold winter nights, and bridges had to be built across the rivers.

The work was tedious, dangerous and not financially rewarding. The Chinese workers were paid $1.00 per day.

But they also had to pay for their equipment and food out of that money.

The European workers earned $1.50 to $2.50 per day and did *not* have to pay for food and equipment. Good ole America!

Just like the ill treatment of African slaves during and after the hard, back-breaking work of slavery, the Chinese, upon completion of the railroad, were met with violence from murderous, white mobs.

At least the Chinese were paid a $1.00 a day. That's a $1.00 more than what the slaves were paid. When the "white" society is finished with you, you get thrown onto the garbage heap.

That appears to be the American way. It happened to me a few times after building the ratings at various radio stations, only to be unceremoniously dismissed of duty.

The Chinese were not the only group to make massive contributions to our railway system. Many African Americans did as well. Here are a few.

Elijah J. McCoy (May 2, 1844–October 10, 1929). He was an inventor and engineer with fifty-seven U.S. patents. He invented the lubrication of steam engines that allowed a train to travel longer distances without stopping to be lubed.

William Henry Cling (October 1866–February 25, 1937). In 1905 he invented the Railway safety device which was designed to prevent head-on, or rear-end collisions of two trains moving on the same track, by providing the setting of the emergency brake.

Andrew Jackson Beard (1849–May 10, 1921). He introduced two improvements to the automatic railroad car coupler in 1897 and 1899. He was inducted into the National Inventors Hall of Fame in Akron, Ohio in 2006.

Frederick McKinley Jones (May 17, 1893–February 21, 1961. This man had innovations in refrigeration which brought great improvement to the long-haul transportation of perishable goods. He co-founded Thermo King and was a winner of the National Medal of Technology, and an inductee of the National Inventors Hall of Fame.

Granville Tailer Woods (April 23, 1856–January 30, 1910). This man held more than 60 patents in the U.S. One of his notable inventions was a device he called the Synchronous Multiplex Railway Telegraph, a variation of induction telegraph which relied on ambient static electricity from existing telegraph lines to send messages between train stations and moving trains. His work assured a safer and better public transportation system for the cities of the United States.

CHAPTER 6

COLOR!
Aren't All People, People of Color?

I f you're not telling the truth, you're telling something else. What is it you're telling? In some of my research in various art books, Wikipedia, Google and other search sites, I ran into the following passage.

> "Black is the absence of light...Some consider
> white to be acolor, because white light comprises
> all hues on the visible light spectrum. And many
> do consider black to be a color, because you combine
> other pigments to create it on paper. But in a
> technical sense, black and white are not colors.
> they're shades."

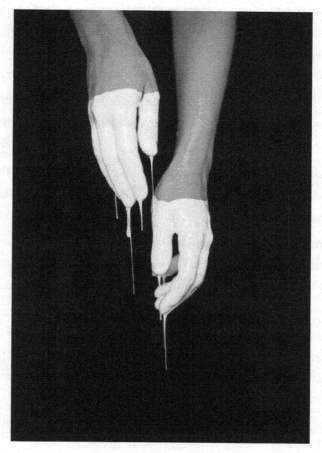

Only white is white. It has been twisted and misrepresented.

If you think you are white, get a regular sheet of blank paper and place it on a surface. Then place your hand upon the paper. If your hand looks like the sheet of paper, then you are white.

If your hand does not look like the paper, then perhaps you can see one of many lies that have been perpetuated and bought into our culture. If any lie is spoken often enough, soon individuals will begin to believe it. Ask Hitler, ask drumph.

I am an adjunct college professor. I teach radio, television, acting, voiceovers, (voice acting) and public speaking. One of the courses I have taught for more than twenty years is called Media Performance and Presentation.

One day one of my students gave the best speech they had ever given that semester. The speech was on race and race relations in America and my class was of very mixed-race. As she was returning to her seat, I asked her to go back to the front of the class. I then told the class to look at her, just look.

After several seconds of silence and everyone experiencing a level of discomfort, I asked the young speaker to raise her right hand high in the air. Then place that hand over her heart.

I reminded the class to please continue looking at her. I then asked the class what color was the sweat shirt. Everyone said, "black." I then asked the class what color was her hand. Many of the students said, "ooooohhh."

They realized that the speaker's sweat shirt was black but her hand was brown which made them realize the inconsistencies, lies and untruths that are so very much woven into the fabric of our language and culture.

They called us Colored, Negro, Black, and African American. Black people are not black. People of African Descent, (PAD) is a better, more accurate term. They are called White and Caucasian, but white people are not white, People of European Descent (PED), again, is a far more accurate definition.

Jane Elliot once said:

"I am not a white woman, I am a
faded black person. My people
moved far from the equator,
and that's the only reason my
skin is lighter. That's all any
'white' person is."

COLOR: AN ARTIST'S PERSPECTIVE.

I am really interested in the definition of color from the perspective of a professional artist, not our society's perspective or of that of a dictionary. But rather from the perspective of an individual who analyses, mixes, selects, and applies color to various surfaces for a living.

Color is her life. *She* is color*ful*. Gayle Gibbons Madeira is an internationally recognized multi-award-winning artist, a contemporary artist in the tradition of classical realism (www.gaylemadeira.com).

I had the fortunate opportunity to interview her by phone during the horrible COVID-19 Coronavirus pandemic in the summer of 2020.

Batt: My first question is: What is the name of the kind of art that you do?

Gayle: Well, it is realism. It's contemporary realism which would be defined differently from classical realism in a few ways. One is that we have different colors that we use-although my paintings are actually more similar to classical realism because I use the colors that they used back then.

The era of the 1600s, the time of Rembrandt, basically. I don't use modern pigments. So, I'm a weirdo...I'm very old fashioned, as you know.

Batt: The main thing I want you to talk about is color from the perspective of a professional artist. You and I have talked about the fact that black people are not really black and white people are not really white. I want to share some of our conversations with others. So, what is black and what is white?

Gayle: I'm sure everyone has seen those things online where there would be an object on the screen and the text would say something like: "Do you see grey and green in this sneaker, or do you see white and pink?"

And your answer would tell you something about yourself. And there was a big controversy as to what was what. Everyone was arguing. "No, it's grey! No, it's blue."

So, a lot of color, is in the beholder and it has to do with genetics and the fact that a lot of men are color blind to some degree or another. So, they often don't see red as other people. That's the most common problem color from what I remember. You know everybody is going to see your work differently.

It's very important to have really good structure in your values, the lights and darks and the composition because a lot of people see colors in different ways.

But in terms of color itself, like if we were to take somebody who was average, who doesn't have color-blindness of any type, who is average, the colors of everything depends on what they are next to when you are going to paint them.

So, if you were going to paint a very light skinned Caucasian person next to a very blue, royal blue background, you'd have to use a different choice of paint than you would if it were a black background, or a yellow background or a hot pink background. You would actually choose slightly different colors.

So, if you took the color Mars Brown for example, I'm staring at this painting I'm doing right now of an African American dude. He is a mid-orange. I add a lot of blue to knock down the chroma so it's not so bright but it still has depth.

There's a lot of purple in there. A lot of African American skin tones have a lot of purple in the turning to the shadow or often, it depends on what the person is around.

"White" people's skin from the Mediterranean, you would see hints of green often, more than purple. Someone with very thin, translucent white skin, really, really white skin from like Ireland or Norway would have some blue in the turning.

That's where you get into the interesting other colors that are in there. The base of all of them is just *orange*.

In general, what you start out with is a shade of orange. No matter what the person, no matter where they are from, except with two exceptions. On the very outside edges, or on the far edge with Caucasian skin there's something like a pink tone.

Like it's so light that it's translucent and you see more blues and more pinks. But you would actually still start with a very light orange and you would tint it with different colors.

And then on the other side of the spectrum you see darkest black skin, you can have a lot of blue in it. But again, it is still used as a base of orange. Everybody is orange.

Batt: I guess that pretty much sums it up! We are not black or white, we're orange. Hahahaha.

Gayle: Yea! We're orange! We're orange!

Gayle Gibbons Madeira's work has been exhibited at the MEAM Museum (Museu Europeu d'Art Modern), Sotheby's in Los Angeles, The National Arts Club, Salmagundi Club, Williamsburg Art and Historical Center, Principle Gallery, Abend Gallery, Foundation Gallery, and the New York Hall of Science, among others. Her paintings have appeared in various magazines, books, and films.

Ms. Madeira studied at SUNY Purchase in Purchase, New York, the Art Students League, Grand Central Academy, New York Academy of Art, and the School of Visual Arts.

Thank you, Gayle.

CHAPTER 7

The Un-Supreme White Supremacy

First, they're not white and they're not supreme. They are the majority, for now, the un-white-white. While having dinner with a non-African American friend, this subject came up.

I told him to lift his hand. I moved his napkin closer to him and then asked him to put his hand on the napkin. I asked him if his hand looked like the napkin. He said, "No, but that's semantics." I said, "No, that's the *truth*." Few people want to hear the truth.

Chris Rock once said, "In America, we're told to remember everything but slavery. Remember the Holocaust, remember 9/11, hell even remember the Alamo. But mention slavery, people lose their damn minds."

I am not an expert in social justice or social change. I studied sociology in college and earned a Bachelor's Degree in Social Theory, but I have never used any of what I studied in a professional context, or toward my Master's Degree.

My social comments contained within this manuscript are based on my experiences, observations and empirical knowledge, and not what I learned reading books by C. Wright Mills, Karl Marx, and Max Weber.

I did, however, read once that racism began with the ancient Greeks. But I believe the idea that most of us are most familiar with, is the separatism brought on by the Spanish Inquisition. This occurred in Spain and all of the Spanish colonies, territories, and possessions in North, Central, and South America around 1478.

They were murdering people who they believed to be of certain religious beliefs, but they could not tell what an individual's religion was by simply looking at them.

This is much the same situation that our U.S. Army, Navy, Air Force and Marines, found themselves in when we were involved in the Vietnam War. One could not tell the enemy Viet Cong from our allies, the Vietnamese. They looked the same because they *were* the same, but you could not tell what was in their minds and their hearts by looking at them.

Beautiful, innocent-looking Viet Cong children were placing bombs and hand grenades in the pockets of American GIs on seemingly safe streets and neighborhoods in South Vietnam. (These are not Viet Cong children. This is a stock photo)

The Viet Cong were highly armed, communist political revolutionaries in South Vietnam and Cambodia, our main enemies while we were in the Vietnam War.

Those in the Spanish Inquisition had to find another way to identify those they were going to kill, so they used skin color as the determinant.

Is there a Caucasian genetic predisposition or an unnatural propensity for violence? Let's ask Vladimir Putin.

Rain beats a leopard's skin, but it does not wash out the spots.

Ashanti proverb

How many international countries have the blacks of the world invaded, marauded, pillaged, raped, enslaved, and or destroyed, outside of the continent of Africa? There are about eight-hundred U.S. military bases in over seventy countries around the world, ready to fight. They are ready to fight anyone at any time.

As I mentioned earlier, Jane Elliott is an internationally recognized Caucasian American diversity educator and human rights activist. If you have never seen her speak, you should (YouTube).

She once said, *"...what we call education is actually indoctrination. It takes from the ages of five to the age of eighteen to thoroughly indoctrinate people so that they will believe in the myth of white superiority-and it is a myth."*

That is not all Jane Elliott had to say. This is her return email to me.

Dear Batt,

You absolutely have my permission to use that quote, because it is even more relevant, today, after four years of Trumpmania, than it was when it was first broadcast. There have also been studies done that prove that the longer we stay in school, the more bigoted we become, because every year we are reinforced in what we learned K-12.

The Columbus Myth is one of those that need to be expunged from our curricular materials, since Africans arrived on these shores from 10,000 to 20,000 years before Columbus was even a gleam in his father's eye. Think about what you've never been allowed to think about, and it will drive you batty, which, in view of what you're doing, and who you are, isn't a bad way to be, eh?

Happily,

Jane Elliott

This is my favorite Jane Elliott moment where she conducted a lecture in an auditorium filled, with what appeared to be, all young, "white" women.

Jane said, *"If you white folks want to be treated the way blacks are in this society, stand…(no one stood, raised their hand, or even moved.)*

You didn't understand the directions. If you white folks want to be treated the way blacks are in this society, stand…

Nobody's standing here.

That says, very plainly that you know what's happening, you know you don't want it for you.

I want to know why you're so willing to accept it or allow it to happen for others."

These words, and words like them, are *far* more powerful to the listener, viewer or reader when they are said by someone who is NOT black. You are less likely to think that they are simply attempting to advance their own agenda and the agenda of their people.

What is white supremacy? What makes a group of people supreme, superior? The Jews are God's chosen few, no? What does that mean? There are countless Jewish people walking around with this false sense of superiority granted to them by…God? Is this why white supremacists hate Jews? Don't they know that Jews are white people too? Well, except the Black Jews of Ethiopia, but you can bet they hate them too, of course, they are black AND Jewish. A double whammy, a double dose of hate coming their way.

The more one looks at this idea of racial superiority, the less sense it makes. White supremacists are operating on a weak, faulty platform of insecurity, lies, ignorance and stupidity. White supremacy is a state of mind, a concept, an idea, a myth. It is not real.

Just take a look at the jackasses who stormed, broke into, and raided the Capitol Building of the United States in Washington, D.C. on January 6th 2021. What is superior about these idiots? I guess they do have brains. They must, they have managed to live this long without walking in front of a speeding bus.

When I think of the words supreme and superior, no person or group of people come to mind. I see things like Mt. Fuji, the Grand Canyon, Mt. Kilimanjaro, the Pacific Ocean, the sun, an elephant, these things are superior.

These groups have an overinflated sense of self. Where did that come from?

I was in a taxi going to substitute teach a theatre class in 2013 or 2014 at Westchester Community College, and the driver was listening to sports talk radio. One of the guests was basketball legend, Charles Barkley.

Charles said, "One of the greatest racial levelers is sports. Sports teaches you teamwork, sportsmanship, and how to be humble. In sports you *have* to learn to play together, you *have* to get along, otherwise, you won't have a team and you're going to *lose*. Losing is not something an athlete is interested in.

Question: How can an individual or group of individuals, hate another individual or group of individuals who have done nothing against them, their families or humanity? What has the black man done to make so many people so angry with us? I am waiting for an answer to that question.

Try to draw a logical through line between hating someone because they murdered your mother or father and hating someone because they do not look like you.

The racial dynamic in America is so illogical, so upside down, so wrong, that I have never been able to lower myself, lower my standards to conform to these trite American norms.

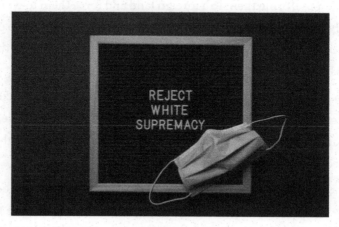

The hate of white supremacists comes from a desire to control something that does not belong to them, including the life of people who don't look like them.

They want to be the leader, the king without having the bloodline or the crown. This idea, along with so many others is insanely illogical.

"There is no vaccine for racism."
Vice President Kamala Devi Harris, Wednesday, August 19th 2020.

In 1690, Connecticut had a law that forbade red or black people from walking beyond the town's limits without a pass. Wait a minute! Who are YOU to tell the people whose land you are walking upon, whose land you stole through violent murder and genocide, that they cannot walk on the land, their own land, the land that is rightfully theirs, any time they wish? It belongs to them.

Compare that to someone saying that you cannot breathe with your own lungs anytime you want without having OUR permission. Screw YOU! Even the name Connecticut is Native American. It comes from the Algonquian word "quinnehtukqut" which means "beside the long tidal river."

How arrogant can a group of people be? Who are YOU to kidnap a group of people, bring them to a foreign land and force them to work under extremely harsh conditions created by them, the oppressor, for no pay, feed them poor food, some of it rotten and inedible, and strip them of their dignity? WHO DO YOU THINK YOU ARE?

To this day, many African Americans only eat well-cooked food because of the stories from our ancestors being fed rotten, inedible, subhuman scraps the slave owners called food, getting them sick and they were still forced to go out in the fields and work.

The slaves had to over-cook their food to kill the bacteria so they could stay alive. The slave owners didn't want the slaves to die, because that was their source of income, but they always had to show the slaves who was boss.

European Americans do NOT like to hear these stories. I understand that. But they are all true.

The slave owners, white nationalists and white supremacists operate under the flag of fear by intimidation. The Ku Klux Klan tried to look like ghosts to scare the black population because they thought they were afraid of ghosts. They even put hoods on their horses.

Get out of here or we'll kill you.

Get out of here or we'll burn down your house.

Get out in that field and work or I'll beat you.

Get out in that field and work or I'll kill you.

Get out in that field or I'll kill your wife, that is, after I rape her right in front of you.

If the framers of the Constitution, past Presidents, and creators of our great nation, as we know it, were so intelligent and noble, how could they think that *owning* people and forcing them to work for free was a good, fair and equitable idea? How?

Many Americans of European descent think they can do *anything* and get away with it.

That is the thinking of the individuals involved in the insurrection on the Capitol Building on January 6, 2021. They are no different from any other group of people in that they do *not* want to hear of, or admit to, any wrong doing by anyone in their group, especially when it comes to racism.

They do *not* want to admit that they are descendants of murderers, rapists, and spreaders of disease. Even when they are doing it in front of the world. We are not stupid! We hear, we cogitate, we react, we attempt to resolve; resolve for the greater good of humanity.

I remember Friday, November 22, 1963, when John Fitzgerald Kennedy, the 35th President was assassinated. I was a student at Abraham Lincoln High School in San Diego, going from my math class to my social studies class when a passing student told me the unbelievably bad news. I was too young to understand the gravity of this situation but I knew it was bad.

I remember, so vividly, my very first thought was, *"Oh, my God, I hope it was not a black person who did it!!!"* That was my VERY first thought. When the social studies class started, the only thing we talked about for the entire class was the assassination of President John F. Kennedy, of course.

Since white supremacy is so ingrained within the fabric of this society, it comes as no surprise to have the ultimate being of supremacy, God, look like the general, Caucasian society. Has anyone ever seen God?

In the Bible in Genesis 1:27, it says: "God created man in his own image."

Then they turned that around by creating God in the image of man and installed a blond haired, blue eyed man as the representative icon of God.

Famous American boxer, humanitarian, and activist, Muhammad Ali (1942–2016), once said: I used to ask my mother, how come everything is white? Why is Jesus white with blond hair and blue eyes? Why is the Lord's Supper all white men? Even the Angels are white.

Mary had a little lamb, fleece was white as snow. Snow White and Santa Claus was white, and everything bad was black. The little ugly duckling was a black duck and the black cat gave you bad luck, and if I threatened you I blackmailed you.

So, I said, mama why do they call it black male, white males they lie too? The angel food cake was the white cake and the devil's food cake was the chocolate cake.

I always wondered why is Tarzan the king of the jungle in Africa, and he was white. I saw this white man swinging around Africa with a diaper on, hollering, beating on his chest. So, Tarzan is beating up all the Africans and breaking the lion's jaw. And he could talk to the animals. The Africans been there for centuries and they couldn't talk to the animals, but he came along and all of a sudden, he could talk to the animals.

I always wondered why Miss America was always white. Mr. World was always white. Miss Universe was always white. The President lives in the White House. Then they got some stuff called White Horse cigars, White

Swan soap, King White soap, White Cloud tissue paper, White Rain hair rinse, White Tornado floor Wax, everything was white.

I went downtown to a restaurant after I won a Gold Medal in the Olympics. Things were segregated then and black boys couldn't eat downtown at this time. So, I went in, sat down and ordered a cup of coffee and a hot dog. The lady said, "We don't serve Negroes." I got so mad, I said "I don't eat 'em either. Just give me a cup of coffee and a hot dog!"

America, a lie!

There are enumerable photographs, drawings, paintings, sketches, lithographs, and etchings of the baby Jesus looking like the Gerber Baby Food baby. Jesus did not look like the Gerber Baby Food baby, at least not according to the Bible.

THE BIBLE, REVELATION 1:12-18

Then I turned to see the voice that was speaking to me, and on turning I saw seven golden lampstands, and in the midst of the lampstands one like a son of man, clothed with a long robe and with a golden sash around his chest.

The hairs of his head were white, like white wool, like snow. His eyes were like a flame of fire, *his feet were like burnished bronze, refined in a furnace,* and his voice was like the roar of many waters.

Wait a minute!! That sounds like someone who has a LOT of black blood in them, but I speculate. Forgive me, for I find this concept very interesting. My church going, God fearing, God believing mother, never told me about THIS! We all have to remember that many, many black folks were afraid to speak their truth, or speak of any belief for fear of extreme, brutal retaliation from "the white man."

Retaliation such as killing the Africans, burning down their homes and raping their wives and children…maybe even raping the husband as well. I don't have any research to back up that statement, but it would not surprise me if homosexual acts did occur by those savages.

This is real American history whether you know it, believe it, acknowledge it, like it, or not. Right-wing domestic terrorists are terrorists…period. I have read where al-Qaeda and the Islamic State refer to themselves as the "Army of God," created to *kill* in the name of God. That's just crazy talk.

Sociologist Stephen Klineberg of Rice University in Houston, Texas, once stated that U.S. immigration laws prior to 1965 clearly declared that "Northern Europeans are a superior subspecies of the white race."

Please do not forget who is writing the history and who is doing the research. This is white people fighting white people for the role of the "ultimate superior white group of people." How is superiority proven? What is the test? Who created the test?

When speaking of the Black Lives Matter movement, someone will inevitably say, "all lives matter," or "white lives matter," or "all lives matter" or some derivative thereof. This is just another example of the colorless society trying to discredit, minimize, diminish, deny, and steal from the African American community, again.

This is an attempt to cover up all of the ill deeds perpetuated upon the black community by the invading Europeans. I believe that most people in our society, black, white, red, yellow, and brown, are racist but they do not know it or act upon it.

When I was married, we often had dinner parties. Lisa was a fantastic cook and loved doing it. The dinner conversation would often steer toward background, race, and genetic origin. Not once did the conversation come to me with questions of my genetic lineage. Not once!

I would think that since I was the only African American in the room, hearing my input would be interesting to them. I was always the one individual at my dinner table who had more *American* blood than anyone because of the Native American genes of my grandmother. I find this lack of exchange to be rude and fueled with basic ignorance, and an unwitting air of white supremacy.

I am NOT saying that these individuals were white supremacists by any stretch of the imagination. But I will say that they have been damaged by the outlook of our society on race in America.

I learned, as an actor, when auditioning, that I had to *ask* the casting director what kind of character I was auditioning for. Was the character the mayor of a city? Was he a street thug? Was he a regular Joe? Was he a black All-American kind of guy? Was he a college graduate? I had to know in order to bring to the character what they were possibly looking for.

The "white" casting directors all seemed afraid to offer that kind of information to me up front. They were afraid to mention anything about race or class, just like all of the Caucasians at my dinner table. This is because we have all been brainwashed to believe that "white," Caucasian is first and anything after that does not really exist or matter.

I believe Jessie Owens wanted to display his African American superiority as a track star who won four Gold Medals in the 1936 Summer Olympics in Berlin. He was competing against many German athletes as Adolph Hitler watched in the stands in disgust as the superiority of the black athlete was evident to all who watched (https://www.youtube.com/watch?v=jB0n35UIv-s).

In a separate display of black supremacy, Jessie Owens ran against a race horse, and beat it (https://www.youtube.com/watch?v=IlfCLnxtew8). White supremacy? Ask Michael Jordan, Magic Johnson or Muhammad Ali about "superiority." LeBron James, professional basketball player and multi-championship title holder once said, "We're built differently." I wonder exactly what he meant by that?

If white supremacists are supreme, are superior, why do they commit such atrocities against humanity? Killing countless millions of individuals does NOT make you superior. It makes you a murderer, a thief of life, taking something that does not belong to you. If they were superior wouldn't they be working to *build* our species? Their supremacy is superior in numbers only…for now.

The U. S. Census population estimates as of July 1, 2019, show the white population to be 76.3%, Latins at 18.5%, and the black population at 13.4%. All of these numbers are changing and the U.S. "white" population is expected to no longer be the majority in the year 2045, decreasing to around 49.7%.

These statistics can make many in the American Caucasian population very uncomfortable. Could those statistics be attributable to the rise in white nationalism and white supremacist groups in America?

The complexion of the American societal landscape is morphing, quickly, as we see more and more people of measured color quotient come into power in significant positions in our "fair" halls of American government.

I know the founding fathers never thought that there would be so many people of high melanin content in such high positions in government across our land. A black President, a black Vice President? But wait, this is not the end.

In the end, it is not about the shade, tone or tint of your skin, but rather your willingness to advance the general human agenda. I don't care if you are a Republican, Independent, Democrat, or wear a pink tie on Wednesdays. I just want to leave this world in a better place than it was in when my great grandmother and great grandfather were here. There is no adversity in diversity.

THE BLONDE MYTH

You know, blonde hair is considered a mark of beauty in many cultures around the world and the U.S. is no exception. It is also considered a sign of superiority.

Why do brunettes' dye or color their hair blonde? I have heard from many of my close "white" friends that blonde hair makes you look more "pure," whiter. As an actor, I used to hear a lot about blonde hair making one look less ethnic, more "All-American," as a "type," therefore more marketable. Sounds like Hitler to me.

These days black people, women and men, are dying their hair blond. You even see an occasional Asian with blond hair.

I think they do it as a fashion statement, rather than an attempt to completely fool you into thinking that they are a biological, and not a bottle blonde.

But why? Often the individual, usually a female, was blonde in her youth and she wants to maintain that hair color. But the dark line down the middle of the scalp is not so attractive. Is it the reverse skunk look? Is that a thing? Do your roots, girl!

Why do women newscasters' dye or color their hair blonde? When I was doing more television, one of my anchor newscaster friends tried to convince me that she went blonde because when the television studio lights are on, her blonde hair reflects the light better, thereby creating a brighter, more pleasing picture for the viewer. I told her that was bullshit.

Why does Donald Trump's hair appear gray, white, blond? Why does he dye his hair blond? Why does he suntan? If he is white, and white is right and superior, why is he trying to get black, brown, chocolate, caramel like the people he hates? Throw away your tanning bed.

I have applied many years of thought, research, and listening to my Caucasian friends to arrive at these findings.

The American culture is no different from any other culture when it comes to myths and stereotypes. We generally have two types of images for the blonde female. We have the dumb blonde and we have the sexy bombshell but we do not have a standard image of the blonde intellectual, the blonde mother, yes, but not the blonde intellectual, unless she has glasses. Isn't this all sounding rather silly? But it is all true, whether you believe it or not.

The image of the dumb blonde applies to men as well, like the dumb surfer dude and the dumb, athletic jock. Hey, dude!

In the movies, the blonde bombshell is more common than the dumb, ditsy blonde. Marilyn Monroe, Mae West, Brigitte Bardot, Mamie Van Doren, and Jayne Mansfield brought the sexy blonde image to the forefront in the 1950s and 60s American cinema, and that image has not left our consciousness.

Actor Reese Witherspoon starred in the 2001 film, *Legally Blonde*. She played a Harvard Law School student who was blonde, beautiful, and the opposite of dumb.

Country music superstar, singer, songwriter, businesswoman, Dolly Parton said it best when she said, "I'm not offended by all the dumb-blonde jokes because I *know* I'm not dumb. I'm also not blonde.

I remember greeting someone on the street whom I had recently met at his place of employment in a local coffee shop. I said, "Hey, how are you?" He said, "I'm good, I'm good. I mean, I'm tall, I'm white, I'm blond, I'm a male…I have privilege. What more do I need?" I thought, he really believes that. If he has privilege why is he working for minimum wage in a subterranean start-up coffee shop in a lower middle-class neighborhood that is not quite developed? What the hell are you talking about?

If all he has going for him is being born "male, tall, blond, and white," I think he is a loser. If because of that he thinks he has it made, in my eyes, he is a loser. He is of no use to the advancement of this country or the world. He is a narcissistic, brain washed, societal impediment and a buffoon.

I had a co-worker once say to me, "As long as I have blonde hair and blue eyes, I have the boss wrapped around my little finger." What a pitiful thing to say, think, and actually be.

When one does not have "white privilege" and continue to fight the oppressor, one gains strength, savvy, knowledge, awareness, understanding, and uncanny insight that others do not possess. I can see it as plain as day.

If Caucasians are the superior "race" why did they go to Africa to kill, kidnap and enslave the people who lived there? That sounds like a group of murders to me. Don't we have a place for people like that? Let's start with Sing Sing, Alcatraz or Rikers Island. A "superior" people would never do something like that, if they are truly superior.

If Caucasians are superior, why didn't the slave traders use Caucasians to work in the fields from sun up to sun down? If Caucasians are superior, why do they need sun block to shield them from God's greatest resource, the sun?

Let me get on the other side for a moment. Let's say I am a greedy, wealthy European who wants MORE. What do I do? I want to discover, conquer, and steal (they would never use the word steal, but that is what it is) new land to expand my empire. Remember what President Vladimir Putin of Russia did to Ukraine.

I need help. What do I do? Go to China and kidnap some people to work for free? Go to Sweden and kidnap some people to work for free? Go to Japan and kidnap some people to work for free? Go to South America, Germany, Australia, Bolivia, Antarctica, Canada, France, Israel to get some people to work for free?

The European oppressors tried enslaving the Native Americans but they would escape and since the Native Americans knew the land so very well, the invading Europeans could not find them to recapture them. Africans did not know the land, landscape, or the language of their captors or the language of each other because they were separated from their tribe before being loaded onto the slave ships.

The slave traders of Portugal decided to go to Africa to get people they believed were "superior" in many ways. Strong, intelligent, good bones, good teeth, good genes, and passive. Only these people, of all the peoples of the world, could work from sunup to sunset, be fed lousy food, some of it rotten, sustain daily beatings and whippings and still survive and work hard daily. Of all the peoples of the world, only the Africans could sustain such prolonged maltreatment.

We cannot choose our parents or do anything about being born into privilege but we can choose what we do with the privilege we have been given. I once read that in twenty-five years "white people" will be a numerical minority in the United States. That is one of the factors driving the fear and overt racism of the far right today, that and the fact that the president elected in 2016 foments racist, immoral behavior.

Think about this for a second. How do you think it would feel to live in a "free" society when the president wants to kill you and anyone who looks like you, because you don't look like him?

I wonder if the tide will turn one day and those targeted for oppression will *not* be those of darker skin tone but those who wear darker shoes or those who have a dog with brown furry feet or even left-handed individuals. It is all pretty silly, isn't it?

As a man of major color in America, I used to think that when I heard a person of no color with a southern accent, that he was automatically a "red neck nigger hater." But I realize that is like saying all people of major melanin content are criminals, can sing, dance, play basketball and are well endowed. Good night.

CHAPTER 8

Black Bodies-Black Brains: Part 1

A FEW SIGNIFICANT AFRICAN AMERICAN INVENTORS

African Americans have made massive contributions to our country and to civilization. But the way our education system, system of government and society are designed and operate, many of the contributions by African Americans are hidden.

European Americans fear the African American, they fear our strength in all of its forms. This is going to sound racist and stereotypical but, can you imagine a world without athletes of African lineage? I wonder if the game would be as boring as I am imagining. Oops, now *that's* racist.

"Almost always, the creative dedicated minority has made the world better."
-Dr. Martin Luther King, Jr.

"Bear" Bryant was the head coach of the University of Alabama football team for twenty-five years. During this time, he won six national championships and thirteen conference championships. He is often considered the greatest college football coach of all time. But he wasn't always such a winner.

One day, someone asked him, "Why don't you ever have any black players on your teams?" Coach Bryant said, "I'll be dead in mah grave 'fore I git a nigger." For some reason, one day he started using some African American players. He was then asked, "What happened? Why do you have African Americans on your team?" He said, "Well, I wonted ta win."

The power of black.

Can you imagine music without the influence of Africa? By listening to the jazz of Charlie Parker, Dizzy Gillespie, John Coltrane and Miles Davis, you can hear the high intellect of the African American musician.

While on these shores, African Americans are constantly creating new, different and exciting music forms such as rhythm & blues, better known as R&B, rock and roll, reggae, ska, calypso, rap/hip-hop, spirituals, ragtime, gospel, blues, doo-wop, soul, boogie-woogie, disco, and others.

African Americans have made contributions to the world in areas other than sports and music.

There have been many more inventions by individuals of African descent than are listed here. Many of them had their inventions either stolen by the white society or the creator was not given a patent because they were African American.

If you are white, how does this make you feel about having the blood of such cruel, inhumane, and dishonest individuals, racing through your veins? I often wonder how powerful our nation could be if we treated all of our men and women with fairness, honesty and encouragement.

SOME BLACK BRAINS THAT WE DON'T GIVE ENOUGH CREDIT TO

Alexander Miles (May 18, 1838–October 11, 1887). He was awarded U.S. Patent #371,207 for automatically opening and closing elevator doors.

Garrett Morgan (1877–1963) He patented several inventions, including the traffic signal and the first automatic three-way traffic signal system, which he eventually sold to General Electric. He also made tremendous improvements on the sewing machine, invented a hair-straightening product, and a respiratory device that would later provide the blueprint for the WWI gas mask.

Philip B. Downing (1857–1934). Mr. Downing was an African American man who received a patent for his invention, the modern-day mail box.

Madam C.J. Walker (1867–1919) She created specialized hair products for African American hair care and was one of the first American women, not black woman, American women to become a self-made millionaire.

George Washington Carver (1864–1943) Contrary to popular belief, George Washington Carver did not invent peanut butter, but discovered over three-hundred uses for peanuts including chili sauce, shampoo, shaving cream and glue.

Lewis Howard Latimer (September 4, 1848–December 11, 1928) An American inventor and patent draftsman for the patents of the light bulb and telephone. He improved Thomas Edison's original invention by patenting the use of a carbon filament which made possible the widespread use of electric light in public and at home.

Marie Van Brittan Brown (1922–February 2, 1999) She was the inventor of the home security system in 1966, along with her husband Albert Brown. In the same year they jointly applied for a patent, granted in 1969.

Patricia Era Bath (November 4, 1942–May 30, 2019) An American ophthalmologist, inventor, humanitarian, and academic. She was an early pioneer of laser cataract surgery.

Otis Frank Boykin (August 29, 1920–March 13, 1982). His inventions include improved electrical resistors used in computing, missile guidance, and pacemakers.

Sarah Boone (February 1832–1904). On April 26,1892, she obtained United States patent rights for her improvements to the ironing board. Boone's ironing board was designed to improve the quality of ironing sleeves and the bodies of women's garments. The board was very narrow, curved, and made of wood.

Thomas L. Jennings (1791–February 12, 1856). In 1821 he was one of the first African Americans to be granted a patent for his method of dry cleaning.

Jan Ernst Matzeliger (September 15, 1852–August 24, 1889. He invented a lasting machine that brought significant change to the manufacturing of shoes.

Benjamin Banneker (November 9, 1731–October 19, 1806) was an almanac author, surveyor, landowner and farmer who was part of a group that surveyed the original borders of Washington, D.C.

Norbert Rillieux (March 17, 1806–October 8, 1894. Mr. Rillieux was an American-French inventor who was widely considered one of the earliest chemical engineers and noted for his pioneering invention of the multiple-effect evaporator. This invention was an important development in the growth of the sugar.

Sarah E. Goode (1850–1905). She was born a slave but became an inventor and entrepreneur. She was the first African American woman to be granted a patent in 1885 by the U.S. Patent and Trademark Office, for her invention of a folding cabinet bed.

Alfred L. Cralle (September 4, 1866–May 3, 1920) was an African American businessman and inventor of the ice cream mold and disher. He was awarded patent 576,395 on 2 February 1897.

Percy Lavon Julian (April 11, 1899–April 19, 1975) was an American research chemist. His work laid the foundation for the steroid drug industry's production of cortisone and birth control pills.

Samuel Raymond Scottron (1843–1905), an inventor, best known for his invention of the curtain rod.

Lyda D. Newman (1885–April 18,1820). She was a patented African American inventor and involved activist for women's suffrage. She is known for the invention of a durable hair brush that could be taken apart for cleaning.

Robert F. Flemming, Jr. (July 1839–February 23, 1919). Mr. Flemming invented a guitar he called the "Euphonica" that he believed would produce a louder and more resonant sound than a traditional guitar. The U.S. Patent Office granted his patent (no. 338,727) on March 30, 1886. He also received a Canadian patent.

Richard Bowie Spikes (October 2, 1878–January 22, 1963) He invented the beer tap, automobile directional signals, the automatic gear shift device for automobiles and other motor vehicles and a safety braking system for trucks and buses.

Lewis Temple was born in Richmond, Virginia (1, October 1800–5 May 1854). An American "negro whalecraft maker," blacksmith, abolitionist, and inventor. He invented a harpoon that greatly improved the success rate of the American hunt.

Leonard C. Bailey (1825–September 1, 1918) He invented and received patents for a series of devices, including a folding bed, a rapid mail-stamping machine, a device to shunt trains to different tracks, and a hernia truss adopted into wide use by the U.S. military. Bailey had to escape from a military camp after there was an attempt to capture him as a slave while he was dropping off his inventions.

Ellen Eglin (1849–after 1890). She invented a clothes wringer for washing machines that is still used today, but for mops.

Bessie Blount (1914–2009) was a physical therapist who worked with injured soldiers during World War II. She recognized their need and desire to do more on their own, so she invented an assistive device that permitted people who had lost limbs to feed themselves.

David N. Crosthwait Jr. (May 27, 1898–February 25, 1976) His expertise was in air ventilation, central air conditioning, and heat transfer systems. He was responsible for creating heating systems for larger buildings such as Rockefeller Center and Radio City Music Hall, both in New York City.

Mary Beatrice Davidson Kenner (May 17, 1912–January 13, 2006) This African American inventor was most noted for her development of the sanitary belt. Racial discrimination prevented its adoption for thirty years. She invented an adjustable sanitary belt with a built-in, moisture-proof napkin pocket. In 1956, she was finally able to save up enough money to get her first patent on it. However, the company that first showed interest in her invention, the Sonn-Nap-Pack Company, rejected it after they discovered that she was African American.

More information on this subject may be found in the book, *"Black People Invented Everything"* by Dr. Sujan Kumar Dass. In it, he talks about the deep history of *"indigenous creativity"* possessed by those of African descent.

HIDDEN FIGURES

Katherine Goble Johnson (August 26, 1918-February 24, 2020. NASA mathematician and human computer.

Dorothy Vaughan (September 20, 1910 – November 10, 2008) NASA mathematician and human computer.

Mary Jackson; (April 9, 1921– February 11, 2005) NASA aerospace engineer and mathematician.

These three African American women conducted extremely complicated mathematical computations for NASA, thereby making massive contributions to the American/Soviet Union space race.

Without the use of computers, they found flaws in the computations of the new, at the time, high-tech IBM 7090 computer, purchased to possibly replace them.

These women calculated trajectories, ideal launch times, emergency return paths for Earth orbits, the Apollo 11 launch that first landed humans on the Moon, the Space Shuttle program, and plans for a mission to Mars.

Their work helped launch astronaut, John Glenn, the first American to orbit Earth three times,

Alan Shepard, the first American in space, Commander Neil Armstrong, the first to walk on the moon, and lunar module pilot Buzz Aldrin, the second person to walk on the Moon.

In spite of these women's amazing contributions to American society and culture, their contributions to the U.S. space race, had gone unrecognized and hidden because they were African American. They were forced to work in a unit segregated by race and gender, and forced to walk half a mile to use the nearest bathroom assigned to "Colored" people. This is in the "United" States of America.

In 2016 there was a movie, *Hidden Figures*, released about these three African American math geniuses. It was a commercial success, grossing $236 million worldwide, one of the most profitable of 2016. It was nominated for an Academy Award, won a Screen Actors Guild Award, and many other awards since.

Black Bodies, Black Brains

MY CHILDHOOD INVENTIVE MIND

I have never worked in an office, or held any traditional job. I have always used my creative gifts to feed myself, pay my rent, and pay my mortgages. Not too bad, so far!

As a child, I was very curious, a dreamer, creative and inventive. I always looked at what was there and said, "Now what?" When I saw something that didn't work well the way it was designed, created or manufactured, my brain would automatically figure out a better way to do it, make it, or us it in a different way.

I used this skill often on film and television commercial sets. I could often spot problems and figure out a solution when the director could not. Sometimes I shared my insight, usually I did not. Film directors often have very big egos and do not want to hear another opinion when he or she may be stuck...especially from an actor. Keep your mouth shut and act!

I understand that. The director has an extremely difficult job. First, a sheet of paper or a computer screen filled with words is not very interesting to look at.

A series of visual scenes without sound, speaking, and or music, is also not very interesting.

What the director has to do is take a script and a storyboard (drawings) and make it come to LIFE! If you have the right cast, it is easy. If you don't, well . . .

As a child of about nine or ten years of age, I was in love with cars. That is not unusual for a Southern California kid in the late '50s and '60s. I loved modified hot rods. I used to buy all of the hot rod magazines and read them from cover to cover several times over before the next issue was published.

I had pictures of hot rods on my walls. Of course, I had surfing pictures too. I always wanted to own a 1929 Tall "T" Ford or a 1934 Ford (with suicide doors where the front door opens from the front), four door sedan with a Corvette engine, duel quads (two four-barrel carburetors) and Racemaster slicks as the rear tires.

The following is a series of thoughts/ideas/inventions/creations that I had, I drew them up but only a few were actually created.

SOME OF MY CHILDHOOD INVENTIONS:

Outside rearview mirror for night vision.

Let's say you are driving down a dark, country road and there are no street lights. What do you do? You turn on your high beams or your bright lights so you can see better, correct? Then another vehicle appears behind you. Obviously, they have their high beams on as well. Their bright lights are now reflecting into your eyes through your rearview mirror. What do you do? You adjust the rearview mirror to the "night vision" setting, right? This is like sunglasses for your mirror so the bright lights behind you don't impede your vision.

But, what about the outside rearview mirror? The bright lights are still shining in your eyes from that mirror. Why don't they have a night vision setting for that mirror. Well, twenty or twenty-five years later, I saw that Mercedes invented one for their cars.

Headlight wipers.

I remember sometimes after a rain (which didn't happen very often in Southern California), my dad used to clean his headlights because the cars in front of him would kick up the rain and dirt onto our car. When your headlights are dirty the beam does not go as far and I suppose it could even be dangerous.

So, my nine or ten-year old brain devised windshield wipers for your headlights. Guess what happened? Yep, many, many years later Mercedes came out with windshield wipers for their headlights.

Rear window wipers.

I came up with the same thing for the rear window of a car but I don't think Mercedes was the first to use that idea.

Lateral car parking.

When learning to drive an automobile, often the most challenging thing to do is parallel park. I takes a lot of practice but I must admit that is easier than parking a tractor trailer or a car with a trailer or a boat behind it. You have to turn the steering wheel in the opposite direction to get the trailer to go in the opposite direction…or is it the same direction…I forget, it's so confusing.

Why don't they have a locking/unlocking mechanism on the axle of the car that would allow the wheels to go left and right as well as forward and backward? Then all you have to do is drive up to the space, unlock the wheels and drive the car left or right, right into the parking space.

Yep, many years later, the Japanese created such a mechanism, later an American manufacturer created one but I'm not sure if it is in production.

Rear mounted car engine.

I am not an engineer. I was just a child with an overactive imagination. One day, as I was daydreaming or night dreaming lying on my bed before sleep hit, I had a thought. I wondered if by putting the engine in the rear of the car, you could get more horse power to the rear wheels. This would eliminate the driveshaft. You might have to reconfigure the issue of the transmission.

Well, one day while walking around the streets of Tokyo and Kyoto, Japan, I saw my first Honda. I didn't know that they were going to revolutionize the automobile industry many decades later. This was between 1966 and 1968. It was a small, two-seat, soft top convertible with what appeared to be a rear-engine mounted, chain driven car. On this trip, I saw many of them. I thought, "Why didn't I think of that?" Oh, I did, but it is too late.

Wheeled battery cart.

When I was in elementary, junior high, and high school, I worked at my dad's gas station on the corner of 16th Street and National Avenue to get money to buy my school clothes for the next year. My dad only paid me a dollar a day, but I was a kid. I didn't really need money, but as I grew older, he eventually gave me more money.

I guess the car batteries in those days were not very good because someone's would often go dead and we would provide them with a jumper battery. Car batteries are heavy, very heavy because they have many lead plates inside. We had to carry them to the location, or to our car to drive to the location of the customer's dead battery.

These batteries had muriatic acid or hydrochloric acid inside and sometimes there would be some on the top or the sides of the battery. When you carry it, you would often get some of it on your clothes. After you wash the clothes there would be holes where the acid was. We lost a lot of pants and shirts.

I created a wheeled cart from scraps I found lying around. You just put the battery on the cart and push or pull it to your destination. From then on, my father and I saved a lot of money on work clothes. My dad loved that little red cart that I made. It was highly functional.

Automatic car brakes.

You're driving down the street and a child darts out between two parked cars chasing a ball. You immediately put on the brakes. But that takes time. In a situation such as this, a milli-second is very important.

My idea for this could save lives. It is a device that automatically applies "some" pressure to the brakes as soon as you take your foot off of the gas pedal, thereby slowing down your car immediately. Yes, I do see television commercials advertising something very similar to this over fifty years later. The 2022 Nissan Sentra and the 2022 Subaru Forester now have an automatic braking system built into their automobiles. What took them so long?

Parachute for airplanes.

They say, "You are safer in an airplane than you are in a car." But, if your car runs out of gas or the engine stops for some unknown reason, you won't automatically die. As a child, I was always deeply saddened and perplexed whenever a jet airliner went down and hundreds of people perished. Does that have to be?

Here goes another idea from a ten-year old. What if you rigged a parachute to the top of the plane? Then attached a giant balloon to the bottom of the plane that could only inflate half way. Both would be deployed by the pilot. If the airplane loses power, the pilot can deploy the parachute, which would slow the descent of the plane. The giant, half inflated balloon would act as a cushion when the aircraft reached earth. Makes sense to me.

Well, many years later as I was browsing the magazine section at a drug store, I picked up a Popular Mechanic magazine, which I read regularly. On the cover was…you guessed it, a small, single engine airplane, descending with a parachute attached to it.

SOME OF MY INVENTIONS AS AN ADULT:

A rear mounted car horn.

I came to New York City in the summer of 1977, right after serial killer, Son of Sam was terrorizing neighborhoods with his .44 caliber hand gun and murdering people. This was also the summer of the massive blackout on July 13–14, 1977 and the bombing of One Police Plaza, two Federal office buildings, and the Federal Courthouse in Brooklyn during a 90-minute period. These bombings were being performed by the F.A.L.N. (Fuerzas Armadas de Liberación Nacional or Armed Forces of National Liberation). This was a Puerto Rican liberation terrorist organization. Bad times in New York City, but I didn't know. I thought it was always like that. I had just moved here.

New York is a very different kind of beast. It is a City with a very different culture from any other. We do many things differently here. We stand in the street to cross the street. In other cities you stand on the sidewalk. It wastes too much time.

In New York, you stand in the street. One day, I was standing about one or two steps off the curb, waiting for the light to change so I could cross. In the distance I heard a car horn. In New York you hear a thousand car horns a day, no big deal. I happened to glance to my right and I saw a car backing up, almost hitting me. Obviously, I immediately jumped out of the way.

That car horn I heard a few seconds before, was this car's horn. The problem was that his horn was located in the FRONT. I was in the BACK, so the horn was a soft, faint sound as if it were a half a block or more away.

Ah, ha! Another idea, put a horn in the back of the car, van, truck or bus. Here we go again. A few years later, trucks emitted a beep, beep, beep sound when they backed up. Now, they all have it. Stop stealing my ideas!

Guitar stand.

When I was working on the radio in Kansas City, Missouri, I started playing guitar. I saw it as a way of getting the music that was in my head, into the ears of other people.

One night I went to a music club with friends. The guitar player played an electric guitar, a mandolin, a dobro, which is an acoustic a guitar with a metal face and several small sound holes. After playing each instrument, he would unstrap it, return it to the stand, pick up the next instrument, strap it on and began to play.

Later that night, I thought wouldn't it be great if a multi-instrumentalist like this, had his instruments on stands facing the audience.

All he would have to do is simply walk up to the instrument and start playing it. No unstrapping or re-strapping. So, I started designing it as a basket type device that the body of the guitar would sit in. There would be an arm extended to hold the neck of the guitar and it would be mounted on a microphone type stand that telescoped up and down to accommodate the height of the musician. I'm thinking, "brilliant!"

I had been in New York for a short period of time.

I went to the Bottom Line one night after I interviewed Pat Metheny on the radio earlier that day. He is a professional jazz guitar player, nice guy, loves his instrument. The Bottom Line was a professional music industry showcase club. Only the best of the best could play there.

Jazz guitarist Pat Metheny (L) before a show in New Jersey with Batt Johnson (R) as MC and host of the show (1980).

The coat check was straight ahead and the stage was to the right of that. I walked in, waved hello to some friends who were seated on the right. As I turned to go to the coat check, guess what I saw standing in the center of the stage. Yep, my guitar stand/holder idea. The difference was Pat's holder was a vice grip and you could see that once someone tightened it a little too tight because there was a tiny crack on the face of his acoustic guitar.

Later that night it was abundantly clear to me that there was no such thing as an original idea. After the show I told Pat about my idea. He laughed and said, "Yeah, I know. I stole that idea from one of your dreams one night in Kansas City." We both laughed because Pat Metheny is from Kansas City, Missouri and I moved to New York from Kansas City.

A multi-guitar carrying case on wheels.

Sometimes roadies (the people who carry the musician's instruments and sets them up on stage when they are on the road on tour) have horrible, backbreaking jobs. Especially when the band has a lot of equipment. One night I saw a roadie carrying six or seven guitars. It looked heavy, uncomfortable, awkward, and I'm sure his fingers didn't appreciate it.

Ping!

I had an idea, as I often do. It would be a piece of "luggage" made out of the thin, black material that drum transport cases are made of. It is light but strong. It would be cut at an angle (slight triangle) so the guitars would be easy to remove. The mobile guitar kit, the entire thing, would be placed on casters so the roadie could wheel it around instead of physically lugging six or seven guitars at a time by hand, no?

Ceiling mounted carrying straps for a standup acoustic bass in a van.

I used to manage my brother-in-law's jazz band called, "So What." Actually, I was more of a booking agent. The four of them were friends from Columbia University, all of them were named Steve, except Rob, my brother-in-law.

Steve Shebar on drums, Steve Bargonetti on guitar, Steve Skinner on keyboard, and Rob Aldisert on bass. The band would always rent a van when they had gigs to transport the equipment. When Rob brought his big, standup acoustic, double bass, there was a lot less room in the van for people. So, I created a device that basically consisted of bungee cords to strap the bass to the ceiling, leaving more room on the bottom for they guys.

Sounds like a good idea, right? Well, this is one I did NOT see Mercedes come out with. In fact, I don't think anyone did. What can you do? They can't all be gems.

Tunable clave sticks

Clave sticks are the two sticks that you often see musicians in Latin bands clapping together. Clave also means key in Spanish, the key around which salsa music is written.

Late one night I was playing my clave sticks to something other than Latin music. It was very late and although the walls of my building are very thick, I didn't want to take a chance of disturbing any of my neighbors. So, I put one of the sticks under my bathrobe to mute the loud clack, clack sound.

This muted the sound like a trumpet or trombone player does when they use the rubber end of a toilet plunger to soften their sound. Then I thought, "Heeeeeyyyy!

I like this, I might be onto something."

I don't want to give away too much for someone to steal my idea. But the idea is to have a removeable and rotatable cloth, soft plastic or other material to soften the sound and also create new clave sounds so that every click clack of the clave is not the same.

I'm working on it now.

I guess I should start writing these ideas down and DO something about them the next time one comes up. I want to be on "Shark Tank!"

CHAPTER 9

Black Bodies-Black Brains:
Part Two: Music

A BRIEF LOOK AT AFRICA AND ITS MUSICAL CULTURE

Because of extensive archaeological work by Dr. L. S. B. Leakey in the Olduvai Gorge in Tanzania, it is believed that the human race was born in Africa. For centuries it was known as "the Dark Continent." Africa is now known as the place humankind first received light. Ancient Africans were considered "primitive," but it is now known that they are creative contributors to Egyptian civilization and builders of powerful communities.

Africans were the leaders of the world for over 600,000 years. They were the first to use tools, paint pictures, plant seeds, and worship gods; many believe that they were the first to make music. The book, *They Came Before Columbus* by Ivan Van Sertima is a must-read book on the presence of Africans in North America hundreds of years before the arrival of Columbus or any other Caucasian.

Music was an important part of everyday ancient African life, as it still is today. With such a historically rich musical background, it is surprising to discover that African music and most African languages were not written or read, but instead were only spoken and played.

It is the griot, or storyteller, who passes on African traditions, stories, history, culture, and song. In my interview with West African drummer/percussionist Idy Diop for my book, *"What is This Thing Called Jazz?"* he said, "The one who sings is called a griot. The griot is one who sings praise; he is the one who knows practically everything about the history of our ancestors."

Most African compositions are played, sung, chanted, clapped, or stamped and have been handed down for many generations. The music is not written down and is often performed in a group with *everyone* participating. This is unlike the Western world, where the artists perform on a stage while the audience listens, sometimes quietly, in preassigned numbered seats.

In some African music, there are tones that cannot be written by using standard Western musical notation because symbols do not exist for some of these sounds in our system of musical notation. European classical music is written based on the range of the instrument. In much of the African music, sounds and instruments are made to replicate the human voice.

Many of these musical tones are derived from African speech inflections and song. These tones are referred to as "blue notes." Blue notes are named from the mournfully sad tonal qualities of the major and minor thirds of the scale.

These notes were sung by the African slaves as they grieved for the homeland they were forced to leave behind as they picked cotton and dug in the soil to plant crops for free to help build a new country called America. This note, or series of notes, are a critical link between Africa and most of the popular music we listen to today.

African American slaves used music to help ameliorate the feelings of their horrid living conditions, to help them forget, to give them hope for a better future.

After the Civil War (That's an oxymoron. How can the act of killing be civil?), many African Americans got jobs playing European music in military bands. This led to the creation of some of their own musical artforms like ragtime, cakewalks, Dixieland, jazz, spirituals, gospel, rhythm and blues, blues, rock and roll and many other musical genres. These creations had massive, long-lasting musical and cultural impact world-wide.

When I returned to the United States from my Army tour of duty in Korea, I wondered how and why this new music I was hearing on KPRI-FM radio, fit so well into my inner ear. I thought it was all brand new. I had never heard it before or at least I "thought" I had never heard it before. All the while I had fallen in love, all over again, with the blues my parents used to listen to.

ROCK AND ROLL

I once read that the term "rock and roll" was African American slang for sex around the 1940s. Then a record store owner in Cleveland started using the phrase to encourage white teenagers to by rhythm & blues records or race records as they were known, without racial prejudice.

There is another definition and origin of the word rock & roll.
It was a term used in the African American church in the south in the 1920s.

Call and response is something the slaves used while picking cotton in the fields, work songs, field hollers or slave songs were used to remind the Africans of home, to help raise morale. The captors used them to keep the Africans working in rhythm.

Call and response is when the lead, lead singer, leader in the cotton fields, or the preacher in the church, calls out a word or phrase and the congregants or workers repeat the word or phrase or use a different word or phrase in response.

Usually the congregants would be simultaneously clapping in rhythm with one another and rocking from left to right. They called this swaying, rocking action rockin' and rollin'. THAT is where the term came from.

Chuck Berry's hit song that he wrote and recorded in 1957 called "Reelin' and Rockin' " was a constant reference to dancing. So, rock & roll is an African American term and an African American music form that has taken over the world.

Babyface, whose real name is Kenneth Brian Edmonds, is a prolific African American singer, songwriter and record producer. He has won 11 Grammy Awards and produced more than twenty-six number-one hits.

As American history will tell you, it is common for the African American not to be given proper credit for his or her accomplishments in the music industry and any other industry, for that matter.

Very few individuals knew that Babyface co-wrote, co-produced and sang back-up vocals on Madonna's Bedtime Stories album which featured the number one hit song, "Take a Bow." This song shared the billing with another Babyface number one song, "Change the World" by Eric Clapton. That is not an Eric Clapton song, that is a Babyface song. I'll bet you didn't know that.

Babyface produced Ariana Grande's first album, "Yours Truly." He collaborated with Barbara Streisand on her "Partners" album and performed a duet on the song "Evergreen" with her.

After Hillary Clinton's speech at the 2016 Democratic National Convention they played the song "Stronger Together" which was co-written by Babyface.

There are thousands and thousands of songs that were written, produced, mixed and remixed by black artists for white artists that you do not know about like: "Manic Monday" by The Bangles (Written by Prince), Nothing Compares 2 U" by Sinéad O'Connor (written by Prince), "Human" by Human League (Produced by Jimmy Jam & Terry Lewis), "Let's Dance" by David Bowie (Produced by Nile Rodgers), "All I Have to Give" by the Backstreet Boys (Produced by Full Force), "Armagideon Time" by The Clash (Written by Willi Williams), "The Reflex" by Duran Duran (Remixed by Nile Rodgers), "Baby" by Justin Bieber (Written by Tricky Stewart and The-Dream, an African American songwriting team), "Justify My Love" by Madonna (Music by Lenny Kravitz and Andre Betts), "Like a Virgin" by

Madonna (Produced by Nile Rodgers), "Lady" by Kenny Rogers (Written by Lionel Richie), and the list does not stop.

White pop stars like Justin Beiber, Ariana Grande and white rappers like Post Malone, Iggy Azealea and the first white rapper, Vanilla Ice, have all enjoyed earth-shattering record sales on the backs of the African American community. In an interview I heard Justin Beiber admit to using the affectations of the black man to his bankrolled advantage.

Someone once said, "Isn't it interesting that the world's greatest golfer, Tiger Woods, is black and the top selling rap artist, M&M, is white?" I think more change than THAT is yet to come.

Elvis Aron Presley was named the King of Rock and Roll but could not read or write music, was not a good guitar or piano player and never wrote one, single song in his life. Nashville based African American songwriter, Otis Blackwell, whose son was one of my students in my voice acting class at the Weist-Barron School of Television in New York, wrote many hits for Elvis.

Blackwell wrote over a thousand songs, including "All Shook Up," "Don't Be Cruel," "Fever," and "Return to Sender." "Hound Dog" was also a big hit for Elvis. It was written by Johnny Otis who was not African American but in August, 1952, four years before Elvis' success, African American rhythm and blues singer, Ellie Mae Thornton, better known as "Big Mamma" Thornton had a massive hit with the original version. It is said that Elvis stole it from her.

When I was a home shopping host on Q2 Television, the representatives of the Elvis Presley organization chose me to be the sole Elvis Presley product sales representative (How that happened, I do not know). I was sent to Nashville to film some segments at Graceland for a couple of days. Of all of the Elvis songs we sold on Q2, "Hound Dog" was the one song everyone wanted on the CD set they purchased.

Today, there is a music category called goth. This category often promotes black lipstick (on the men and women), black fingernail polish, black dyed hair, etc. Bands like Bauhaus and The Cramps, even Alice Cooper in the 70s, were all inspired by the original, Screamin' Jay Hawkins, who had a hit with "I Put a Spell on You" in 1956. The African American opera singer turned r&b singer and shock stage artist decided this was a better career path.

This song has been covered by many artists including, Creedence Clearwater Revival, Annie Lennox, Nina Simone and Jeff Beck. Screamin' Jay, or Jalacy Hawkins, his real name, used a skull on a stick and wore rubber snakes and bones in the 1950s before most of these other artists were born. Well, not Alice Cooper, he was born on February 4th 1948 and used a live snake in his act. When I worked at KRIZ radio in Phoenix, Alice's dad used to call the radio station and request his son's songs.

I must admit, Led Zeppelin is one of my all-time favorite bands, since their first album which was released on January 12, 1969. I was there, I bought the very first album and others, and I still listen to them to this day. In fact, I was listening to them on the treadmill in the gym just the other day.

Willie Dixon was a Vicksburg, Mississippi born African American blues musician who was born in 1915. He played upright bass, guitar, sang, produced, wrote over 500 songs and was an arranger as well. Many of Mr. Dixon's songs were recorded by rock musicians, many of whom are English, like Cream, Led Zeppelin, and Eric Clapton and many others.

There is a very real reason Led Zeppelin sounds so down and bluesy. It is because they had been stealing from the best, black American blues artists. Zeppelin's "Whole Lotta Love" is quoted from a song written by Willie Dixon, sung by Muddy Waters in 1962. No credit was given so, Willie Dixon sued twenty years later, and is now getting his credit. Whole lotta love? Whole lotta stealin' goin' on.

On the Led Zeppelin II album, there is a Sonny Boy Williamson blues song written by Willie Dixon called "Bring It on Home." The lyrics to "The Lemon Song are from black bluesman, Robert Johnson's "Traveling Riverside Blues." But in reality, it is from Howlin' Wolf's "Killing Floor." Of course, no credit was given on the Led Zeppelin II album. Howlin' Wolf sued and got credit as co-author under his real name, Chester Burnett. I think when the band knew they were taking something without permission, they would list the author as "Traditional," which is a pseudonym they used for Jimmy Page.

On Zeppelin's Physical Graffiti album there is a song called "Jesus, Make Up My Dying Bed." Blind Willie Johnson was the first to record it in 1927. Bob Dylan recorded it in 1962 and called it, "In My Time of Dying." Neither artist gave credit to Blind Willie. There was no law suit because the song is in public domain. I am not sure who wrote the song but some of the lyrics come from the Bible.

My first rock concert was Jim Morrison and The Doors. Their debut album was called Back Door Man. Of course, that is the name of, yet, another Willie Dixon song. Howlin' Wolf recorded a version as well.

Kansas Joe McCoy and, Memphis Minnie we're an African American blues team who wrote a song to remember the Great Mississippi Flood of 1927. It caused massive damage and forced the migration of many African Americans to the Midwest. The song is called, "When the Levee Breaks," recorded by Led Zeppelin as well.

Zeppelin has also borrowed other Willie Dixon tunes from the recordings of blues musicians like Otis Rush and Muddy Waters. "I Can't Quit You Baby" and "You Shook Me," are two examples which were on the first Led Zeppelin album.

I am not saying that Zeppelin was a band of thieves, I am NOT saying that but I would love for you to listen to the group, Spirit's song called "Taurus" from the album simply called Spirit. They sued claiming it was stolen and used on "Stairway to Heaven". Please listen to "Taurus" for yourself. It is on iTunes.

1930s African American singer & guitarist, Robert Johnson wrote"They're Red Hot, "which was recorded by the Red-Hot Chili Peppers around 1991.

In 2004 Eric Clapton recorded an album called Me & Mr. Johnson. It consisted of all Robert Johnson compositions. When you credit the artist and source of your inspiration and material, you cannot call it "stealing." Clapton recorded "Love in Vain" on this album. The Rolling Stones recorded it on their 1969 Let it Bleed album and were consequently sued for not crediting Mr. Johnson. Robert Johnson is an artist I have had in my library and enjoyed for many years.

The Allman Brothers recorded Statesboro Blues but Blind Willie McTell wrote it and recorded it in 1928. The Brothers slide guitar work was also inspired by McTell.

Of course, country music cannot escape the touch of black, remember where there is music, there is Africa. The Carter Family was one of country music's most celebrated families in the 1930s. June Carter Cash was a member of this group. She was a five-time Grammy Award-winning singer, songwriter, actress, dancer, comedian and author. She was also the second wife of singer, songwriter Johnny Cash. The Carters got some of their most popular songs from a one-legged African American guitar player named Leslie Riddle who was born in 1905, in Burnsville, North Carolina.

His role was so significant that filmmaker Ken Burns, featured him in his documentary "Country Music." If Ken Burns put him in the movie he MUST be important. Many other country music stars had African American songwriters and collaborators who helped them become wealthy, but were kept in the background, not getting credit, not getting paid. These artists include Hank Williams, Johnny Cash, and Bill Monroe.

Not only did Leslie Riddle have one leg from a cement factory accident, but he was also missing the middle and ring fingers on his right hand from a shotgun accident. Accident prone?

Like the great French, jazz guitarist Django Reinhardt who had three frozen fingers on his left hand injured from a fire accident, both individuals re-learned to play with astonishing speed, dexterity, clarity, and emotion.

Of course, one cannot speak of African Americans and country music without mentioning Charlie Pride, the first black American artist to have commercial country radio and record sales success.

I met him in the WKHK, Kick-FM studios in Times Square on 43rd Street and Broadway. We went into the production room and recorded some promos for the station.

As with Willie Nelson, Charlie Daniels, Rosanne Cash, Bobby Bare, and the list goes on, we had them record a standard line like: *Hi, I'm Charlie Pride, and when I come to New York, I always listen to WKHK, Kick-FM.*

He passed away as I was writing this on December 12th, 2020 of Covid-19 complications. He was 86 years old.

He has sold more than seventy million records, he has twenty-nine number-one hit records and a Lifetime Achievement Award from the Recording Academy. Charlie Pride was the first African American performer to appear on the stage of the legendary Grand Ole Opry since Deford Bailey in the 1920s.

He was a professional baseball player and became the best-selling artist for RCA Records since Elvis, and was inducted into the Country Music Hall of Fame in 2000. This is one black man who got his just due and of all places, in country music.

I could go on for days about the African American influence on the world's music, but I think my point has been made. In the world of music, you cannot go far without encountering a black person or their influence. In pop and rock music around the world, the mark of the black creative, the black spontaneity, the black ingenious, is ever present. The black man is the inventor, creator and progenitor of all things musical. I wouldn't be surprised if they found some black in Beethoven.

After I wrote the above statement, I thought, well, who knows? Let me dig deeper, research further, who knows? There could be some black in Beethoven.

This is what I found.

It is said that Ludwig van Beethoven was born of Flemish parents but some have said that his mother might have had an affair with a Spanish person with African ancestry or Moor (northwestern African Muslim people) blood because he was not as "white" as the others.

THAT PART IS CONJECTURE. THE FOLLOWING PART IS FACT.

After visiting his sick mom in Dresden, Germany, twenty-four-year-old George Augustus Polgreen Bridgetower arrived in Vienna in 1803. His mother was German/Polish, his father was a black West Indian, probably from Barbados.

Young Bridgetower had been invited by Prince Lobkowitz, one of Beethoven's patrons, to play an event. He became an instant hit for he was a master of his instrument and became the first violinist of the Prince of Wales's band. He was called the "very first master of the violin."

Beethoven and Bridgetower became instant friends. After Beethoven heard him play, he wanted to write something for them to play together. On the day of the concert the piece had not been completed so Bridgetower was sight-reading his part. The legend has it that Beethoven had given Bridgetower and opening solo, that he executed beautifully. He then surprised Beethoven by expanding on a portion of the piano part in a way Beethoven had never heard before. He then jumped up, ran across the stage, hugged Bridgetower crying, "My dear boy! Once more!"

After the performance, Beethoven presented Bridgetower with his tuning fork and wrote a dedication to him on the music score: "Sonata mulattica composta per il mulatto Brischdauer, gran passo e compositore mulattico." Which means "Mulatto sonata composed for the mulatto Bridgetower, great lunatic and mulatto composer."

So, perhaps there *IS* some black in Beethoven. Where there is music, there are or have been black people. I will bet that George Augustus Polgreen Bridgetower had *some* influence on Beethoven *somehow*. It is irresistible, it is powerful, the power of black.

CHAPTER 10

Africa Journal: In Search of Music Education & Culture

This was my first trip, of two, to Africa. The purpose of this trip was to interview preselected individuals to be included in the book I was writing at the time, *"What Is This Thing Called Jazz? Insights & Opinions from the Players"* with a foreword by Wynton Marsalis. (Writer's Showcase, an imprint of iUniverse.com, Inc ISBN: 0-595-15166-3) Available on Amazon.

SEPTEMBER 19TH, 1980 10:20 PM

The final episode of "Shogun" is on NBC tonight. Richard Chamberlain is getting so much work these days. He has two major TV specials running a few days apart. The new special he's on-he's a blonde.

Lisa and I are excited as little children. Excited because we are on our way to Africa, Dakar in Senegal, West Africa. What?

Dakar is the capital of Senegal where some English is spoken, most speak French, and Wolof is the native tongue. It also happens to be a member of the Organization of World Heritage Cities.

After Dakar we will go on to Abidjan, which is in the Ivory Coast (Cote d'Ivoire), south of Senegal, and then on to France. We will drive to Marseille,

Nice, and Cannes. Then back to Paris to return our car, then back to NY. And of course, we'll be driving so we will hit many, many little towns in between, which is by far, one of my favorite things to do in France. Now onto San Remo, Italy and if WRVR-FM hadn't changed the format from jazz to country music, I would have gone to Portofino, Italy to check out the Splendido Hotel which is also the name of guitarist, Al Dimiola's new album.

We will double back and go up through the Loire Valley of France, famous for its world-class wines, yum. We will eventually end up in Paris, then back to NY. I'm really glad I know Lisa (this is one year before we were married). She is such a fantastic traveler-except when she goes to sleep when I'm driving. I hate that.

THE NEXT DAY. SEPTEMBER 20TH 1980
6:50 PM NEW YORK CITY

The big day. It is 8:15 pm or so. Check in time at Kennedy International Airport. Mostly Africans lined up at the Air Afrique desk. Our turn finally comes. The lady puts the wrong tag on our luggage which would have sent it to Abidjan, not Dakar. We both noticed it. Lisa says "Excuse me, does this mean that our luggage goes to Abidjan?" The blonde airhead Air Afrique desk clerk says "Oh, I made a mistake." Then she puts the wrong seat and row on our boarding passes. She gave us seats 10A and 11B. "Wait a minute I think that's wrong." The counter lady says "No, that was not my fault," blaming it on the computer. I'm thinking, all of this is going wrong and we haven't even left the airport.

Am I making a mistake going on this trip as a black man with a white woman into deepest, darkest Africa? I know nothing of the racial or political climate in this country? What if they hate me? What if they hate her? What if they hate us together? What if we get attacked by a mob? What if we get thrown in jail? What if they kill us? What if? What if?

Why didn't I check the conditions through the United Nations? The headquarters are right here in New York. Why didn't I go to the U.S. Embassy or the Senegalese Embassy in New York? Looking back on my decision, I feel it was somewhat irresponsible and somewhat shortsighted. But, she wanted to go and would not let me go alone. Ok, here we go. Once the decision was made, I never looked back or had a single regret.

We finally boarded the plane. I noticed it was a very nice, clean, possibly a new plane. As we start down the aisle to find our seats, then the lights go out and the engines stop. We're standing there in the dark. There were some low lights on in the back. So, I instantly grabbed my pen light and flicked it on.

Naturally we are not very comfortable in this plane with the lights going out before we even reach our seats. Is the Lord trying to tell us something? Of course, we're thinking, "Is this thing going to crash?" I asked Lisa three times. "Do you want to get off? Do you want to get off the plane? Do you want to get off the plane?" We'll catch another plane and we'll be able to read about this one crashing in the middle of the Atlantic Ocean (I thought it but did not dare say it).

We landed in Dakar as two little African boys on the plane began to cheer. Just minutes before that, they were entering into a call and response. One brother who was about 9 years old would say "bla do, bla do, bla doo doo." And would punch his brother in the ribs sayin "yu bla do," encouraging his big brother who was about 11 years old to respond with "bla do." It was very cute.

So, we get off the plane and it's warm, muggy, humid, sticky. Looks and feels like South Florida. Except everyone is black. THIS is a new experience. Even Harlem isn't this black.

We went through customs, then everyone wants to carry your bag... for a tip, of course. We say no and carry them ourselves to a taxi. We are approached by another four or five guys. We jump into a cab. The driver puts the luggage in the trunk.

We know in advance how much the ride to the hotel will be. We get in and ask how much it would be. He said 2500 francs. We say, "Oh no, that's too much. It only costs about 1000 francs to the Croix Du Sud Hotel." He said, "Well I can't take you there for that amount." I say, "Okay, forget it."

I opened the door, and we got out. He got out and opened the trunk, he took out the luggage and by that time we had a slight crowd of cab drivers crowded around us.

Some big guy who looked like he was a boss, asked us how much we wanted to pay and how much the other guy was asking. We finally settled on 2000 francs, or about 10 dollars with this guy.

The ride to the hotel was enjoyable. Rather short. About 15 minutes in length at most. We arrived at the Croix du Sud Hotel at Amadu's suggestion. Amadu Thiam was a person I met at WRVR radio in New York about a month before our trip.

He gave me the name and number of a few people to contact to interview for the jazz book I was writing. The book is called *What is This Thing Called Jazz?* That was the purpose of this trip, to get some African authenticity into the book.

The price of the Croix du Sud Hotel was much too high so we asked if they could suggest an alternative that was perhaps a little cheaper. They recommended the Hotel Atlantic which was only a 2-star hotel but it had air conditioning and was only twenty-five dollars a night which was a lot better than fifty dollars a night.

So, we took it, dropped our stuff off and went to Gorée Island to see where they housed the slaves before shipping them to the Americas. (This is the place President Barak and Michelle Obama visited many years later.)

Before boarding the ferry boat for Gorée Island, we went to the train station to see if we could exchange some money. The exchange office was closed, so we went to a different counter and bought a bottle of cold, Schweppes orange soda, for 110 francs.

With this, we took our daily anti-malaria pill because we didn't want to drink the water here. We left the train station sipping our bottle of Schweppes orange as a kid called to us as we walked away.

We stopped, turned around and he asked for the bottle when it was empty. We gladly gave it to him. I think he was joyed as well as surprised as he yelled "walaahhhh!" as I handed him the bottle.

We boarded this nice ferry boat. The skies were blue and there was a slight African breeze cooling us off somewhat. I started thinking, I know conditions weren't exactly like this when they took the slaves to Gorée Island. But exactly how was it? I know there were at least 400 times this many people stacked on top of each other, sad, lonely, frightened, sick, without their families and so forth.

About midway I decided to move to the front of the boat so that we could see the approach to the island. It was beautiful. It was just marvelous. The bay from which the ferry leaves is kind of dirty from all of the industrialization, the oil refineries and so forth. But approaching Gorée it gets much clearer.

Children swam out to the boat, asking us to throw a coin into the bay so they can dive for it.

They also climbed on board and dove off the boat. Just having so much fun splashing in the water and making money at the same time, they were adorable.

We got off the boat and several yards away, under a tree was a peddler who was all set up with his trinkets to sell. I stopped and look at a wallet. I did not want to barter or buy. I just wanted to look. What did I do that for?

As soon as I left there were two or three little kids around me offering their services as a guide, or as they say "geed" We refused them. We refuse them all.

We took off down the path but everywhere we went we would see little boys, and only little boys offering themselves as guides or just plain begging. So, we continued to stroll and discover Gorée Island. Lisa was tired and getting a little crabby... so we got into a few fights.

We went to the slave house which was a lot smaller than I had imagined. But when you stack hundreds of people, one on top of the other, the place holds a lot more than it looks like it does.

Inside the Slave House. The center photo shows the famous "door" from which countless millions of slaves were shipped to North, Central and South America.

The area around Dakar was settled in the 15th century. The paved streets of Dakar, looked like Mexico to me. The Portuguese moved onto

GoréeIsland and used it as a base for the Atlantic slave trade. The "House of Slaves" or the Slave House was built on Gorée Island in 1776. Today it is a museum dedicated to the Atlantic slave trade and is a UNESCO World Heritage Site. (UNESCO is an acronym from *United Nations Educational, Scientific, and Cultural Organization*).

The Slave House on Gorée Island, Dakar, Senegal, West Africa.

I apologize for the photo quality. These were taken before I studied photography.

I was struck by how small the pink, stucco, two-story spiral stair-cased structure was, where hundreds of slaves were kept at one time. The top floor is one single open room where hundreds of individuals were piled on top of one another awaiting a ship to take them to the new land. Hundreds of men and women urinating and defecating for days, weeks, upon one another from the top down. On the ground floor there are a few jail cells and smaller cells (cages) for children that were built into the walls with dirt floors. As a joke, I put Lisa, who is Italian American, into one of the cells so she could feel the sensation.

The Slave House on Gorée Island, Senegal, Dakar, West Africa

Walking straight to the back of the building there is a door opening, which is called "The Door of No Return", with the Atlantic Ocean fewer than three feet from the door. Above the door were the words, *"From this door, for a trip with no return, they went with their eyes fixed upon the infinity of suffering,"* written in French.

Research has shown that the Portuguese arrived at the Bay of Dakar in 1444 as slave raiders. France commanded the island in 1677. Following the abolition of the slave trade and French annexation of the mainland area in the 19th century, Dakar grew into a major regional port and a major city of the French colonial empire.

In February of 1794, France abolished the slave trade. Napoleon reinstated it in May 1802, then finally abolished it permanently in March of 1815. Despite Napoleon's abolition, a clandestine slave trade continued at Gorée until 1848, when it was abolished throughout all French territories.

To replace trade in slaves, the French started peanut cultivation on the mainland. While walking around Dakar I would see many men with what appeared to be old, metal raw milk containers from a dairy farm, being carried on their heads. I finally learned that those containers were used in the production of peanuts.

We climbed to the top of the small mountaintop where they had huge old cannons. I made some spectacular photos there. We sat and composed some musical questions for my interviews that I was hoping to get the next day. Then we went back down the mountain, caught the ferry and went back home. What a great day in Africa.

We went back to the hotel to clean up and check our possessions. Then we went for a meal at a Vietnamese restaurant. Walked in through the bar. Our previous waiter recognized us and greeted us. We went to the back where the restaurant is. We sat, waited for the waiter and the menu.

I had no idea it was a Vietnamese restaurant. I thought it was Chinese. We, for the first time, ordered an Algerian wine. It was red and it was chilled. Wait a minute, cold, red wine, how tacky?

The high point of the meal was when they brought Lisa's appetizers. Something that looked like a thin egg roll. The waiter brought it, set it down and cut it with a pair of scissors. How weird, a pair of scissors to cut your food. What do I know, I'm just an American? Lisa ordered some shrimp configuration thing. I ordered some beef with vegetables and something. Both came with rice. Yum.

We arrived at the hotel, spoke to the desk clerk, then proceeded to climb the 3 flights of stairs to the 4th floor. It's a good thing we live in a 3rd floor walk-up in New York or we'd be completely out of shape for this stair climbing stuff in Africa every day.

We went to room twenty-eight, opened the door, turned on the light and every ant and roach in Dakar was in our room. So, naturally we started stomping. The bright thing to do was to agree to leave the light on all night to keep the insects away. All during the night I would wake up, look around and wonder, "How in the hell did I get to Africa?

NEXT DAY, TUESDAY, SEPTEMBER 22

7:30 AM I awaken and set the alarm for 8:30, then 9:30, then 10:30. I get up because I had to go to the bank, which closed at 11: 30.

We just made it. There were three people behind us, then they closed the door. I got my money, Lisa got hers, but there was a weird moment when I was getting my money. Some guy with a dark green suit, white shirt and green tie was standing next to me. Not in line but next to me, leaning on the counter.

He saw how much Lisa got. He saw how much I got. She exchanged almost one hundred dollars. I got one hundred-fifty. He did not try to rob us, but I had my New York antenna up. We got the money and split out of the back door because the front door was locked. It was neat walking through this bank as all the Africans worked counting money, clicking and clacking on typewriters and speaking French and Wolof.

Next stop, the marketplace. Wow what chaos! Lisa was very funny as gangs of young Africans tried to sell her their wares. "How much you give me for this? I make you good price, I make you good price." I saw some wallets that I wanted so I picked one up and tried to put my international driver's license, passport, credit card, and shot record of immunization in it.

Huh, no deal, wouldn't fit, too small. So, this kid, whose name turned out to be Guilles (Zheel), went to get me a larger wallet. Beautiful tan, iguana skin wallet. It was beautiful. I loved it. I saw it and I said to myself, "Self you want that wallet. Start negotiating." I had a leather bag of American record albums with me because before I left New York, I was told they love American music.

"Okay Guilles. I will give you one record album for this wallet. Better yet. This album is worth 8000 francs. You want 3000 francs for the wallet. Take the John Klemmer "Cry" album, give me 5000 Francs change, take 3000 francs for the wallet and you have a deal.

He said "What's the matter with you? Are you crazy?" I said no! We looked at each other then I tried to walk away. No way. They hounded and pitched and hounded and pitched. Hard-sell tactics these guys had. Somehow, we got away. Silence at last. We saw another vender with some nice necklaces.

Oh no, here they come again. But different young peddlers this time. "Hey this is nice." "How much you give me for this." "Give me 2500 francs and you can have it." "2500 francs?" "2500?" "Okay, I make you good price. It's nice. Very nice. 2500 francs, 2500 francs, 2500 francs."

"Lisa, let's get the hell out of here." They follow us. We stopped around the corner and I aggressively chased the little vendors away. Across the street at the market I saw some guys carrying butchered halves of cows on their backs. Interesting. Very interesting. I've never seen anything like that before.

We went back to the hotel to drop off some stuff then to the Government of Senegal Building Administration of Culture to locate my music contacts to get some interviews for my book. Mr. Bingey helped me out tremendously with telephone numbers and addresses. In fact, I'm writing this on the steps of the building right now waiting for it to re-open so I can thank him with an album. Success. Mr. Bingey was there. I gave him the album and he was elated, to say the least.

He wanted my address in Dakar at the Hotel Atlantic. I also gave him my card in the United States for Batt Johnson Productions. We went back to the hotel to drop off the mask that we bought at this artist village called Soumbédioune, which is on the western seacoast. Beautiful, beautiful spot.

We bought a big beautiful mask for our home, some necklaces for my sisters and friends of Lisa's. Nice stuff. Most of them were made of shark vertebrae mixed with beads. We made our way away from the solicitors to a nice, quaint, open-air bar-restaurant overlooking a bay.

There were some men there with pant legs rolled up with big kitchen pans, panning for gold. Our waiter said they find some every day. A little bit here, a little bit there.

WEDNESDAY, SEPTEMBER 24TH 1980

So much has happened. As usual, I'm getting lost and behind in the writing of my journal notes but it is extremely difficult to vacation, take photographs, have experiences and write about them in detail at the same time. Today I did a lot of walking. My black and white Oxfords or saddle shoes as they are sometimes called, were all run over now and they look like hell. I'm run over, I look like hell. Lisa's run over, she looks like hell. No, just kidding.

Back at the hotel, feeling somewhat uninspired with the excitement of Africa rapidly wearing off, we sat and played cards, then napped for about 30 minutes. We got up and went in search of the University of Dakar and the Senegalese Conservatory of Music to learn more about African music, instruments and culture.

We found both but we had to be driven to the conservatory. We stopped at the "Ministre du Environment" to once again, ask for directions.

As usual, the guard at the door didn't know. There was another person there, so we asked him where the conservatory was. He sent us in the wrong direction for the twentieth time, but we are used to it by now. We decided that this weird water has gone to their heads.

After trying to give us more directions as to where it was, we weren't going for it. This really nice man at the Ministre du Environment got a car and a driver and drove us to the Conservatory. He said the Conservatory du Arts is just around the bend. Sure, it is. We've been led on enough wild goose chases in Africa. No more. So, he took us.

Now to the bus. We find a dispatcher. We ask what bus goes to the University of Dakar. He says number twenty-eight. We said, great. We go to the stop, wait for number twenty-eight. It comes in about fifteen minutes. We arrive at the University. We walk for a few minutes. We stop for an orange Fanta drink and we sit at the bus stop. As African students walk by we ask where the "Itan" building is. He says "Hmm Itan I don't know." We think, "Oh no, if there is no such building, I am going to kill somebody."

I show him my notes and it turns out to be "IFan" not ITan. It's Amadu's writing that we cannot understand. He gives us directions with much trouble because he speaks neither French nor English. He speaks the native language which is called Wolof. We get the directions finally. He drew them in the dirt for us. It was a long walk. But the directions were correct.

I WENT ON THE RADIO IN AFRICA

We took the bus back to the main part of the city and got off at the radio station. It was so early for Kalile and his radio show called, "English Magazine," so we sat on the steps and I wrote notes. He come at about 6:38 or so, for a show that started at 6:40. It is a twenty-minute show every day.

So, we walked up three flights of stairs and into the control room. Not much there in the way of equipment. Even WRVR-FM is better than this and that was bare bones. I don't believe it, but I do. They have an old Gates control board, two old, outdated turntables, and two old pre-440 Ampex tape recording machines. They have no cart machines for commercials.

The show consists largely of British and American Armed Forces news tapes, with records and talking, live news tape introductions and so forth. Kalile sat me down and put me on the air. I was surprised. I was excited and slightly nervous because I wasn't sure how wild or conservative I could be but I had heard the show from my hotel room before.

Batt Johnson on the radio in Dakar, West Africa with a John Travolta t-shirt on.

I always travel with a mini-radio station in my bag; AM-FM, shortwave radio with a recording device attached, pens, notebooks, camera, film, a traveling journalist. So, Lisa was enjoying it. He interviewed me briefly then I tape my segment consisting of reading some news stories and introducing a couple of records. I took some pictures, and before we knew it, the twenty-minute show was over.

So, we were back in front of the building with Kalile and his friend Abass who is a journalist. We go across the street for Perrier and an interview. It was good. I enjoyed it. Kalile is a pretty smart guy and speaks pretty good English. The best we've heard since we've been in Africa. One hour and fifteen minutes later we bid each other good-bye and we departed. A few seconds later they call and run back to us. Kalile asked me for some money because he's going on a brief jaunt with his drummer friend who I am supposed to interview before he calls NY tomorrow. I give him 1000 francs which at that time was about 5 dollars.

We said goodbye and went to the hotel Croix du Sud restaurant. Remember, we were supposed to stay there, but it was much too expensive. More than Amadu said it would be. In fact, not many of the things Amadu said, were true.

So, Greta said, "This restaurant has about the best French food in all of Senegal." We'll see. The food was good. The rose was not so good. The service is even worse. We left no tip and went home to bed before our big day of three interviews tomorrow.

THURSDAY SEPTEMBER 25TH, 1980

We get up at 7:15 AM. Wow, I can't believe I'm up this early and I'm on vacation. We showered and went to the Boia Bank to exchange about 190 dollars. We walked up Ponte Avenue to Republic to catch the number ten bus for the University of Dakar to interview Amar Samb who is the director of the museum which is farther in the city.

Well, fortunately for us, we went the day before to exactly see where the IFAN building was because the Senegalese will give you the "Wawa" or send you on a wild goose chase. "Wawa" means West Africa wins again, is what I was told. We arrived at the University. We had the guard call Mr. Samb. We went up to his office. It was locked. Yes, that's right. It was locked. So, I said, "let us try this door." The secretary to the director. Great! it was open.

We asked for Mr. Amar Samb. He was not there but he left a note attached to his University catalog. The note said that Yaya Mame would answer any and all of my questions. Okay, okay we're here, so we might as well check it out.

We went to Yaya's office. He says he knows nothing about music. He is a sociology professor. They have no music department at the University. If we want to find out more about African Music we have to go to Zaire.

What!? Zaire?! Screw you. I'm not going to damn Zaire. Now I'm pissed. We came thousands of miles across the Atlantic Ocean, spent thousands of dollars on plane fare, hotel, food and so forth to get here and this fool is sitting there in his almighty incompetence telling me we have to go to another country.

Well, that just put the icing on the cake. I'm steaming. I'm pissed off. You can fry an egg on my head. We went outside and I blow it off on Lisa. Boy, did I. Yep, we got into another fight. I was in a surreal world. I was hysterical, schizophrenic. Laughing, crying, pissed off, laughing, shouting, pissed off, apathetic, happy, pissed off, hot and sweaty.

Okay that's enough for him. We board the number ten bus for the Conservatory of Music to interview Abdu Arhakman Diop. He is the director. We got there forty-five minutes early, and we sat in the lobby of his bungalow.

The secretary was sick, I think. She kept her head on the desk. It took about twenty-seven rings to answer the phone and every few seconds she would wrinkle her brow, like something inside really hurt. Yellow fever?

We had an eleven o'clock appointment. At eleven-ten or eleven-fifteen, Mr. Diop came out and said "just a minute." He came back and we went next door because his wife or someone is having family problems.

We began the interview. I slate the tape, ask the first question and we're off. Lisa takes over in French and does an outstanding job. What a pro. She's got it together. She is translating from English to French for me. We end the session. I take his photograph. I thank him, shake his hand, give him two albums and we're off to the next interview with another Diop, (The name Diop is like Smith or Jones in America) the drummer friend of Kalile, the DJ at "English Magazine" radio show.

We only have to go up the street and around a couple of corners to the Senegalese British Institute, where Kalile learned English. They had to call New York to hook up studio time, musicians, a tour and so forth for Idy Diop, the drummer. They made their phone call then we went to the next room. We sat down and the interview began. Once again, I slate the tape, ask the first question and it takes off, only this time, Lisa has a much better handle on things and the interview is one and a half hours in length and it was excellent. This guy knew a lot.

We finished, we said goodbye. They invited us to their house and Idy Diop invited us to his gig at ten-thirty that night. Kalile doesn't have my 1000 francs and I'm pissed. I think he thinks I gave him that money. It was a loan.

We now have three interviews because we have one with Kalile. Back to the hotel for a brief rest for water and air conditioning. It's overcast today and not really that hot. We went to Carmel market for more shopping and back to the original mask place near the hotel. We negotiate one doll for Greg, Lisa's brother, three elephant tail hair bracelets, six good luck charms for 2100 francs. Not that great of a deal but let me tell you what happened.

I knew I had good negotiation and barter skills because I learned at an early age going to Tijuana, Mexico often. It is a barter country. My tactic is, before I leave home, I put a one-dollar bill in my upper left pocket, a five in the upper right pocket, a ten in my left front pant pocket, and a twenty in my right front pant pocket. My mother would not be happy if she knew I was doing this. Sssssshhhh!

So, let's say the item costs twenty dollars. I would reach into my upper right pocket and pull out a five. The key to the whole "negotiation" is, they have to *see* the money.

I then put on a sad face and say, "Oh, heck. I only have five." Then I start to walk away. Once they *see* the money, you've got 'em. They fall for it every time. Africa is no different. Well, it is a little different here in Senegal in that you browse around the store, selecting various items. You put them on the counter and negotiate for the *whole pile*, not individual items.

I finished my browsing and shopping and created a pile on the counter. We negotiated and agreed upon 2200 francs. I handed him some of the money as I looked for the rest. He kept the 100-franc coin in his right hand. He put the 2100 francs bills on some magazine paper, then he placed the trinkets on top of the money and wrapped them all up together in the pages from the magazine because they don't have paper bags.

Well, on the paper there was a photograph of an outdoor scene with green and brown, foliage and earth. He put the money on the paper and the trinkets on top of that. I guess the money blended in with the scenery of the paper.

I stood there watching all of this happen before my very eyes. I couldn't believe it. I thought to myself. "Hurry up! Hurry up." I took the package and hauled ass down the street, twisting, turning, weaving and bobbing like a halfback for the Dallas Cowboys who smells the victory of the goal line with no one in front of him to stop him.

Poor Lisa, bless her heart. She was running behind me knowing something was up. I know she is thinking, "Now Batt, what the heck is up? Slow down! Stop!" After about four blocks of this mad, dashing pace she said "HEY! SLOW DOWN!

Where are you going?" I figured, well, we're far enough away so I let her in on what just happened. Her eyes got as big as a 25-franc piece.

Now, don't judge me. I was young, dumb and looking for adventure. I didn't think that I could end up in an African jail, but I guess I could have.

I don't think her father's position as a United States Federal Judge could get us out of a West African jail very easily or very quickly.

We darted off to a distant bar for a Flag beer. In fact, two, because the first was not cold. These beers are very thirst quenching because they are not filling, nor are they very strong. I refused to drink the water here, eat lettuce or put ice in a drink. We must watch out for our health. Remember, we didn't do much research before leaving New York.

So, we sat and let the heat wear off. Then we went shopping again. Damn, we did more shopping than we've ever done in our lives. Then back to the hotel to dump the gifts, back to the nice shrimp restaurant for dinner and rosé and then back to the hotel Atlantic for the last time. I didn't believe it, but it's true. We divided the gifts on the bed, analyzed what we've purchased, grinningly so. We then tucked in for our last night in Dakar.

FRIDAY MORNING 6 AM.

The alarm went off but I think we were both awake in anticipation of our departure. We got up, repacked, paid our hotel bill which is 25,435f. We got on the bus for the airport, nodding off, falling asleep, waking up, falling asleep because we haven't had our daily dose of morning coffee. Another plus for Western Africa. The have great coffee.

We arrived at the airport. Someone grabbed our bags off the bus and carried them into the terminal. We give him 100 francs. He says "No! It's 100 francs per bag." Okay we've had it with these people trying to get our money again! I told him we have no more money and proceed to ignore his wishes for more. We got away with it.

It was 8: 30 AM. They called our flight. We boarded. It was 9:15. We took off and said goodbye and good riddance to Dakar, Senegal, West Africa. We may return but I'm just not sure as to when. Overall, I am so happy we made that trip.

Now I have been on the radio in San Diego, Phoenix, Pittsburgh, Los Angeles, Miami, Kansas City, MO, New York, Paris, and Dakar, West Africa. Many years later I discovered my DNA:

Nigeria 43%

Cameroon, Congo & Southern Bantu Peoples 28%

Mali 7%

Senegal 4%

Benin & Togo 4%

Ghana 3%

Eastern Bantu Peoples 1%

England, Wales & Northwestern Europe 5%

Germanic Europe 2%

Sweden 1%

France 1%

Native American, East Asian 1%

CHAPTER 11

Religion

Muslims killing Jews, Protestants killing Catholics, Christians killing Muslims, Hindus killing Sikhs, Islamics killing Buddhists, killing, killing, killing. There are some terrorist groups that kill in the name of God. In many cases religion separates us, not the other way around.

If you are religious and you believe in God, and you believe that God makes no mistakes, why do you think there is something wrong with the color of my skin? Don't punish me for something your God created.

Any religion that professes to be concerned with the souls of men and is not concerned with the slums that damn them, and the social conditions that cripple them, is a dry-as-dust religion.
Martin Luther King, Jr.-1961

Sex, race, religion, politics. If you want to create a heated discussion, all you have to do is bring up any of those subjects.

As you may or may not have concluded thus far, I loved my mother. Perhaps that is why I am an Argentine tango dancer. The embrace, the extreme close embrace of this dance can remind the dancer of their FIRST serious, meaningful hug, the hug from your mother. For me, this tango hug is a religious experience.

Our first hug was probably from the nurse in attendance as he or she whisked us away the moment we were born, washed us, swaddled us, and returned us to our mother.

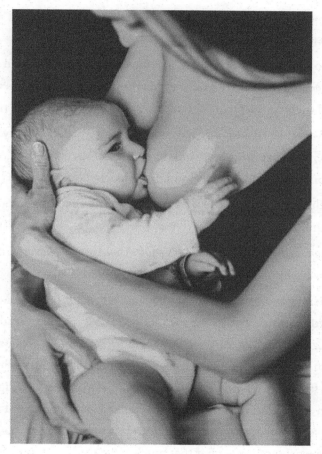

The hug of your mother, was your first LOVING hug with serious intent.

African Americans are religious people, especially the older generations. My mother was a very strong believer in God. My dad did not believe at all. That gave me a clear point of view straight down the middle. I am so thankful for that.

My religion is simple. It is, *do unto others as you would have them do unto you.* As soon as we elected Trump, I saw more ugliness in the streets than ever before. People yelling at each other, rushing to get themselves through a door first instead of opening the door for their fellow human to pass first, and other antisocial behaviors.

Viewing such repulsive conduct brought out the other portion of my self-imposed religion which is, *just be nice to people.*

I moved to New York with a California mentality. I smiled at people on the street, I said hello, I would even compliment random men on how wonderful their tie was, that is, IF it was, in fact, a cool tie. I love ties.

In New York you don't do things like that, if you do, you may be asking for trouble. You keep your eyes straight ahead and keep it moving. I still find this to be inhumane, insensitive, and disconnected.

I believe that if you know what the right thing to do is, you must do the right thing.

When the Europeans came, they said we were non-believers. They denied the validity of our ancient religions. Miriam Makeba-1987

When I was a child, every Sunday morning my mother woke up early, and cooked as she listened to her spiritual records waiting for a radio broadcast that came from Los Angeles. My memory says that it was Brother Joe Mays from his church. Something else in my memory tells me that Aretha Franklin's father, Reverend C. L. Franklin, Baptist minister, civil rights activist, known as the man with the "Million-Dollar Voice," had something to do with this weekly broadcast and or the church as well. I was very young at this time. I'm surprised I remember that much.

My religion is my religion. My people are my people. They are not interconnected. My people are first. I happen to be a Black Jew. I am first Black and the religion I have chosen is Judaism. Sammy Davis, Jr. -1990

Who is God? Where is God? Is God in the sky? Is God a person? Does she/he/it look like a person? Does he/she/it look like a cloud. If God lives in the sky, what does he/she/it eat?

How do we know about heaven? Did someone die, went to heaven, came back and gave us a report about what they experienced? How do we know about hell? Did someone die, went to hell, came back and gave us a detailed report about their experience? These are all the curious thoughts within my six-year old mind as I watched my mother pray.

Religion and religious ideas are all methods of controlling vulnerable people who need help, who can't defend themselves, who have not spent much time thinking outside of the box of their immediate life. One reason is because they didn't know they were *in* a box. Or perhaps they had been in such dire situations that to believe in and pray to God or *something,* was the only way to receive and believe in hope.

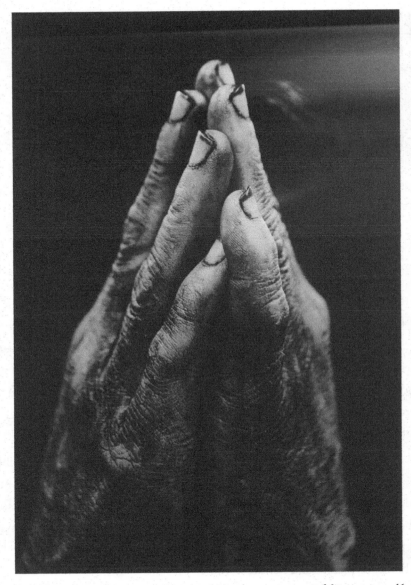

"Oh, Lord, someone, anyone, something, anything, please get me out of this imprisoned hell hole I am in, and save me from these white devils."

Religion without humanity is poor human stuff.
Sojourner Truth-1877

There are many, many religions in Africa including Judaism, Baha 'I Faith, Hinduism, Islam, Buddhism, Christianity, Muslim, Jehovah's Witness, Vodun, Brazilian Vodum, Cuban Vodu, Dominican Vudu, Louisiana Voodoo, Hatian Vodu, Seventh-day Adventists and some Chinese religions, to name only a few. It is a very large and diverse continent with countless languages and dialects, complex cultures and philosophies.

Religion, faith, belief, and hope are all things that helped the slaves survive their abominable situation on American soil. African American history did not begin with slavery in America, it began in Africa.

Religion in the African context is an understanding of nature.
Clarence Glover-1987

When I was a high school athlete, we would always pray before the game or track meet. We would pray to God to give us the strength to help us win but we lost anyway. Then I started thinking…does the other team pray too? If so, why did God choose to answer *their* prayers and not ours?

Does God answer the prayers of the team which prays the hardest? How do you pray harder? What does that mean? Do you pray louder, pray longer, pray before the game, pray during the game? In high school many of my African American male friends were on the football and or track team with me.

Glen "Big Molly" (long story) King, Charles "Bucket" (Because he had a head as big as a bucket) Smith, Charles "Bimbo" Davis (aka Bim. Actually, Bim was misnamed. He was so named because he had big ears like "Dumbo", the charming Disney elephant character), Joe Lowery, Ernest Bryson, Willard Bryant, and many others. These were some of the guys I played football with, hung out with, and laughed with.

Praying, church, and religion are all standard fare in most African American households so this was natural for us. On the bus going to an away game or in the locker room before the home games, we had a little call and response song we always sang.

Gonna beat 'em…Yeees, Lord!

Gonna beat 'em…Yeees, Lord!

Gonna win tonight…Yeees, Lord!

Gonna win tonight…Yeees, Lord!

I have known Glen King since elementary school. He was in my 7th grade Spanish class at Memorial Junior High School in San Diego with our teacher, Ms. Luna with the flat ass and clickity-clack high heel shoes. We could hear her coming to class a mile away. Clickity-clack, clickity-clack, click-click. "Buenos dias clase!"

Later, Glen King was on my football team in high school. As a matter of fact, he is the first and only person to make me see stars and hear birds chirping, although it was night.

Please allow me to elaborate. We were playing Saint Augustine High School in a night football game. They had a hot-shot running back. I was on defense with Glen.

Saints, the opposing team called a running play and there I was, face-to-face with their star running back. This was my golden opportunity to tackle the hell out of him and put him on the ground for a few minutes.

Juuuust as I was about to lay the hammer down…BOOOOM! Big Molly (Glen King) hit me at the same time I hit the competition's running back. My head rang and I saw stars and I heard birds chirping, just like in the cartoons. I got up off the ground and walked toward the *wrong* huddle.

I always wondered what it would feel like to be jogging down the lane and have a freight train hit me head on? Now I know. Big Molly was big! Yeeeessss, Lord, and that night, it hurt like hell, and I saw God. Yeeess, Lord!!!

There are a few things in this life that anger me beyond belief. One thing is guns, gun violence, and weak gun laws and lack of enforcement. The other thing is pedophilia. The thought of someone harming the beauty and stealing the angelic innocence of a child infuriates me to the point that *everything* I see is red.

Just the other day there was another case of a member of the Catholic Church being accused of the sexual abuse of a child. The children, boys and girls, have been known to be as young as three years old.

The Church is equally as guilty by constantly covering up these heinous crimes by these sick and depraved individuals. Why does the Catholic Church attract pedophiles? What is the lure, safety, protection, automatic cover-up?

Often after being caught, the violators are sent to other parishes where the abuse continues with an entirely new group of children. This is not just in the United States. This is a problem in much of Europe, Australia, South America, and Canada. The investigations between the years 2001 and 2010 involved as many as three-thousand priests. The number of children they harmed is astronomical.

Pope John Paul II launched an apology in 2001 in which he called sexual abuse within the church "a profound contradiction of the teachings and witness of Jesus Christ."

If these individuals are such "men of the cloth," why are they committing such immoral acts?

These sick hypocrites should be placed in a dirty prison cell like the kind of dirty prison they have placed the emotional and mental health of the young victims they have scarred for life. They should be imprisoned, and receive deep psychiatric counseling.

This kind of behavior causes religious and non-religious individuals alike, to wonder about the credibility and presence of God.

While watching a cable television program I saw an ad for the "Clergy Abuse Helpline." If something like this is on *television*, it shows our society is in a very deep state of decrepit decay.

I only saw my father, who was a non-believer, in church one time in my entire life. He once said, "How is the preacher able to buy a brand-new car every year when he says the money you put in the collection plate every Sunday goes to God? How does the money get to God? Does God fly down every Sunday night after church is over and pick it up? Does the preacher mail it to him? Son, I think religion is a hoax."

I think they want me to believe there is a man who lives in the sky.

In December 2019, Pope Francis executed many changes to create a greater sense of transparency. But transparency is not necessarily what is needed. What is needed is arrests, convictions, psychiatric counseling, sexual predator registration and lifetime monitoring. Then perhaps sexual predators will attempt to seek refuge elsewhere, possibly where they can be discovered and apprehended more quickly, and easily without the protections of the church. If priests believed there was a God, they would not harm his innocent, angelic creations.

CHAPTER 12

My Parents

My father, William McKinley Johnson, was a quiet man, not super social, and not particularly well educated but he loved and was serious about supporting the three children he created and the woman he married. So, basically, I grew up in a household of women. I love women. They make so much sense to me…usually.

My dad was always at work. He had two jobs, always. I think that is where I got my hard work ethic, even though he thought I was lazy (I am). He, upon occasion, would say, "Boy, you're lazy. You don't want to work." His idea of work was hard, manual labor. I always wanted to work smarter, not harder. For me, if I was sweating while working, something was wrong. That is probably why I decided on a career of talking for a living. Hahahah. How lazy.

My dad owned and operated a gas station and a restaurant on the same piece of property at 16th Street and National Avenue in San Diego, by day. By night he worked in an aircraft factory.

Mom & Dad at Johnson's Cafe

When I was a child, in the summer, I went to work every morning with him to make money to buy my school clothes for the next year. I would always go to Los Angeles to visit my cousins and buy my school clothes so no other kids would have the same clothes. I was vain, even at ten years old.

One morning while driving to work with him he said, "You know son, I don't know what the colored man did to the white man to make him hate us so much." Wow! That was such a powerful statement that still resonates within me today. I would love to see that answer. What *did* we do?

There are many ways to think about the race issue in America. It is not Latins hating Asians. It is not Middle Easterners hating Polynesians. It is not blacks hating anyone. It is always whites hating blacks, or whites hating Muslims, or whites hating someone. I wonder what kind of race dynamic this country would have if Europeans never "imported" the African people. The Africans would be a lot happier, that's for sure, and so would the Native Americans.

MY MOM

My friends loved my mother. They would come to my house many days a week. Not so much to see me, but to see my mother. She would always have something good to eat, cake, a pie or a whole dinner. She would make them laugh, play ball with us. She had this special ability. She could throw a tennis ball into the air until it disappeared. This was sunny Southern California, so there were no clouds for the ball to get lost in. This was more impressive than anything their ten-year old little eyes had ever seen.

My mom had many talents and skills. In addition to being able to throw a ball into the air until it disappeared. On Christmas or her birthday, she could shake her gifts, listen to it, and tell *exactly* what it was. She was also a good shot with a rifle (of course, she was a country girl). She also had an extremely keen sense of smell and could not wear a wrist watch because she had too much electricity in her body which would make the watch stop.

She could also wring a chicken's neck until she was holding its head in her left hand while the body flopped around on the ground. Don't forget she was a country girl. You have to kill the chicken before you eat it, right? What I didn't know was where she got live chickens in the middle of the city in San Diego.

These are all things I knew about my mother since childhood. What I did NOT know until I was an adult over sixty years of age, is that she was a swing dancer. I think she was a Lindy hop style aerialist. You know, the fast swing dance where the woman gets thrown into the air repeatedly. AND she knew Count Basie!

WHAT? Why didn't anyone ever tell me that? I guess when you are the youngest and only the boy in the family some things just don't trickle down to you. But, but I was in the music business! You would think that at some point that would have come up for me, no?

While I was still doing research for my *What Is This Thing Called Jazz?* book, I went to the world-famous Village Gate club on Bleeker Street in Greenwich Village to hear Count Basie. For some reason, our promotions or sales department didn't get any free tickets, the owner of the club, Art D'Lugoff, who always let me in free, was out of the country. I couldn't get any free tickets from my other sources so, I had to stand in line, and it was a long one, around the block, and buy tickets.

As I was standing in line with a friend, Count Basie and a couple of guys walked by. I thought, "Oh, great, this is it. This is my chance!" (Sometimes I feel like such an opportunist. But that's my job, to make it work and be ahead of the game.) I left the line and my friend and caught up to the Count and his gang.

"Excuse me, Sir. Excuse me, Mr. Basie. Uh, my name is Batt Johnson and I am on the jazz radio station here in New York, WRVR-FM, and I was wondering if I could interview you for a book that I am writing.

So far, I have Ray Charles, Buddy Rich, Percy Heath, Jimmy Heath, Larry Coryell, Milt Jackson, Elvin Jones, Joann Brackeen, Chet Baker, Ron Carter, Herb Ellis, Barney Kessel, and I also have blah-blah-blah, and blah-dee-blah."

It would be fantastic if I could spend just five minutes with you." Mr. Basie said, "Wellll, I don't think so this time around. Catch me the next time I'm in town." I said, "That I will do, Mr. Basie. That I will do." We shook hands, I shook the hands of the other fellows and we walked away.

I took about three steps and thought, "I should have asked him if he ever had sex with my mother!"

Of course, that was a joke. I would never do such a thing, but it would have been a very funny moment. Sometimes I do things just for the laugh. You know, sometimes ya just gotta live!

As a child, my mother would often come into my bedroom and tuck me in, making sure I said my prayers. (Now I lay me down to sleep, I pray to the Lord, my soul to keep. If I should die before I wake, I pray the Lord my soul to take. God bless mommy. God bless daddy, my sisters, my friends and all my other relatives. Amen.) I said that *every* night before getting into bed!

On these little nighttime tuck-in visits she would also tell me a little story, I guess to help me grow up and prepare me for what is to come as an African American man in America.

I remember her telling me about South Africa being white, minority ruled. WHAT? White people rule South Africa? WHAT? There are white people in Africa? I was too young to know South Africa from any other part of Africa. I thought all of Africa was black with jungles and wild animals, until I went there.

I didn't know that Morocco in North Africa was Arabic, until I went there. Most of the people look like Latins from the Bronx.

My mother told me that I didn't know how lucky I was to have friends like Ronnie Murakami, Matthew Qzaki, Rick Ejima, George Fakuda, George Romero, Danny O'Keef, Jessie Ortega, and Paul Valdez.

Forget about the Japanese friends for a moment. She said that when she was a kid growing up in Texas, she or anyone who looked like her, could not walk down the street with a Mexican person. If they did, the police would stop them, question them and possibly take them to jail or just beat the hell out of them and leave them lying there in the street. Is this what constitutes white superiority?

Mom said that it was more illegal to kill a chicken in the street than it was to kill a black person. Hhmm, that sounds like America with drumph in office.

THE BLONDE MYTH

You know, blonde hair is considered a mark of beauty in many cultures around the world and the U.S. is no exception. It is also considered a sign of superiority.

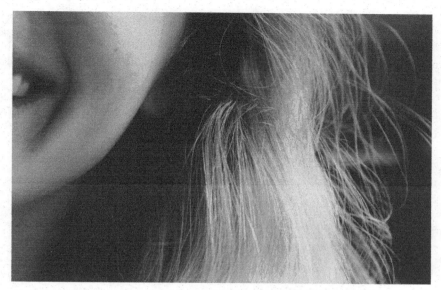

Why do brunettes' dye or color their hair blonde? I have heard from many of my close "white" friends that blonde hair makes you look more "pure," whiter. As an actor, I used to hear a lot about blonde hair making one look less ethnic, more "All-American," as a "type," therefore more marketable. Sounds like Hitler to me.

These days black people, women and men, are dying their hair blond. You even see an occasional Asian with blond hair. I think they do it as a fashion statement, rather than an attempt to completely fool you into thinking that they are a biological, instead of a bottle blonde.

But why? Often the individual, usually a female, was blonde in her youth and she wants to maintain that hair color. But the dark line down the middle of the scalp is not so attractive. Is it the reverse skunk look? Is that a thing? Do your roots, girl!

Why do women newscasters' dye or color their hair blonde? When I was doing more television, one of my anchor newscaster friends tried to convince me that she went blonde because when the television studio lights are on, her blonde hair reflects the light better, thereby creating a brighter, more pleasing picture for the viewer. I told her that was bullshit.

Why does Donald Trump's hair appear gray, white, blond? Why does he dye his hair blond? Why does he suntan? If he is white, and white is right and superior, why is he trying to get black, brown, chocolate, caramel like the people he hates? Throw away your tanning bed.

I have applied many years of thought, research, and listening to my Caucasian friends to arrive at these findings.

The American culture is no different from any other culture when it comes to myths and stereotypes. We generally have two types of images for the female. We have the dumb blonde and we have the sexy bombshell but we do not have a standard image of the blonde intellectual, the blonde mother, yes, but not the blonde intellectual, unless she has glasses. Isn't this all sounding rather silly? But it is all true, whether you believe it or not.

The image of the dumb blonde applies to men as well, like the dumb surfer dude and the dumb, athletic jock. Hey, dude!

In the movies, the blonde bombshell is more common than the dumb, ditsy blonde. Marilyn Monroe, Mae West, Brigitte Bardot, Mamie Van Doren, and Jayne Mansfield brought the sexy blonde image to the forefront in the 1950s and 60s American cinema and that image has not left our consciousness.

Actor Reese Witherspoon starred in the 2001 film, *Legally Blonde*. She played a Harvard Law School student who was blonde, beautiful, and the opposite of dumb.

Country music superstar, singer, songwriter, businesswoman, Dolly Parton said it best when she said, "I'm not offended by all the dumb-blonde jokes because I *know* I'm not dumb. I'm also not blonde.

I remember greeting someone on the street whom I had recently met at his place of employment in a local coffee shop. I said, "Hey, how are you?" He said, "I'm good, I'm good. I mean, I'm tall, I'm white, I'm blond, I'm a male…I have privilege. What more do I need?" I thought, he really believes that. If he has privilege why is he working for minimum wage in a subterranean start-up coffee shop in a lower middle-class neighborhood that is not quite developed? What the hell are you talking about?

If all he has going for him is being born "male, tall, blond, and white," I think he is a loser. If because of that he thinks he has it made, in my eyes, he is a loser. He is of no use to the advancement of this country or the world. He is a narcissistic, brain washed, societal impediment and a buffoon.

When one does not have "white privilege" and continue to fight the oppressor, one gains strength, savvy, knowledge, awareness, understanding, and uncanny insight that others do not possess. I can see it as plain as day.

If Caucasians are the superior "race" why did they go to Africa to kill, kidnap and enslave the people who lived there? That sounds like a group of murders to me. Don't we have a place for people like that? Let's start with Sing Sing, Alcatraz or Rikers Island. A "superior" people would never do something like that, if they are truly superior.

If Caucasians are superior, why didn't the slave traders use Caucasians to work in the fields from sun up to sun down? If Caucasians are superior, why do they need sun block to shield them from God's greatest resource, the sun?

Let me get on the other side for a moment. Let's say I am a greedy, wealthy European who wants MORE. What do I do? I want to discover, conquer, and steal (they would never use the word steal, but that is what it is) new land to expand my empire.

I need help. What do I do? Go to Sweden and kidnap some people to work for free? Go to Japan and kidnap some people to work for free? Go to China and kidnap some people to work for free? (Well, perhaps the Chinese could do it, after all, they built the Great Wall) Go to South America, Germany, Australia, Bolivia, Antarctica, Canada, France, Israel to get some people to work for free?

The European oppressors tried enslaving the Native Americans but they would escape and since the Native Americans knew the land so very well, the invading Europeans could not find them to recapture them. Africans did not know the land, landscape, or the language of their captors or the language of each other because they were separated from their tribe before being loaded onto the slave ships.

The slave traders of Portugal decided to go to Africa to get people they believed were "superior" in many ways. Strong, intelligent, good bones, good teeth, good genes, and passive. Only these people, of all the peoples of the world could work from sunup to sunset, be fed lousy food, some of it rotten, sustain daily beatings and whippings and still survive and work hard daily. Of all the peoples of the world, only the Africans could sustain such prolonged maltreatment.

We cannot choose our parents or do anything about being born into privilege but we can choose what we do with the privilege we have been given. I once read that in twenty-five years "white people" will be a numerical minority in the United States. That is one of the factors driving the fear and overt racism of the far right today, that and the fact that the president elected in 2016 foments racist, immoral behavior.

Think about this for a second. How do you think it would feel to live in a "free" society when the president wants to kill you and anyone who looks like you, because you don't look like him? I wonder if the tide will turn one day and those targeted for oppression will *not* be those of darker skin tone but those who wear brown shoes or those who have a dog with small ears, or even left-handed individuals. It is all pretty silly, isn't it?

As a man of major color in America, I used to think that when I heard a person of no color with a southern accent, that he was automatically a "red neck nigger hater." But I realize that is like saying all people of major melanin content are criminals, can sing, dance, play basketball and are well endowed.

"I could stand in the middle of 5th Avenue and shoot somebody and not lose any voters."
-Donald J. Trump

Mom once said, "Son, you're colored which means that you have to be twice as good as the white man to get your deserved recognition." Obviously, I didn't know what she was talking about but I think those nighttime bedside stories and chats, fueled my drive for success. Perhaps when one is "privileged" you don't have to work as hard, you don't have to be gifted, or even talented.

I remember, every day when I got out of school in junior high and high school, I would rush home, eat dinner, because mom always had dinner ready, change my clothes from my school clothes to my play clothes and race the half a block to the city park to play basketball.

It was there, in Mountain View Park on Ocean View Boulevard that I first heard of Lou Alsindor (Kareem Adbul-Jabar) from Jet Magazine. It was a story about a kid in New York who was growing so fast that his parents had to constantly buy him bigger beds.

As many of you may know, this young man grew up to become a six-time NBA Most Valuable Player, a record nineteen-time NBA All-Star, a fifteen-time All-NBA selection, an eleven-time NBA All-Defensive Team member, a member of six NBA Championship teams, and was honored as one of the Fifty Greatest Players in the history of the National Basketball Association. Not bad for a tall, skinny New York City kid, huh?

When I played basketball as a kid, I always wanted to guard the tallest guy.

Why, Batt? You're an idiot! I think I always wanted to prove something. Something within me created a huge competitive streak. Maybe that is what led me to creation and invention. If there is a hole, put something in it. When there is a problem, solve it.

Perhaps there is something within me that says, most people aren't that smart. I must admit, I find that comment to be arrogant and self-serving, self-aggrandizing but I do believe it to be true.

Playing basketball every, single day of my life, is the way I pursued dancing. When I love something, I totally dedicate myself to it. I studied every day, I practiced every day and I went out to dance every day. I later learned that my wife hated that. But I didn't understand because we started dancing together. I thought she loved dance. Actually, what she loved was going to the ballet to watch *others* dance. I did too, however "I" wanted to dance too. We just eventually drifted to different dance forms. More on this later.

On another visit to tuck me in at night, my mom said, "Son, I don't care what you do, what you become or what you do for a living, but please son, please be the best!"

I always hear my mother in my head. I believe that anything worth doing is worth doing well.

WORK HARD

Just before I started my radio career, I used to spend most of my gas money, most of my rent money and most of my food money on the latest albums. I HAD to have them. I HAD to listen to EVERY song over and over, note for note. I used to study the ENTIRE album. I studied the cover. If it was artwork, I would study every brush stroke. If it was a photograph, I would study the lighting, the composition, the foreground, the background, *everything*.

I would study the back of the album with the same precision and passion. I would study who wrote which songs, who played drums, who played bass, who played keyboards, who sang lead vocals, who sang backup vocals, who played rhythm guitar, who played lead guitar, who were the horn players, who was in the string section, who produced it, where was it recorded, who, who, who.

I was hungry for music, hungry for information. How can I be the best if I don't have a good knowledge base? I think that deep down inside I was in competition with myself to make my mother proud of me.

Years later, when I decided I wanted to become an actor, I worked my butt off with the same kind of intense studying. I bought tons of books, I took many classes in a couple of different schools, and I studied movies, television and television commercials like I never had before.

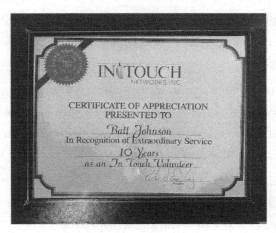

I became a volunteer reader of books, magazine articles, and newspapers for "InTouch Networks." This was a closed circuit and satellite delivered radio service for sightless and print impaired individuals in many locations around the world. I volunteered here for over fourteen years, once a week, every week. We received a certificate of appreciation every five years after ten years of service. I didn't get my fifteen-year award.

I wanted to give back and at the same time, I wanted to work on my cold reading for my acting. I would never pre-read anything. I would always read everything sight unseen, the ultimate challenge.

I would read for fifty-seven minutes and thirty seconds, straight, without stopping. Because I woke up at 2:44 that morning and already did a three-and-a-half-hour radio show, sometimes I would fall asleep while reading, *in the middle of a sentence!*

Fifty-seven minutes is a long time to read non-stop. The constant drone of my voice would put me to sleep because I had to be serious, no laughing, no loud gestures, no jokes, just read it as written.

Do you remember, as a student, falling asleep in class while writing something and when you woke up, there was a long line drawn down to the bottom of the page when you fell asleep? Same idea, only I stopped talking. Yep, once I was even snoring.

The engineers were all sightless but their hearing was extremely acute. They would bang on the studio glass as they were laughing their heads off. WAKE UP, BATT!!

Wait a minute, I'm a professional. That's not funny to me. I had such a great time working with a whole office filled with sightless people. They taught me a lot. They had nothing against me, they didn't know I am black. They couldn't see. (Not meant as a joke.)

I also volunteered for the Screen Actors Guild outreach program called "Book Pals." They sent actors to various elementary schools to read to the children. This was also a lot of fun and it helped my acting.

Both of my parents instilled within me the idea that I could do ANYTHING. I could do anything I wanted but first, I would have to WANT it. I would have to work hard to achieve it. I could do anything I wanted but I would have to really want it. Also, they said I could marry whomever I wanted.

"Son, you can marry a horse if you want to, I don't care. It doesn't matter because you are going to have to take care of her. (Remember, they were simple, country people. My mom was from Wichita Falls, Texas, and my dad was from Huntsville, Texas).

Mom could be tough when she wanted to be or when she had to be. My two sisters don't remember her the way I remember her. They remember her as a mean woman who wouldn't let them go on dates at teenagers.

My sister, Gloria (left), my mother, (center), my sister, Connie (right). My mother made these dresses. I never realized how beautiful the women in my family were until I grew up.

Mom and I were really good friends, in fact I really loved her. I remember one day she called me in from playing football in the street with my friends. She wanted me to go to the store, which I had to do all the time. I *hated* it!

She came outside and called me from the front gate. I came and she said, "I want you to go to the store. Here's the money. Get a half gallon of milk, a loaf of bread, and a dozen eggs." I was upset because I had to stop playing football. I said, "You make me sick!"

POW!!!

She was left handed and all of that left hand landed on the right side of my face. It sounded like a thud, a fire cracker, and a bomb combined. She slapped me so hard my teeth rattled, my spine shook, and my heels wiggled around in my shoes for a millisecond. Guess what, I went to the store, and I never said THAT again.

RACE MASSACRES

My mother was the source of many stories and historic, educational information for me during our bedside chats when I was a kid. Now that I think about it, I wonder why I didn't have nightmares about some of the things she told me?

I think that if I were a "white" American, I would be ashamed of my forefathers for the ill, cruel, vile deeds they performed on the black, red, brown and yellow people of this country.

Much of the information was kept hidden and away from the general public. I believe it was because of guilt and "possibly" legal action of sorts. Some of that guilt the white society should have had for their continuous barbaric, animalistic, inhumane treatment of the American black person then, "may" be redeveloping today.

During the many, many international street protests against police brutality in the summer of 2020, and the murdering of far too many African American men by the police, many historical American stories were revealed in the news coverage. These were stories of racial hatred, bigotry and disgust.

Before the protests, these stories were not common knowledge. The proceedings that brought more life to the Black Lives Matter movement, were Donald J. Trump, racial and social injustice with the killing of unarmed black men in the streets of America, and of course, COVID-19. All of these events contributed greatly to the chaos in the summer of 2020.

In all of this turmoil and confusion lies the possibility for a better sense and execution of justice and a better society in which thriving, not just surviving, for more, is possible. Many of my friends, black, red, brown, yellow and white, had never heard of these stories. The stories were kept secret, that is why. But why were they kept secret?

White guilt is one reason. The desire to make those who do not look European, feel inferior is often the goal of the oppressor. The (Black Wall Street) Greenwood, Tulsa, Oklahoma massacre and the Rosewood, Florida massacre are only two of the most well-known of those grisly stories. There are more, many more. Shooting, killing, destroying African American homes, businesses and lives was a *sport* in America, and it still is but to a lesser degree.

GREENWOOD, "BLACK WALL STREET" TULSA, OKLAHOMA MASSACRE.

From May 31 to June 1, 1921, one of the most devastating and horrific race riots and massacres in U.S. history occurred.

Greenwood, also known as "Black Wall Street" in Tulsa, Oklahoma, was one of the most successful and prominent concentrations of African American business in the United States. There were many attorneys, real estate agents, entrepreneurs, and doctors, many of whom died on that gruesomely horrifying day and a half in May.

Wherever you have African Americans, you have worship, and Greenwood was no exception. It was a very active religious community with numerous black-owned churches, Christian youth services, and other religious organizations.

Greenwood was burned to the ground because the police accused a black shoe shine boy of "assaulting" a white woman. Because of this, more than three-hundred African American men, women and children were massacred, more than eight-hundred injured, and over five-thousand were left homeless.

Evil enters like a needle and spreads like an oak tree. Ethiopian proverb

This is an historic event, not just because it was a horrible race riot and a major portion of an American city burned to the ground but how it was done is what brings more historical significance to the story.

Many believe the first time Americans were bombed and terrorized by an aerial assault was the attack on Pearl Harbor on December 7, 1941. Actually, it was twenty years earlier with Americans dropping "bombs" on Americans.

Six airplanes circled in the Greenwood skies during the morning hours of May 31, 1921. Of course, planes flying low over a neighborhood would have a huge psychological impact upon its residents, the same as when Donald Trump sent the helicopter to hover low over the protesters in Lafayette Park next to the White House during the protests of the summer 2020.

Officials said the small aircraft over Greenwood, generally thought to be two-seat, single-engine Curtis "Jenny" biplanes, dropped incendiary devices to start fires. Molotov cocktails might have been used, or "turpentine balls" which are rags soaked in flammable liquid and wrapped around the head of a stick.

Whatever the method, it was successful, creating one of the saddest days in American history. Perhaps it is events like these that caused African Americans to account for the highest increase in gun purchases of any group of Americans during the first six months of 2020.

You can poison our water, build sewage plants in our neighborhoods, and place poisonous fast food restaurants where many of us reside. You can make it difficult for us to buy real estate in neighborhoods where not many of us live, and make it increasingly difficult for us to vote. But you will *never* erase us from the face of the earth. We are here!

THE ROSEWOOD, FLORIDA RACE MASSACRE

There were many race riots and massacres in the U.S. over the years. The Rosewood massacre was not as large or as devastating to property as Greenwood, in Tulsa, Oklahoma, but it is equally as important.

Near the Gulf of Mexico about nine miles east of Cedar Key, Florida lies the town of Rosewood which was settled in 1847. It was named for the proliferation of Cedar trees and when cut for milling they displayed a reddish color interior.

From January 1st to January 3rd, 1923, another racially motivated massacre of black people and destruction of a black town took place. The town had two general stores, a Masonic Hall, three churches, a turpentine mill, a sugarcane mill, a school and a baseball team, the Rosewood Stars.

As with the Greenwood, Tulsa, Oklahoma massacre two years earlier, this massacre started when a black man was accused of assaulting a white woman. The man was found and lynched, setting off three days of rioting as a gang of white men roamed the countryside looking for black people to murder as they burned their homes to the ground.

I must oppose any attempt that Negroes may make to do to others, what has been done to them. James Baldwin

The death toll of this riot was not as great as Greenwood with about twenty-seven deaths but some say as many as one hundred-fifty deaths, and many injuries.

As with many of these incidents, the victims remained silent out of fear and shame while the oppressors remained silent as they sat in their superiority. They didn't feel the need to talk about it and no one did until sixty years later in the early 1980s when journalists started researching the event.

In the 1990s the survivors and their descendants organized to sue the State of Florida for failure to protect the Rosewood black community. Because of that, Florida became the first U.S. state to compensate individuals for damages due to racial violence. In the year 2004, the state designated the site of Rosewood as a Florida Heritage Landmark.

In 1997, Los Angeles born actor, director, producer, and screenwriter, John Singleton directed the film Rosewood. He was also nominated for the Academy Award for Best Director for Boyz n the Hood, the first African American and youngest at 24, to have ever been nominated for that award.

Throughout American history, many African American towns have been erased by being submerged in water. Yes, drowning an entire town.

LAKE LANIER, FORSYTH COUNTY, GEORGIA

This lake was named after poet Sidney Lanier, and was once called Oscarville.

It was a vibrant community with a barbershop, which is a traditional, cultural meeting place for African American men. It had more than 15 other businesses, a church, a school, many cemeteries, and over 250 families.

In 1912, two African American teenagers were accused of rape. On the same day of their arrest, their trial was held. They were found guilty and given the death penalty.

After the boy's execution, a mob of crazed Caucasian men, who called themselves Night Riders, terrorized and murdered all people of African descent in the entire area. The county went from having over 1000 residents in 1912 to 0 in 1920.

They flooded the area and literally covered the entire town with water, creating a reservoir.

Now, people go swimming, boating, water skiing, and fishing with no awareness of the skeletal remains of murdered human beings under the 156 feet of water, which cover 59 square miles.

Just think, the fish the families of the local fishermen ate, had been breathing rotting human remains. I know the thought is despicable, but so are many moments in our American history.

COLEGIA, (KOWALIGA) ALABAMA

This African American community had literally hundreds of family homes and is now under Lake Martin, a 39,000-acre reservoir.

It had an African American college, Kowaliga Academic & Industrial Institute, it had the first African American railroad, which was owned by William E. Benson. All gone.

SUSANNAH, OR SOUSANA, ALABAMA

This African American community was also flooded by Lake Martin. At least this time they removed the bodies from the cemeteries before flooding the town that also had a gold mine.

VANPORT, OREGON

In the 1940s, Vanport, Oregon was the center of a booming shipyard industry in support of World War II. It quickly became the second-largest city in the state. But as the war progressed, Caucasian males were drafted to serve overseas.

This created a tremendous labor shortage, thereby causing a massive migration of African Americans from the south to work in these newly federally desegregated, wartime defense industries.

The secretary of the Portland Urban League, Edwin C. Berry, described his city as a 'northern' city with a 'southern' exposure.

This influx of new workers needed housing. In the Portland area, in the 1940s, Vanport, also known as Albina, Vanport City, and Kaiserville, was the only neighborhood in which African Americans were legally allowed to live. I feel I should say that again, *LEGALLY allowed to live.*

At its peak, Vanport had 40,000 residents, of which 40 percent, were African American.

The spring of 1948 saw an unusually rainy season and a large gaping hole developed in the railroad dike that was blocking the Columbia River. This created a massive flood, and local officials neglected to warn residents of the danger. Many didn't evacuate in time and were killed, and the town disappeared–all within one day!

Today, that area is known as Delta Park and the Portland International Raceway. Just another little-known American historical fact for you.

Despite its loathsome past, African Americans love their country. It is the only country most have ever known.

SENECA VILLAGE, NEW YORK, NEW YORK

Historically there is something very special on New York City's Upper West Side from 82nd Street to 89th Street. This area is now known as Central Park West.

In the year 1825, it was an area called Seneca Village, populated, predominantly, by free, property owning, African Americans. At the same time Irish and German immigrants lived there as well.

By the 1840s, half of the African Americans who lived there owned their own property–a rate five times higher than the city average.

In 1857, Seneca Village was torn down for the construction of Central Park.

There is a commemorative plaque there–but it wasn't erected and dedicated until 2001.

YORK HILL, NEW YORK, NEW YORK

Another well-kept secret is that Central Park used to have another African American community within it called York Hill. The City of New York destroyed York Hill so that they could build the Central Park reservoir. Yes, yet another drowned African American community that no one talks about.

What does this say about our American traditions, culture, history, and norms? I hope by reading this, you will want to be a better person, a better American.

I know, I know, you never knew of many, if not all of these occurrences. In which case, you MUST ask yourself, why? Then answer yourself with an HONEST answer.

You and I didn't know of these American tragedies because our local and federal governments, and historians, did not want us to know about them.

Historians often tell a truth that makes them, and their people look good. Why? Because they always want to look like the good guy, the entity who is protecting us, (as they steal money and property from us and lie to us to our faces!) I think it is time to for us to wake up!

My mom didn't tell me ALL of that but you get the picture.

PART II

The Form That Became Me

CHAPTER 13

Radio & Television- Love at First Sight

This is the absolute beginning of my professional broadcasting career, at least this is when the light bulb came on about radio while I was in the U.S. Army in Seoul, South Korea.

In winter, South Korea gets punishingly cold. This day was one of those days. I was lying on my bunk, listening to the radio, dozing off and on. The record ended, another one started. That record ended and a voice came on. It said, "You're listening to AFKN, Armed Forces Korean Network, and I'm Harold Greene."

Harold Greene? Harold Greene? Red Greene? (I used to call him Red Greene because he had red hair and red freckles but his name was Greene.) Harold Greene, my buddy from my hometown, San Diego? Naaah, it couldn't be. It couldn't be the same Harold Greene I was in basic training with at Ft. Bliss in El Paso, Texas . . . or could it?

Wait a minute, I remember he was into media and was a newscaster. Maybe that IS him. I'm going to call the radio station and find out.

I called.

Ring...ring...ring.

The voice on the other end said, "AFKN, may I help you?"

Batt: "May I speak with Harold Greene, please?"

Harold: "Speaking."

Batt: "Is this Harold Greene from San Diego? Red Greene?"

Harold: "Who is this?"

Batt: "It's Johnson from San Diego and basic training in Ft. Bliss, Texas."

Harold: "No shit! I think about you all the time. I wondered where they shipped you. I thought you were sent to Vietnam and got shot. Where are you?"

Batt: "I am on Yongsan compound, 8th Army Headquarters, in Soul, Korea."

Harold: "Me too. You should come to the station one day, say hello."

Batt: "Ok, how about today?"

Harold: "Come on up. I am on the hill where all of the radio and TV towers are."

Batt: "I'll be there in fifteen minutes."

I arrived at the mountaintop studio, entered and found Harold while he was still on the radio. He invited me into the studio with him to watch him finish the rest of his radio show. This was my first time being in a radio and television studio. I was excited to see Harold Greene again and I was excited to be in the AFKN studios, in Seoul, Korea.

I remember when I was very young I thought the DJ on the radio knew *everyone*. I thought he knew all of the musicians in every band on the radio and he was in a giant room so all the bands could fit in it.

The reason I thought that is because I thought the bands were actually in the room *with* him. I also thought the bands were well-rehearsed because the music sounded the same every day. Geez, I was naïve, but at least I was thinking.

In Harold Greene's studio I was surrounded, lovingly engulfed by dials, nobs, switches, buttons, wires, meters, electronics up the ying-yang. I was so excited, I was taken, I was hooked, I was in love.

I didn't know it at the time, but that was the beginning of my long love affair with the media.

When I got out of the Army, my first job was at one of the many aircraft factories in San Diego.

I was drilling holes in metal to make airplanes, a very boring assembly line job. Then I studied electronics, that wasn't working for me. One day I saw an ad in a magazine for the Columbia School of Broadcasting. I later enrolled into the Bill Wade School of Radio & Television Broadcasting. I guess I chose that school because I had heard Bill Wade on the radio in LA before. I enrolled and I immediately felt at home.

Harold Greene had a fantastic career, all of which was in California.

Television newsman, Jack White, a friend of Harold's, was hired as a consultant for the film "Anchorman: The Legend of Ron Burgundy." It starred Will Ferrell, Ben Stiller, Steve Carell, Cristina Applegate, Fred Willard, Seth Rogen, and others. It is said that Jack White was inspired for the look of Ron Burgundy by Harold Greene. Some say that newsman, Mort Crim was the inspiration.

Harold earned ten Golden Mike Awards, the Columbia Graduate School of Journalism Award, two Emmy Awards and nine Emmy nominations, three Edward R. Murrow Awards and twelve Press Club Awards. The crowning Glory? He has a star on the Hollywood Walk of Fame!

THIS is the man who introduced me to broadcasting. Thank you, Harold Greene. Because of your introduction to media to me in Korea, this is what happened.

```
book.   TOP TEN MORNING DJS.  According to Arbitron results from spring
        Ranking by persons 12+ and Metro cume:
        Scott Shannon/WHTZ-FM, New York.  1,517,800.
        Jim Kerr/WWPR-FM, New York.  1,160,200.
        Rick Dees/KIIS-FM, Los Angeles.  1,121,300.
        Jay Thomas/KPWR-FM, Los Angeles.  976,500.
        John Gambling/WOR-AM, New York.  952,800.
        Bob Collins/WGN-AM, Chicago.  878,200.
        Howard Stern/WXRK-FM, New York.  855,100.
        Harry Harrison/WCBS-FM, New York.  769,800.
      ✓ Batt Johnson/WLTW-FM, New York.  747,800.
        Dave Herman/WNEW-FM, New York.  715,200.
        You may want to aircheck the ones you haven't heard lately.
```

From the introduction to broadcasting in Seoul, Korea around 1967, to making the top ten morning show radio DJs almost twenty years later. There are approximately 13,769 radio stations in America with 51,558 broadcasters on staff. I was #9 of the top ten, and the only African American on the list. This is from an article in Radio & Records Magazine in the mid 1980s.

I LOVED KOREA

I had a group of friends who lived on my floor of a multi-floor barracks complex. We would go out drinking almost every night after work. Why not? We're young men who are countless thousands of miles away from home on the other side of the planet. We are away from our mothers, who love us, our families who miss us and our fathers who have just one more lesson for us. We're adults. Let's party!

One of the guys, Charles Patoky, was from Los Angeles and loved to play poker. One day the big rumor around the base was that Gary Lewis, the singer in the group Gary Lewis and the Playboys, who had the hit record, *This Diamond Ring*, and was the son of comedian Jerry Lewis, was in the barracks in the building next to ours. He also loved to play poker. A few nights a week we would go just to hang out with Gary Lewis. Patoky would play, and we would watch. Maybe Gary's dad would get his son's Army buddies a movie contract, hahahaha.

Private First-Class Johnson at my barracks in Seoul, Korea

Patoky was an extra in the move, *What Did You Do in the War, Daddy?* It stared James Coburn and Dick Shawn. Patoky thought he was a movie star, but I loved him. He was a wild guy.

The movie came to our base one day on movie night and we all went to see it. In his scene, he was a soldier (how ironic), leaning against a lamp post smoking a cigarette. You can't make this stuff up. Well, I could, but I am not.

I loved living in South Korea. To this day, I still have a soft spot in my heart for Korea and her people. Today, I really enjoy going to my neighborhood dry cleaners because they are Korean and I can practice my language skills, such as they are.

When I was there, many of the white soldiers would curse the Koreans and call them gooks, slant eyes, chinks, slopes, yellow fever and other derogatory names.

I would hang out with the Korean soldiers. They were called KATUSAs, which is an acronym for *Korean Augmentation to the United States Army*.

I had befriended some of the KATUSA soldiers. One of my best Korean Army buddie's name was Kim. Kim is a *very* common last name is South Korea. In that country the family name, the last name, comes first.

One day we were studying at the library on the Army base in Yongson Compound. I was watching him take some notes. As a joke, I said, "Why do you write with that chicken scratch?"

This was during a time much before political correctness was even a thought. Again, I had many Asian friends at home. I knew them, I understood them, I loved them. I was even made an honorary Japanese. I would never say something derogatory, hateful, racist, or mean spirited toward them, their language or culture.

I think Kim was somewhat insulted. He got up from the desk, walked over to a large map on the wall, and with a long, wide sweeping motion of his hand across Asia, he said, "Do you see *alllll* of this land mass? All of these billions of people write with that "chicken scratch."

I then realized that my statement was insulting and racist. I felt two feet tall.

I learned to speak, read and write some of the Korean language, I learned about their food, culture, their history, and I traveled by land to see more of that incredible country. Why not? I was there, why not learn and grow? I also got a chance to see some of Okinawa and Japan.

While stationed in Korea, I took a quick, free military stand-by flight to Okinawa, Japan to visit the identical twin brother of a good Army buddy of mine whom I met while stationed in Korea. They were from Michigan. I love twins. But what I don't like about twins is when I think I'm talking to one twin when I am actually speaking to the other.

You can often catch their body language or facial expressions when you are speaking of something that your twin friend would know, and the other twin to whom you are speaking, is not responding in the appropriate manner. Then you know you are speaking to the other twin. I know, I know it all sounds very confusing as it can actually be. But I love twins.

MY FIRST HEARTBREAK!

Japan is the birthplace of my nephew, Darrell Lamar Barnes. Darrell was the first baby born in ALL of Asia on January 1st, 1960 in Yokosuka, Japan at the U.S. Naval Hospital at 12:00 midnight…and he is African American. Yep, the first baby born in all of Asia that year was black.

When I say, "all of Asia," this includes Okinawa, Thailand, China, Vietnam, Philippines, Borneo, Indonesia, Malaysia, Cambodia, Taiwan, Laos, Papua New Guinea, Afghanistan, Armenia, Azerbaijan, Bahrain, Bangladesh, Bhutan, Brunei, Burma, East Timor, Georgia, Hong Kong, India, Iran, Iraq, Israel, Jordan, Kazakhstan, Kuwait, Kyrgyzstan, Lebanon, Mongolia, Nepal, North Korea, South Korea, Oman, Pakistan, Qatar, and a few more. I think he got me beat with my first African American baby born in a hospital title.

I know, I know it sounds like something from Ripley's Believe it or Not or a Dave Chapelle comedy skit, but it is true.

I will let my sister, Connie Rae Johnson, the mother, tell her story.

Batt: Where did you meet Ronald, your ex-husband?

Connie: I met Ronald in San Diego. My girlfriend and I were at the park one day, which was only a quarter of a block from our house, as you remember. I guess he used to talk to her. I don't know what the situation was between them but one day he asked me for my phone number and I gave it to him. Much later, we started talking and I invited him over one evening and he and mom had a great time. She just fell in love with him. He and our older sister, Gloria, were friends and it took off from there.

Ron took me to dinner. That was the first time I'd gone to a Chinese restaurant. At that time, he had been in the service for about four years, then he had gotten out. He was about eight or nine years older than I, so of course, he had world experience from being in the service. So, he took me to my first Chinese restaurant, which was absolutely wonderful.

My sister, Connie with her husband Ronald D. Barnes E-6 Ship Serviceman 1st Class, U.S. Navy (around 1974).

I didn't know any different so it was wonderful. From there we just started going out. We would go to drive-in theaters, the drive-in restaurants.

That to me was really fun because I'd never gone to one until I met Ron. Keep in mind I was seventeen when I met Ron. He was twenty-five or so. Everything was all new experiences.

He decided to go back into the service. When he made that decision, that's when he asked me to marry him. He wanted to get married before he went back into the service. He went into the service and right away got his orders. He was being shipped to Japan. I stayed in California, worked, saved my money because the military would not pay my way to meet him in Japan. I had to pay my own way so I worked in a laundry, saved every penny I could put my hands on, and that's how I got to Japan.

Batt: This is my memory. I was standing on the dock in San Pedro, California (Long Beach). I remember the ship had two big smoke stacks that were cut at an angle. The stacks were tall in the front and lower in the back, cut at an angle toward the back of the ship and they were painted red.

Connie: The name of the line was President Lines.

Batt: Yes. I remember you were walking up the ramp, onto the ship. I was crying my head off. I was so sad. I was heartbroken and this was my first heartbreak at ten or eleven years old. You represented so many things to me.

You were my friend, you were my sister, you were my brother, you were my pal, you were my dance partner. When you left, Connie, I was so sad. The ship took off and I was waving and crying and waving and crying. I was a mess. You owe me for that.

Connie: That was our first time being separated.

Batt: Yes, and it was not fun. It was not good, I was so sad. How long did it take to get to Japan?

Connie: It took about five days, I believe. We stopped in Hawaii. We were allowed to get off the ship for the day. I had become very close to a young lady who was on the ship. It just so happened that she was going to Japan to meet her husband who was in the Navy as well.

When we got to Hawaii, we got off the ship and just kind of walked around a bit and had lunch. And then back on the ship. The closer we got to Japan, the sicker I became because there was a typhoon. I have never been so sick in my life. That was an experience, a horrible experience. Ron was waiting for me when I arrived. He called me "okusan," which means wife in Japanese. That was the first word I heard in Japanese.

Batt: I remember you wrote me a letter telling me about Hawaii and how expensive it was. You said a Coca Cola cost five dollars or something. Who else did you meet on the ship going over?

Connie: I met the Harlem Globetrotters (the world-famous American comedy basketball team). I met Goose Tatum, one of the stars of the team and his wife. That's the only name I can remember. He was the only one who was traveling with a woman. All of the other guys were single and we had a good time dancing, we danced a lot, and just having a great time. That was quite an experience.

Batt: So, you made it to Japan. How long were you there before you had Darrell, your first child?

Connie: When I got to Japan, Ron had already applied for Navy housing. Your spouse had to be there a certain length of time before they would allow you to go into military housing. We lived on base for about 2 or three months.

Probably two years later, I became pregnant and my due date was on Christmas Day. One evening I was coming down the stairs, we had the two-story Navy style housing.

I was going down the stairs and I slipped, fell, and tumbled down the stairs. I started going into labor, so they rushed me to the dispensary (the military hospital) but I didn't go into labor. They sent me back home. A week later, there it was, labor, labor, the working pains of labor. Back to the dispensary I went. That's when Darrell was born.

Darrell was the first baby born. He was a New Year's baby. At that time, Asia was called the "Far East." Now it's called Asia. At that point in time, he was the first baby born in the entire Far East.

Batt: So, it was January 1st, 1960. And in all of the Far East, in all of those countries…China, Japan, Taiwan, Korea, Indonesia, Vietnam, Cambodia, Singapore, Hong Kong, and others…of all the births that day, the first baby born was black.

Connie: Exactly!

Batt: That's so funny. That's crazy.

Connie: He's gotten rid of several things that I had given him over the years, but the one thing that I always wanted him to keep was his newspaper article. I need to check with him, I hope he still has it. I think it was Stars & Stripes, the American military newspaper. It was probably in the Japanese paper as well, but we couldn't read that.

Batt: I have to get my newspaper clippings too. I was the first black baby born in St. Peters Hospital in Olympia, Washington.

Connie: That is absolutely correct, you were.

Batt: We have this special Johnson blood, hahaha. I wonder if kids used to tease him about being black and the first of all babies born in Asia?

Connie: I am certain they did. Kids will tease you for any reason or no reason.

Batt: That's great. That's all I need.

Connie: Not very exciting, sorry.

Batt: No, it *is* exciting! And it's interesting. Thank you for your time and for letting us in on some of your interesting life.

JAPAN, WHERE *EVERYTHING* IS DIFFERENT.

While stationed in Korea, I took advantage of the free military stand-by flight program that was offered by the Army. I decided I wanted to go back home to visit my family for Christmas. For the first time in my life, I was away from my family and hadn't seen them in months. I flew into Tachikawa Air Force Base, located outside of Tokyo, Japan, as a stopover.

When I got off the plane and walked inside the terminal. I saw many U.S. military servicemen sleeping on the floor waiting for the next stand-by opportunity to reach their destination. They were also probably trying to get back home for the Holidays.

I thought that since I was in Japan, I should see it. I should see what my sister, Connie's letters were all about when she lived there.

I got a room in the Air Force barracks and took a nap. I woke up, showered, put on my suit and caught a train to downtown Tokyo. I had NO idea where I was. I saw no street signs.

Everything was written in Japanese, even the neon Coca Cola signs and ads for Suntory whiskey, the oldest brewing company in Japan. Since I had no idea where I was or where I was going, I just got off the train at a random stop. I walked around admiring this *amazing city* that is so vastly different from anything I had ever witnessed in my nineteen-year-old life.

I walked and walked and walked and ran into the Ginza. The Ginza is like Times Square in New York with giant, brightly lit neon signs and many people.

In fact, New York probably got the idea from the Ginza in Tokyo.

I wandered into a bar and had a drink. Then, as if by a miracle, I found the train station and went back to my room at Tachikawa Air Force Base.

The next day I did the same thing. Took the train to downtown Tokyo and got off at some random location.

I wandered around and found an appealing bar. I went in, sat down and ordered a drink. The bartender spoke some English. That was a relief. But it didn't matter because I was on an adventure and I have so much self-confidence, self-awareness, self-empowered thought from my life and way of being that I knew everything would be alright. My thought was that I don't really have to worry about anything, ever.

The drink came, I am enjoying it and then, in a few minutes, another drink came before I am even half finished with the first one. So, my first thought is, oh, no, they are trying to pull a fast one and rip me off like in a Tijuana bar in Mexico. I know how to handle these kinds of situations. I said to the bartender, "I didn't order this." He said, "Oh, I know. He ordered it for you," As he pointed to a gentleman down the bar. I nodded my head and said thank you.

A few minutes go by and the guy came and sat down next to me. I'm starting to get a bit nervous and preparing to defend myself for whatever happens. The guy sat down and said, "Hello, Mr. Johnson." What the ****? I am REALLY freaked out now. I said, "Uh, hello, uh, how are you…and how did you know my name?" He said, "It is right there on your inside suit jacket pocket." I was thinking a million things at this moment.

One of the things was, this guy is gay and he is going to try to hit on me. If he puts his hand on my knee, we are going to have a problem. We chat a bit and he told me that he is an electrical engineer and is considering getting married soon. He then says, "Well, Mr. Johnson, I just wanted to know if you are having a good time in my country." Of course, I said, "I'm having an *amazing* time in your country. Thank you." We shake hands and he got up and left.

THAT is Japan! I found my way back to the train, I don't know how I did that, and I made it back to Tachikawa Air Force Base.

The next day I packed up, checked out of my room and went back into Tokyo. I found my way to the Hotel New Otani and I checked in. This is a very famous hotel and it has a rotating restaurant on the top floor that provides incredible views of Tokyo as it rotated.

I walked around shopping, looking for a Kabuki doll for Ronnie Murakami's mother. Before I left America, she told me that if I got a chance to go to Japan she wanted a Kabuki doll. I walked and looked and walked and looked, and finally found a store that had some. They were not cheap and I was on a military budget but I was on a mission to fulfill a request from my Japanese mother. So, whatever the cost. I bought it. Ouch!

I don't remember if Mrs. Murakami *gave* me these albums or *loaned* them to me. When I moved away, I forgot I had them.

I went back to the hotel to wait for the sun to go down so I could go check out the Tokyo night life. I would love to see some live music or something but that never happened. I wandered into another really nice bar. This is a pretty high-class area of the city. I guess I saved a lot of money for this trip. I don't remember.

Almost the same thing happened as before, only this time it was two guys. I was drinking at the bar alone. They come over to me, we chatted and drank. I discovered they both happened to be electrical engineers just like the first guy I met.

Then they said, "Are you hungry? We are, we haven't eaten yet. How would you like to have dinner with us?" I agreed. As we were walking out of the bar I'm planning my escape in case they try to beat me up and rob me. We caught a taxi, which they insisted on paying for upon our arrival at a nice restaurant.

We were escorted to a private, slightly elevated room where we had to take off your shoes before entering. There was a hibachi kind of stove in the middle of the room where you cook your own food. It was a small room but certainly big enough for the three of us.

Of course, we sat on the floor, there were no chairs. The sliding door was made of very light, thin wood with rice paper covering squares made by the wood. The walls were made of the same material.

It was very quaint, very Japanese and very beautiful. The waitress brought us some salads, soups and raw fish and beef that we cooked on the hibachi pot in front of us. We drank something, I don't remember what, we laughed and had a wonderful time as I told them who I was and what I did. It was a fantastic time.

We finished our meal, left the room, put on our shoes and went to the front to pay our bill. They INSISTED they pay for dinner. We left the restaurant, the three of us got a taxi and they INSISTED they pay for it, and they escorted me back to my hotel. Wow! What an evening in Tokyo, Japan.

CHAPTER 14

Radio Changed My Life

Many years ago, I was told in a staff meeting at NBC that "You get a good job by doing a good job at the job you have." With my family upbringing and learned lessons of discipline and accountability from being an athlete and from being in the military, I attempt to do everything at my highest level. I am a believer in, "anything worth doing, is worth doing well."

I took those lessons to my selected life and lifestyle of choice. I had a long, fairly successful career as a music radio broadcaster, actor, voiceover artist, model, hand model, TV newscaster, media trainer, professor and television home shopping host. I never achieved superstar status but some of those who did, knew who I was.

I was considered to be the first African American to work in pop, rock 'n roll, country, r & b, smooth jazz, and big band radio in New York City (probably in all of the United States, probably ever), and I was, at one time, the only African American country music radio DJ in a major market in the United States. I was also one of the only rock 'n roll, African American radio DJs in the United States. Quincy McCoy, Walt "Baby" Love, Chuck Leonard, and Mark McEwen were also in that exclusive club.

BLACK SABBATH, JANIS JOPLIN

The first big rock 'n roll/top 40 radio station I worked for was KCBQ-AM in San Diego, California. A legend in the city, I listened to it when I was a child. I couldn't believe I was a DJ there. Holy cow! I would say something like, "This is a dream come true." But in my wildest dreams, I never imagined being a broadcaster on this or any radio station.

When I look back, I cannot believe that I was able to turn something most people would consider a hobby such as listening to and loving music, into a career of forty years, and against many odds.

The KCBQ studios were located in Santee, California. At the time it was considered the countryside of San Diego. Around 2006 or so, a monument was erected to honor this legendary local broadcasting institution. My name is proudly displayed on the monument. My parents would be very proud.

Our most immediate competitor was KGB-AM, the station Buzz Bennett and I just left, another legendary San Diego radio station. Charlie Van Dyke, the program director was giving away a car a day as their big promotion for the upcoming ratings period. Buzz, being the perpetual, fierce, combative competitor that he was, was NOT going to be outdone by ANYONE. So, he put on a contest giving away TWO cars a day. Buzz really had a lot of faith and confidence in me. In fact, he used to call me *"Battski the Prince of Positivity."*

The on-air staff at KCBQ-AM, San Diego, 1971.
Batt Johnson, Rich Brother Robin, Christopher Kaye, Buzz Bennett, "Shotgun" Tom Kelly,
Lennie Mitchell, Chuck Browning, Dave Conley, and Harry Scarborough.

The beginning of radio ideas that COMPLETELY changed how music radio was being broadcast.

I had enough self-confidence for two people but Buzz gave me even more.

I remember one night I went to see Eric Burdon and the Animals, this was before Eric Burdon started working with the group, War.

The Animals were a big group with such hits as "We Gotta Get Out of This Place", "It's My Life", "Don't Let Me Be Misunderstood", "San Franciscan Nights", When I Was Young", "Sky Pilot", and probably their biggest hit, "The House of the Rising Sun", and many other hits. They were part of the massive *British Invasion* when the Beatles came to America. The British Invasion? At that time, I didn't even *like* the Beatles. I didn't like the Beatles until the Sergeant Pepper album came out. Then, I went crazy. But, I mean, Eric Burdon & the Animals were huge.

I don't know what got into me at that moment, but I saw the band in the parking lot leaving the arena after the show. So, I rushed over to talk to them.

These were huge, international stars who could have easily blown me off and not talked to me thinking, "who is this skinny black kid approaching us? Doesn't he know we are big international rock 'n roll stars from England?"

I had only been in the business a short while, I didn't know what I was doing but I didn't give a shit, I wanted to talk to them. It was at that moment that I realized that I was an equal, and this business was for me.

I don't think it was Buzz Bennett who first gave me courage and self-confidence, I think it was my mother.

A few years later I saw Eric Burdon again, but this time he was singing with an African American funk-rock band from Long Beach, California called, War. They also had a string of hits like, "Low Rider", "Why Can't We Be Friends?", "The World Is a Ghetto", "The Cisco Kid", "Spill the Wine", "Slippin' Into Darkness", and "Summer". They were huge on the Top-40, non-African American industry music charts AND the black charts.

Buzz and Batt at a Hollywood release party for War's new album "Why Can't We Be Friends?"

I later learned that the drummer, Harold Brown and I, dated the same girl, Julia (I forgot her last name). Hhmm, I wonder if it was at the same time. Hhmm. Who's zoomin' who?

A few months later Buzzy told me to go host a show with Stone the Crows as the opening act and Black Sabbath as the headliner. This was around 1970 or 1971, before Ozzy Osborne was Ozzy Osborne. At this time, he was just the vocalist for Black Sabbath, a heavy rock band from England. He hadn't even bitten off the head of a bat yet or achieved the level of "The Prince of Darkness." That's how new he was. I didn't know any of these groups, I was just excited as hell to be asked to go host a major rock 'n roll show.

This was only my second, or third time hosting and emceeing a show with major international talent of this caliber. I was new to the game.

Although I am black, I was green at this game, very wet behind the ears. I don't think I was nervous, that was too long ago to remember that detail.

On stage to host a Black Sabbath concert. KCBQ was giving away two cars a day to combat our competitor who was giving away a car a day. Buzz Bennett, not to be outdone...

I stepped out on stage to a crowd of several thousand people and said, "Gooood evennning ladieees and gentlemennnn. Welcooome toooo the Sann Dieeegoo Sportsss Areeeaaa...and IIII'mmm BLACK SABBATH!!

It was at this moment that not only could you hear a pin drop but you could hear the crickets chirping six blocks away. It got so quiet you could hear the blood flowing through the veins of the person ten feet away from you. Quiet as hell! I thought, what the heck is wrong with these kids.

That was funny, funny as hell. Oh, I get it, they don't want to appear racist or they are too stoned on acid, opium, pot, peyote, mushrooms or

Boones Farm wine for the joke to compute. I know I probably completely threw them off from the beginning when I walked out on stage, a black DJ to host a Black Sabbath rock and roll concert.

I remember going to rock concerts and outdoor festivals in the late sixties. I saw Jimi Hendrix twice, Creedence Clearwater Revival, Sly & The Family Stone, Frank Zappa, Jethro Tull, The Steve Miller Band, Deep Purple, Black Sabbath, Alice Cooper, Cream, the Chambers Brothers, Country Joe & the Fish, Blue Cheer, Jefferson Airplane, I saw them all. Well, I never saw the Rolling Stones or Frank Sinatra. This makes me sad.

I was on stage as the host for concerts with Chicago Transit Authority, Canned Heat, Crosby, Stills, Nash & Young, etc. In fact, I was the host and master of ceremony at a show in San Diego where the main act was Janis Joplin and Big Brother & the Holding Company. I have since forgotten who the warm-up act was.

I was on stage making announcements, then I introduced her to the audience. She came out with a long, multi-color tie dyed dress on, beads and bracelets around her wrists, and something, maybe flowers, in her hair.

As she approached me, she extended her hand and in it was her trade-mark bottle of Southern Comfort whiskey. She said, "Wont sum, bebeh?" In her strong Port Arthur, Texas accent.I said, "No, no thank you."

All the while, the crowd was screaming and applauding. Then she stepped up to the microphone, slapped it and said, "I'm TARED uh dat thang!" I laughed and walked off stage. I can still smell her patchouli oil.

I didn't get a chance to speak to her much in the dressing room because it was almost time to start the show but she was kind, and polite. She was a little bit drunk, and a whole lot of Janis.

"LIVE in San Diego, 1968" is an album that is available in the UK. I was at that concert sitting in the nose-bleed section of the San Diego Sports Arena. I had no idea what was going on musically with this group. It was loud blues sounding rock and roll. The whole concert sounded like one looooong guitar solo. I didn't know who Eric Clapton was.

Because it was such a large arena, the sound angrily bounced all around this massive space. By the time you understood two notes one hundred more would hit your ear. It was NOT a good experience for me. I had been home for only four months, fresh from military duty in Korea. The concept of the rock concert was a very new thing in 1968. This was only my second experience with this new genre.

This is a piece written by Sharon O' Neill of Keymailrecords, England.

Radio Broadcast. San Diego Sports Arena on 20th October 1968. Also available in Vinyl.

Keymailrecords Overview.

Cream were the British Rock trio that oozed talent from every musical angle, albeit they were only together for two years their influence was immense. They could be considered as the first supergroup to become superstars and the first top group to truly exploit the power trio format, in the process laying the foundation for much blues-rock and hard rock of the 1960s and 1970s.

All three of the musicians yearned to break free of the confines of the standard rock/R&B/blues group, in a unit that would allow them greater instrumental and improvisational freedom, somewhat in the mold of a jazz outfit. Eric Clapton's stunning guitar solos would get much of the adulation, yet Jack Bruce and drummer Ginger Baker were at least as responsible for shaping the group's sound, singing most of the material in his rich voice. He also wrote their best original compositions, sometimes in collaboration with outside lyricist Pete Brown.

Cream's short lifespan however, was in hindsight unsurprising given the considerable talents, ambitions, and egos of each of the band members. 'Live in San Diego' shows Cream at their finest during their Farewell Tour. Worn out by touring and personal disagreements, Cream agreed to disband after a farewell tour in October 1968. Recorded in outstanding fidelity for broadcast on KPRI-FM (later became my first real on-air job), this outstanding gig features a cross-section of their best-loved material and clearly indicates why they were regarded as the preeminent rock band of their day.

Track list

1. White Room (Pete Brown)

2. Politician (Pete Brown)

3. I'm So Glad (Skip James)

4. Sitting on Top of The World (Walter Vinson & Lonnie Chatmon, original members of the Mississippi Sheiks)

5. Sunshine of Your Love (Clapton, Bruce, Brown, bass line written after seeing a Jimi Hendrix concert)

6. Crossroads (Robert Johnson)

7. Train Time (Ginger Baker)

8. Toad (Ginger Baker)

9. Spoonful (Willie Dixon)

Almost half of those songs were written by African Americans.

As you can see, her view of Cream was very different from my first experience with Cream. I loved the band and their records but that concert wasn't working for me.

I had a German American girlfriend at the time, Suzy. Whenever she went to the restroom or went to the concession stand to get something to eat at one of the many massive outdoor concerts or rock festivals we went to, I was always amazed at how she could find me in this vast, vast sea of humanity so quickly.

It never dawned on me that mine, was the only black face there. Holy cow was I ever so naive? I thought I was just a guy! I mean, I knew I was black but I didn't think I looked that different. I didn't think it was important. In my mind, I am human first, then I am a man, then I am an African American man. I often say, "MY people aren't necessarily those who LOOK like me. But rather, MY people are those who THINK like me." Yes, that has gotten me into trouble a few times.

I guess my color meant something to Suzy's mother when I went to her home to pick her up one day. I parked my car, walked up to the door, rang the doorbell and her mother opened the door. I said, "Hi, my name is Batt Johnson. Is Suzy here?" BLAM!!! She slammed the door in my face so hard that the number four of her house address fell off onto the ground. Ouch! Geez, was that necessary? That was one strong ass German woman.

Rock 'n roll was not easy when you don't *look* like "rock 'n roll." I didn't have long hair streaming down my back, plus my overall melanin content was higher than all the rest. Believe me, I was rock 'n roll on the inside and I am still rock 'n roll. That is, "if" the music is good. Some may call me a snob. I say, I have a certainnnn, what should I say . . . "taste" in things.

"Big" Bob Foster, a big influence on my radio training.

I spent many years of my life chasing those sensations I felt in those massive rock concerts when the floor or ground was shaking from the debilitating, deafening volume of the music. The light shows on the walls behind the bands showed old silent movies, cartoons or the bubbles of oil and water with a colored light underneath them adding an additional stimulant for your brain through your eyes instead of your ears.

That was hip at that time, that was what was happening then. I can't believe I escaped those times without getting tinnitus, or that constant ringing in the ear sensation that so many musicians have from the continuous listening to loud music. But I wanted to feeeeel the music, not just hear it.

13Q RADIO, PITTSBURGH

"I like hiring vultures. Give a bunch of vultures a cause and look out!"
-Buzz Bennett

13Q was a legendary, creative, one of a kind radio station that both professional broadcasters and the people of Pittsburgh, Pennsylvania still talk about today as they have since 1972. I feel so incredibly honored to be one of the original DJs at this facility. I helped build this legendary radio station in more ways than one.

We caught the attention of the entire city BEFORE we hit the air with a new format and a new concept in Top 40 radio. First, Cecil Heftel bought the NBC affiliate, all-news radio WJAS-AM. Before we changed the format to rock 'n roll, we had the newscasters read promotional announcements about a new station coming that will be giving away $13,000 in cash! All you have to do when your phone rings, is answer it by saying, "I listen to the new sound of 13Q" and instantly win $13,000. This got Pittsburgh's attention.

The Battman has emerged! Time to have some serious fun.

Buzz Bennett and I were creating concepts for the station from his Santee (San Diego), California hilltop home when he was still the program director of KCBQ. His beautiful wife, Lani, always nearby providing love, wisdom, and a helping hand. One of my memories of her was with a beautiful necklace, long white dress, and beautifully painted, white fingernails. (Lani, if that is way off, I'm sure you'll tell me.)

I really didn't know what Buzzy was up to or what was to happen. But I knew "something" was about to happen. Since we were roommates and he was really teaching me the ins and outs of radio at that time, I was very open, attentive, and excited. I listened to everything he said. I HAD to listen, for I was in the presence of a MASTER.

I was at the epicenter of counterculture pop music history and didn't know it. When I was living with Buzz Bennett in his hilltop home in Santee (San Diego), California, amazingly accomplished people would come visit. Freddie Mancuso, a record promoter of major artists in Hollywood, came over one day, but he couldn't stay long because he had to take the Staple Singers to their show that night in Los Angeles. The Staple Singers?! You know the Staple Singers?! They had such hits as: "I'll Take You There" (1972), "Respect Yourself" (1972), "Let's Do it Again" (1975), and many more.

Artie Kornfeld came over often. He was one of the creators of the historic Woodstock Music & Arts Fair, where over 400,000 people gathered on Max Yasgur's 600-acre dairy farm in Bethel, New York. This massive, historic event went from August 15–18, 1969. This is the music festival that all festivals ever since have been compared to and modeled after. Now that I look back on it, I was in the midst of magic music makers. Out of the blue, Artie contacted me on Facebook. We are in touch regularly today (as of this writing, July 2020).

The Amazing Buzz Bennett, the man who started my music radio career (RIP).

13Q had many firsts in American radio history that were later used by broadcasters around the world. We had the biggest cash call contests. We always had our production director, Mark Driscoll or someone else nearby to IMMEDIATELY produce promos of our winners. This was another element that created constant excitement on the air, real people in real moments on the air. Why? Because the PEOPLE own the airwaves (ask the FCC). Most radio stations have forgotten, did not know, or did not know how to reflect the very people they are talking to. It is communication theory 101.

"I'm a success today because I had a friend who believed in me and I didn't have the heart to let him down."

- Abraham Lincoln

We were one of the first, if not THE first radio station in America to use a nickname instead of the actual call letters. The legal identification of the station was WKTQ, we called ourselves 13Q. Before there was a Magic 93, Y-100, Q104 or a Lite-FM, there was 13Q. We were one of the first, if not THE first to actually re-equalize and add a little reverb to each and every song played on the air to emphasize different instruments in the music.

This gave the station a very unique sound. The sound quality was like that of FM radio but it was on AM where you usually get static and hisses. But now listeners could hear things in the same old songs the other radio stations were playing but on 13Q they sounded different, clearer and no one knew why.

Another genius Buzz Bennett programming tactic was to play unorthodox "novelty" records like *Alvin & the Chipmunks, Grandma Got Ran Over by a Reindeer, Shaving Cream, Surfin' Bird, One Eyed, One Horned, Flying Purple People Eater, They're Coming to Take Me Away,* Cheech & Chong's *Sister Mary Elephant*, and many others. There was a very specific strategy to playing these and the placement of them.

Those novelty records we called GOOFS or goofball records. I think they were played at :50 or :55 before our most immediate competitor, KQV, was about to go into the news. The theory was we'd play the goof, the kids would tune out and tune into KQV.

They would hear the news and come back to us because the kids wanted rock. WE wanted to rock too! Well, they didn't tune out, they loved the goofs. These records added an additional layer of protective armor to our programming wizardry.

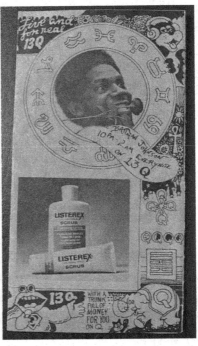

Outside of the weekly 13Q promotional music sheet found in record stores and convenience stores. I compiled these weekly to show our audience what we were playing.

Inside these music playlist sheet. As Program Research Director, I placed phone calls to almost all Pittsburgh are record stores to find out what was selling. Then all of that information would be manually tabulated.

The reason we sounded so different than our competitor was because the program director, Dave Daniels, who was also an engineer, and I, spent three whole days and nights in Ken-Tel Recording Studio in Nashville. This was half owned by Cecil Heftel. This also happens to be where country music star, Roger Miller recorded "King of the Road". Mr. Heftel owned 13Q radio and he also owned a television station, a newspaper, a pineapple farm, all in Hawaii, as well as other mainland radio stations in St. Louis and Y-100 in Miami. He was the first millionaire I ever went out to dinner with.

We were one of the first, if not THE first Top-40 AM rock and roll radio station to play album cuts and not the record company edited single versions of songs. We would take album cuts and re-edit them ourselves thereby giving the listener a totally different sound experience.

We were one of the first, if not THE first to slightly speed up the turntables while recording the music to cart. This made us sound exciting, peppy and alive, while our competition sounded sluggish, sleepy and boring, even though they were playing the same songs.

Buzz Bennett in a major magazine article

We were one of the first, if not THE first to have a fun, unpredictable show in ALL dayparts (Who, of the many radio "geniuses" said radio listeners want to have fun only in the morning?). We believed so much in what we were doing and were so excited that we would come by the station at all hours of the day and night, jump on the air with whomever was on at the time, and proceed to have a ball. We even had three people on the radio at the same time. Let's wake this town up!

The audience had the radio on for a reason and we always gave them a reason to *keep* it on. We had two-man shows all the time. It was a TOTALLY unpredictable radio station and ALWAYS fun...ALWAYS. I cannot believe I have a job where they pay me to party!

13Q was located in glass, fishbowl studios with floor to ceiling windows on two sides of a corner building. It was located on the corner of Stanwix and Forbes in the heart of the Golden Triangle, downtown Pittsburgh, Pennsylvania.

Across the street there was a restaurant, a bus stop and an outside payphone to which we had the number. Every day when we saw an interesting woman waiting for the bus, we would go to the giant studio window, call the payphone, make big sweeping, waving gestures to get her attention, then point to the phone frantically mouthing, "Answer the phone!" Answer the phone!"

I gotta tell you, this tactic worked often. When we got them on the phone, we would invite them up to the studio for a visit. What the heck, we were young, rambunctious, heady, successful, often impetuous, new in town and looking for some "friends."

One day when someone else was on the air, another DJ and I were just hanging out in the studio on a Sunday afternoon. There were two young women waiting for the bus. So, what did we do? Yep, you guessed it, to the phone we went. We got their attention, got them up to the studio and got two dates.

We thought we were so cool. We weren't, we were just bold as hell and immature. This was 1972. My date lasted for over two years as we moved to Los Angeles and then to Florida together. Her name was Linda and she was *lovely*.

Mark Driscoll (RIP) trying to make me flub a live commercial. I think it worked.

That Saturday night, with nothing to do except spend our spare time promoting the radio station, we were back at it. We took some albums that were free promotional copies from various record companies and went outside to that famous telephone booth. We told the DJ who was on the air at that time to announce that Batt Johnson and Mark Driscoll were waiting for them on the corner with free albums.

All they had to do was drive up and say, "I listen to the new sound of 13Q" and they would instantly win. These were simple promotions that none of the other radio stations were doing. It was a city that had been lulled to sleep and our job was to wake them up. And awaken them we did.

So, after about three minutes of waiting, cars started showing up. Then more cars, then more cars, then we had created a massive traffic jam on this small downtown street. After a few minutes we saw some flashing police car lights. Oops, time to get the hell out of there!

Programmers then AND now are so locked into following what had come before, what other radio stations were doing or had done in the past. They were not creative people. So, when someone comes along who IS creative and fun, the audience will soon be eating out of your hands. Many people in our industry do not look at it as a creative medium so they do not hire creative people and that is the main reason commercial radio is so dull and boring today.

Buzz Bennett was "Billboard Magazine's Program Director of The Year" more than once (I think). He created the concept of 13Q. He took the time to HAND PICK each and every individual for each daypart. It was a TOTALLY customized station from each little wire, to the transmitter, to every cart machine, to every recording of everything. It was a tricked-out radio station, totally irresistible, totally seductive to listeners. It was designed for the youth but even grandmas could not resist us.

I had a nightly segment (1972–1975) that I called the *"13Q Tooth Pick of the Week!"* I discovered such songs as "You Ain't Seen Nothing Yet" by the Bachman Turner Overdrive, "Lady" by Styx, "Keep Yourself Alive," and "Bohemian Rhapsody" by Queen, "Life is a Rock" (but the radio rolled me) by Reunion, Sir Duke and Boogie on Reggae Woman by Stevie Wonder, and "Don't Eat the Yellow Snow" by Frank Zappa. This was a track on his Apostrophe album that I discovered while in one of my daily music listening sessions at home.

I was one of those who listened to music *before* work, I listened to music *at* work, because music was the job, and I listened to music *after* work.

The radio station was given an award for, *Don't Eat the Yellow Snow* at a Zappa concert at Carnegie Mellon University one night.

I won a "Black Achievers" award from Talk Magazine in Pittsburgh.

The new music director was called on stage and was given the award for the success of the record. Wait a minute!! "I" discovered that song, NOT him. I should be getting that award. I'm sorry, Batt Johnson, you cannot receive the award, you're black.

Each week Jack Forsythe, my assistant, would help me organize and tabulate the record store research information. I would start on research about 9:00 or 10:00 in the morning, work on it all day, then go on the radio from 10:00 PM to 2:00 AM, then go back to my music research, sometimes until daybreak.

My title was Program Research Director, but in actuality, I was the *music* research director. I had inside music research information as to what was selling in most of the record stores in Pittsburgh and surrounding areas. I also had information as to who was buying which records, singles and albums.

As research director, I learned something on paper that I always knew in my head and that is that African Americans party, dance and buy records much later in life than most other groups.

On a daily basis I would get new records sent to me from the record companies. I would listen to all of them, looking for gems that I thought would either become hits or records I thought would sound good on our station because we were creating a new sound for the city of Pittsburgh. Bohemian Rhapsody was one of those records.

I am extremely proud to have been a member of one of the greatest radio stations in American broadcasting history.

I wrote this for a dedicated 13Q website created by the fans and radio professionals of Pittsburgh.

My Personal Tribute to One of the Best Top-40 Rock 'n Roll Radio DJs I Ever Heard or Worked With

JACK ARMSTRONG WAS THE <u>BEST</u>!

I have worked at many radio stations, in many markets, with many jocks. Armstrong was the best! Fortunately, I had the opportunity to tell him so just two weeks before he passed. I had not spoken to him in almost thirty years when he came to New York to be the "Unknown Jock" on WNBC when I was there. (The Unknown Jock was a take-off on the TV character known as the "Unknown Comic" who used to perform with a bag over his head on the Gong Show.)

My last gig at CD 101.9, New York's Smooth Jazz station, changed formats and went rock. There was Armstrong, on the phone offering con- dolences, making sure I was ok, as if a mutual friend of ours had just fallen on hard times, or died.

That is the kind of guy he was. He was strong, he was bigger than life, he was sincere, he had a heart of gold and really knew how to make your radio jump off the table with his EXCITEMENT! He was Mr. Excitement. He wanted everything he did to be exciting. He was Jack Armstrong.

I met Armstrong in 1972 when the new staff came together in Pittsburgh to create a new kind of top-40 AM rock and roll radio station, 13-Q. Of all the DJs, Armstrong stuck out.

Obviously, the first day on the air was very exciting. But the night didn't know what hit it when Armstrong hit the air.

Night came and Armstrong hit the air...yelling, screaming, laughing and rocking. I never heard anything like that before or since and I had been in the business for several years before that night. Armstrong worked 6-10 PM and I came on after him from 10-2 AM. When I arrived at the station, looking out from our glass fishbowl studios in downtown Pittsburgh, I saw a large group of people listening to portable radios and watching Jack. I thought, "Gee, we are really killing." They LOVE us!

Well, it was ARMSTRONG they loved.

He went off the air at 10 PM, the crowd disappeared. I thought, wait a minute. What about ME? Aren't you going to wait to watch and listen to the Battman? NO! They were gone. That's when I knew he was hot...red hot.

When Armstrong was on the air, you could bet "something" was going to happen. He was excitement, Mr. Excitement and he always made it happen, no matter how he was feeling.

He also had a heart as big as Montana. When we all arrived in Pittsburgh we stayed in a hotel, then we got apartments. I had not found one yet because I had no time to look. I was on the air and I had music research director duties in addition.

When my mother passed away Armstrong came back to the station a couple of hours after his shift was over to tell me my mom had passed and he offered to finish my shift so I could go home to grieve. I said, "no" and I stayed on to finish my shift...because the show must go on!

The summer of 1974 was a very busy time for promotions for the radio station. Armstrong went to Kennywood Park to ride the world famous "Thunderbolt" rollercoaster for an extended period of time with consecutive laps. At the time, this was one of the fastest in the world and one of very few, wooden rollercoasters left. He stayed on it for hours and hours, attracting many people to the park to watch him. They were probably taking bets as to when or if he would throw up.

Jack Armstrong, his wife, Peggy Armstrong & Batt Johnson at 13Q-AM, Pittsburgh (1973)

Later that same summer, someone came up with an idea to have Armstrong do his radio broadcast from one of the most prestigious stores in the entire Pittsburgh area, Hornes Department Store. He was set up in a ground floor display window, on the air, live, from six PM until ten PM (I believe it was for the entire week from Monday to Friday, but I'm not sure. That was a long time ago). But the catch to the promotion was that he was surrounded by a roomful of snakes. Snakes, yes, snakes. Real, live, snakes, complete with teeth, and there were many of them, none were poisonous, however. Yes, he would do anything to further the success of the radio station and boost the ratings.

One night we were on his front porch talking and his wife drove by in their dark green MG sports car with her lights off. Armstrong panicked and said, "Oh, no! There goes Peggy with her lights off, she's going to kill someone. Let's go get her." We jumped into my car in pursuit of her. Half way down the block, I had to make a U-turn because I was parked going the other way. As I did, there was a motorcycle behind us which tried to pass us on the left. As I was turning left, he was trying to go around us on the left, then...KA-BOOM!

Armstrong jumped out of my car to comfort the guy. I was upset, needless to say. Armstrong offered to take me back home to his place and take the guy on the motorcycle to the hospital. Armstrong thought he could do it all...and he could.

He was a hero in his mind AND in real life. He befriended me, he taught me. We had many things in common, mainly: rip roaring radio, rock and roll music, women and laughter.

Armstrong, my dear friend, I am weeping a tear for you. You were the best, the absolute best, I still have many pictures of you and I will NEVER forget you.

I love you,

Batt Johnson, New York

March 27, 2008

Jack Armstrong was born John Charles Larsh on December 4, 1945, in Durham County, North Carolina. He died on March 23, 2008, in High Point, North Carolina at the age of 62. Far too young, gone too soon, boy, what a talent.

Jack's wife, Peggy was also a beautiful soul. They let me stay with them when we all first moved to Pittsburgh, while I found an apartment. Again, this shows their inner beauty, big hearts, and love for humanity.

She did not come to the station very often, but when she did, you knew she was there. She was/is a vibrant personality, not pushy, or overbearing, yet strong. She would have to be, to be the mate of Armstrong. Jack Armstrong was, by far, the best, most potent, most talented jock on staff.

One day he declared himself a candidate for President of the United States when Richard Nixon resigned because of the Watergate scandal.

On the air all week long, Armstrong was declaring himself a candidate for President of the United States. One day, on his morning show (6-10 AM), Crazy Bob McClain decided to call Armstrong to get a quote from the next President of the United States.

He called, Peggy answered. Bob said, "Good morning, this is Crazy Bob McClain from 13Q radio calling to talk to Jackson Armstrong about his candidacy for the next President of the United States.

Peggy simply said, "Aaww FUCK OFF!!" Then slammed the phone down. BLAM!!

Obviously, they put in a delay system in our phone bank the very next day.

Pittsburgh NEVER heard such language on any of their radio, TV, magazine, grocery store flyers, or newspaper outlets before . . . on the street in the worst neighborhoods by the worst people, yes, but on a professional broadcast facility once owned by the National Broadcasting Company, NBC, an American institution? NEVER!

I was very surprised that this event did not make the newspapers, especially because the City of Pittsburgh was watching, and listening to us.

Revolutionary, revolutionaries, that was what Buzz Bennett was all about, counter culture to the core. He wanted to turn the status quo on its ear, and I/was/am with him ALL THE WAY!

The phone call to Armstrong was not intentional, and I'm sure it caused a few more of the people of Pittsburgh to tune in to us. Because, with those people at THAT radio station, who knows WHAT is going to happen NEXT!!

Dennis, Jessie, Batt, Sam, Jack.
ROCK THE BOAT
INSTANT REQUEST LINE
333-9122

Your beautiful Long & Silky hair
can win you a 4-day trip for 2
to Miami, Florida...

AND A CHANCE TO COMPETE IN THE
NATIONAL LONG & SILKY GIRL CONTEST
IN NEW YORK CITY!

SEND 14 Q A PHOTO YOURSELF BY
JULY 81 ALONG WITH A LONG & SILKY
BOXTOP.

Jack Armstrong's wedding day on a boat on the Allegheny River.

QUINCY MCCOY-NO STATIC

Only two of the seventeen radio stations I work for were black formatted stations. One was the legendary WBLS-FM in New York where I did mornings. The other was KGFJ, Los Angeles, as the program director and morning drive host.

As you know, most of the others were "white" rock 'n roll stations. What this meant was, since I was the only on-air broadcaster of color (again, I hear my mother), I had to be twice as good as the white broadcasters. I'm not sure that I was twice as good but I certainly worked hard at developing myself. So, I studied a lot. I studied the music, the players of the music, the style of other DJs at my station, the style of other stations DJs in that city and those in other markets around the United States. I even listened to broadcasters in other countries when I could. When I travelled internationally I *always* had pens, note pads, and a radio with a recording device built into it.

Sometimes I had a shortwave radio, which allowed me to listen to radio stations around the world. I was rabid, hungry for show business knowledge and success.

Quincy McCoy, legendary radio mind and author of the book,
No Static: A Guide to Creative Radio Programming.

Quincy McCoy, radio broadcaster, programmer, brilliant radio mind and author of the book, "No Static: A Guide to Creative Radio Programming" on page 94 he said:

> The first thing I noticed about Batt Johnson on 13Q (Pittsburgh) was how hip he sounded. He was conversational, but he didn't talk too much. He talked like people talked; not like an announcer. "The Battman's" content was right on the money-a mix of street lingo and music information. His vast knowledge of artists and songs quickly made me realize that my show preparation needed immediate improvement.
>
> Then one day John Long, my boss, nonchalantly said, "Batt Johnson may be the best black jock in the country."

That statement caught me completely off guard. I had no idea that Batt was black. I just liked him because of his smooth and cool delivery. Right then I realized two things. First, I was now even more fascinated with the Battman; he became an instant role model for me. But more important was my second realization. John Long's remark solved a mystery that had been puzzling me for years: Why did I love being on the radio so much? The answer was in the anonymity of it, not the celebrity of it.

To be on the radio was to be anonymous. I wasn't black or white. I had the power to be many different things to many different people. It was freedom from the daily trappings of racial stereotyping. Batt Johnson was, simply, an excellent air personality, and I'm sure that, to his listeners in Pittsburgh-in their mind's eye-he took on a variety of different identities. On the radio it didn't matter what you looked like as long as you entertained. I loved that inherent fairness about radio.

I met Batt Johnson for the first time in 1975 when he joined the staff at Y-100 in Miami as our night jock. I told him about studying his aircheck tapes and about my initial reaction to him. I told him about my theory about radio and anonymity. We became fast friends. Batt confided in me about a grudge he had been holding for a while against a major programming consultant who said that black jocks didn't have the same kind of insight as white jocks, and subsequently weren't as good. He was determined to change that mindset. It was a passion he passed along to me. Years later we ran into each other in New York, where he had made a successful transition from radio to acting.

Buzz Bennett, award-winning radio programmer, leader and guru is the person who "discovered" me and really launched my career. Without him

I would not have had a successful career in broadcasting. I'm certain I got hired in places just because I grew up in the Buzz Bennett family of rockers. We were even roommates at one point.

In the book, "No Static" Buzz said,

> "I don't want to build some type of robotic personality so, I've always looked for someone with a solid hold on their identity-someone who knew who they were, where they were going, and had the courage to go for it. I also looked for people who were hungry. I always thought it was cool to hire guys who weren't working. They would do such a great job for you, because they didn't like being out of work. I like hiring vultures. Give a bunch of vultures a cause and look out!"

MY FIRST TRIP TO NY

When I was working at KUPD, and KRIZ radio in Phoenix in 1971 or '72, I met a record promotion man by the name of Bruce Shindler.

Bruce happened to be from New York, but at the time he was working in Phoenix. We became, and still are to this day, good friends.

The drummer for Seals & Crofts (L), Bruce Shindler (M) and Batt Johnson (R) at a 112-degree Phoenix summer heat concert at a baseball stadium.
The show was with Seals & Crofts and Dion Di Mucci.

Teaching myself to play my roommate's bass guitar (1971).
I never became a good musician but I had the passion for it.

After a few months, I got the call to move from Phoenix to Pittsburgh to be an important part of starting an exciting new radio station, 13Q. After a few years, Bruce and I reconnected and I went to New York for the very first time. The purpose was to see Led Zeppelin in Madison Square Garden. Wow! I was so excited. I stayed with him and his mom and dad in Hempstead, Long Island for a couple of days. We went to many clubs and saw many bands. My Father's Place in Roslyn, Long Island was a popular place. We also went to the legendary Max's Kansas City in New York City, the Bottom Line and many other music hot spots. I was in heaven. I had no idea that one day I would be on the radio in this town...New York bleepin' City!

Because Bruce was in the music and record business, he had free tickets to the Zeppelin concert in the Garden. What an AMAZING thing for me because I was, and still am, a huge fan of that band. Back then I used to listen to them every day before going on the air at 13Q. I have many of their albums and I still listen to them in 2021.

I couldn't believe that my first trip to New York was to see Led Zeppelin in concert in Madison Square Garden.

CHEECH & CHONG

My radio guru, Buzz Bennett had many friends at many record labels around the country. Ode Records in LA had a new group. They were not a musical group but a comedy group of two guys, and they called themselves Cheech & Chong. Their humor was counterculture, hippie, free love, and marijuana focused. They are Grammy Award winning artists who recorded six gold comedy albums and starred in eight of their own films.

The cover of the weekly KRIZ music sheet, available in record and convenience stores as a promotion and to show the top records we were playing.

The inside of the weekly KRIZ music sheet

When I was living in Phoenix and working for KRIZ radio, Cheech & Chong came to town. Buzz called me and told me to go pick them up at the airport. We had a contest on the air for the best "low rider" car and whoever won, their car would pick them up at the airport. The winning car was a light blue,1953 Chevrolet convertible, not in particularly good condition.

Our promotional radio station t-shirts were a bright yellow-orange with collar and tie printed on the front with KRIZ going down the tie. We put the top down and taped those bright yellow-orange t-shirts all over the car. It looked like a circus wagon and we got attention and brought about a hundred shirts to give out to people who came to the airport to see Cheech & Chong. I learned so much about promotion from Buzzy. In fact, everything.

Later that year I was working in Pittsburgh at 13Q radio. Cheech & Chong and I had become friends (professional friends), no I never hung out with them smoking pot. One day I read in Radio & Records magazine (a weekly industry newspaper/magazine) that Cheech & Chong were coming to Pittsburgh. I got on the phone to our connection at Ode Records in Los Angeles and got their travel itinerary and concert dates. They were very happy to hear from me because we were the first station in the country to play the new Cheech & Chong routine, it wasn't really a song. It was called, "Sister Mary Elephant" and because we played it, album sales were going through the roof. Of course, the label executive was going to take my call.

I thought I was a rock star, then someone told me I was delusional.

When the date came I went to the airport and intercepted Cheech & Chong and took them to their hotel. I really should not have done that because our competing radio station was sponsoring their show but we were playing a new style of guerilla radio warfare and sometimes you do things a little out of the ordinary, because you're guerillas.

We were writing a new book, method and style for the American broadcasting industry. We thought and felt as if we could do whatever we wanted. We weren't arrogant, just confident and extremely creative.

While hanging out in Cheech & Chong's hotel room after picking them up at the airport, I asked them if I could MC their show. They said they would love that. So, that night, instead of the other radio station introducing Cheech & Chong on stage, I did.

That's when I debuted my black velvet BattMan cape with the white rhinestone trim. I was so ostentatious, but I was a kid and it is showbusiness. I never understood why there were no negative repercussions from that act of artist thievery. How did we get away with that? No one said a thing.

HOLLYWOOD BOUND

When I left Pittsburgh, I went back across country to Los Angeles to be the program director of KGFJ radio. It was a small, but culturally significant institution in the African American community there, as it had been for many, many decades.

One night in the 70s I was at one of my favorite Hollywood music venues, the Roxy. It was partly owned by Lou Adler, who brought the Rocky Horror Show to the U.S; mogul David Geffen who started Asylum Records and Peter Asher of the singing group, Peter & Gordon ("A World Without Love").

The Roxy was also a music industry show-case venue. Some new talent would be featured, but usually the best of the best would play there and the Hollywood glitterati of the entertainment industry we're often audience members.

One night, I spotted Stevie Wonder in the audience seated not far from me. I quickly went over and introduced myself to him and the big burley bodyguard looking guy who was with him.

Batt: "Uh, excuse me, Mr. Wonder. (Mr. Wonder? Well, I didn't want to call him by his real name, Steveland Morris. I KNEW I wouldn't get an interview for SURE if I called him that. I wanted to show respect and not just call him Stevie).

Batt: "Uh, excuse me, Mr. Wonder, uh, my name is Batt Johnson and I'm the program director of KGFJ. I am also the morning show host.

Stevie Wonder: I thought your name and voice sounded familiar.

Batt: Thank you, sir. I want to invite you to the studio for a live, on-air interview with me.

Stevie: Well, you have to talk to my publicist, here. By the way, did you get a copy of Syreeta's Wright's (Stevie's ex-wife) new record?

Batt: Uh, yes, I did. I'm considering adding it. (That was a lie. It was not a good record and no one in the country was playing it, only England was. If my memory serves me correctly, the song was "Your Kiss Is Sweet." She was also singing on a Seven-Up TV commercial at this time. But I think Stevie was saying: no airplay, no interview, without actually saying it.)

The Burly Publicist: Give me your number, Batt.

Batt: I handed him my business card.

Stevie: Nice to meet you, Batt. I'll be listening for Syreeta's record.

Batt: Ok, great. I hope we can hook up an interview.

I think the song was "Your Kiss Is Sweet." Written by Stevie and Syreeta. I never played the song, and nope, I never got to interview Stevie Wonder.

CHAPTER 15

New York Radio

NBC IN MY PEDIGREE.

A few years after my first trip to New York to see Zeppelin, New York radio came calling. New York came to get ME! Wow! I was so thrilled. I was so honored. I was beside myself. I had been asked to perform daily feats of "my" version of American top-40 radio in damn New York City! HOLY COW!

This station is not at the top in terms of ratings or total audience domination, by any stretch, but in America, the letters NBC mean something. I have made it!!

Or had I?

The only thing I ever wanted to do was make my mother proud, still to this day, even though she has been gone for many years. I think she is proud of me.

Working at NBC was a big deal. I loved walking down the halls of 30 Rockefeller Plaza and seeing the cast of Saturday Night Live; Laraine Newman, John Belushi, Jane Curtin, Gilda Radner, and Dan Aykroyd, but I never saw or met Garrett Morris or Chevy Chase.

I saw Katie Couric many mornings as she was coming to work at the *Today Show* with Bryant Gumbel. I stopped her one morning to introduce myself. She was incredibly nice, kind, and gracious.

Then, there was Willard Scott who you would usually *hear* before you saw him. He was large, loud, and full of love and life. When he saw me, he would always address me the same way, "Heeeey there, young fella!!" In his big, loud voice. No wonder he used to be Bozo the Clown. I can see that.

I had some good times at NBC. I got a chance to hang out with and interview people like Greg Lake of Emerson, Lake & Palmer; Bev Bevan of The Electric Light Orchestra (ELO); Maurice Gibbs of The Bee Gees (about one week after Saturday Night Fever was released), Freddy Mercury of Queen, and many more.

In fact, a few years before that I was the first person to play their unusual hit, "Bohemian Rhapsody" on American Top-40 rock 'n roll radio. I know that because we have industry newspapers and magazines that print the new records radio stations add to their playlist each week. As you know, many years later on February 12, 2019, Bohemian Rhapsody became a hit movie. I saw it, I cried.

I was hired to go to New York on August 15th, 1977 from Kansas City, Missouri by NBC to work on WNBC radio. We had two weeks of strategy meetings before our big new format launch on September 1st. This was after I worked at:

KBKB-FM, (KGB-FM) San Diego, CA: Pop/Rock, newscaster
KPRI-FM, San Diego, CA: Rock
KCBQ-AM, San Diego, CA: Pop/Rock, asst. production dir., public service dir.
KUPD-AM/FM, Phoenix, AZ: Pop/Rock
KRIZ-AM, Phoenix, AZ: Pop Rock, music director, research director
WKTQ-AM, 13Q Pittsburgh, PA: Pop/Rock, program research director
KGFJ-AM, LA, CA: Urban Contemporary, (black radio) program director, research director

WHYI-FM, Miami, FL: Pop/Rock
KCMO-AM, Kansas City, MO: Pop/Rock, research director
THEN to NBC and later many other NY stations

I remember arriving at La Guardia airport in Queens, New York on a beautiful, sunny summer day (August 15, 1977) with my girlfriend at the time, Vicky. As we approached the front exit doors, I noticed that we were the only people speaking English. You could probably hear every language under the sun. At that moment I knew I was moving to someplace special.

We came to New York together to pursue our individual dreams. Mine? To work on the radio at NBC. Hers? To go to Columbia Law School.

All the new DJs arrived two weeks ahead of our kick-off date of September, 1st, for a series of strategy meetings to familiarize us with New York because the entire staff of new broadcasters were from some other part of the country. Management wanted us to know that Rockefeller Center was NOT New York. They wanted us to see where the "people" of New York lived.

They hired two limousines and drove us around the New York tri-state area so we could see where the majority of the residents lived. Then they drove us to the Westchester County airport and sent us up in two or three, small, single engine airplanes so we could see New York from above. It was visually stunning, like we have all seen in the movies.

New York City's Manhattan island from the air.

All the while, our General Manager, Charlie Warner was talking about taking us to a place that had the best banana daiquiris in all of New York. Banana daiquiris? Why? Who cares? We are all witnessing the experience of our lives being at the top of the radio heap in all of the United States. DJs around the country, around the WORLD, would kill their mothers to be in our position. It felt good.

As we were going south over the Hudson River in our plane, my girl-friend, Vicki, who was seated in the front passenger seat suddenly said, "What's that? LOOK OUT!!!" The pilot saw another small plane headed toward us, head on. He had time to redirect the aircraft without throwing us out of our seats. But it was a close call. Holy cow! Don't tell me I have been in New York for a week and a half and I'm going to DIE! No way!

All seven or eight of us returned to New York in one piece. We were all living at the Americana Hotel on Seventh Avenue at Fifty-Second Street (It has had many names since). As we pulled up to let everyone out and end our voyage, a handsome cab (a New York horse drawn carriage) pulled up with two guys and two women inside. The guys were yelling, "Hey, wanna party? Come on, let's party!! Follow us!!" It turned out to be Ian Schrager and Steve Rubell, the owners and creators of "Studio 54," the internationally renowned, chic, hip, hot-shot, hot-spot to be seen in, disco joint.

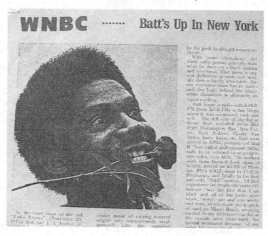

This is from a two-page article in Fred Magazine.

Not everyone could get into "Studio 54". It was one of those exclusive velvet rope clubs. I think our general manager set this whole thing up in advance. How else could something like this happen? Plus, we all got in for *free* and no, I didn't see Mick Jagger, Bianca Jagger or Donna Summer there that night.

I find it ironic that they would let a bunch of ragtag radio people into Studio 54 but they wouldn't let Nile Rogers and his bass playing writing, and performing partner, Bernard Edwards of the mega group, Chic, into the club.

These are the guys who wrote the song, "Le Freak". If fact, many years later, I interviewed Niles Rogers when I was on WBLS-FM in New York and he told me the story of how the song came about. He said that song was written in a jam session in Bernard's apartment after they could not get into Studio 54 on New Year's Eve, 1977 to meet Grace Jones.

They were so upset that they wrote the original refrain as "Aaahh, fuck off!" That was their way of slinging arrows at the doorman for not letting them in. They later changed the lyric to "Aaahh, freak off!", and then finally, "Aaahh freak out!"

"Le Freak" was selected for preservation in the National Recording Registry by the Library of Congress as being "culturally, historically or artistically significant. Niles was honored as the Top Producer in the World in Billboard Magazine.

He had won countless Grammy Awards. Chic has been nominated for inclusion in the Rock and Roll Hall of Fame, a staggering eleven times, and Niles was finally inducted for Musical Excellence.

Chic received a nomination for the Brit Award for an International Group. Nile Rogers has worked with Diana Ross, Carly Simon, Walter Murphy ("A Fifth of Beethoven"), Debbie Harry of Blondie, Prince, Johnny Mathis, The Sugarhill Gang, Daft Punk, Luther Vandross, David Bowie, Madonna, Robert Palmer, Duran Duran, Stevie Winwood, Sister Sledge ("We are Family"), Lady Gaga, Cher, even the Rolling Stones wanted him to produce an album for them. Nile Rogers is a STAR but he couldn't get into Studio 54.

NBC WAS NOT ALL ROSES

I had a few bumps in the road at WNBC, literally. I remember the day I got off the plane at La Guardia airport and Vicky and I were the only two people speaking English, I knew I was in a special place.

New York has a culture of waiting in the street to cross the street, waiting in the street to hail a taxi. This is the place where you ask for change "of" a dollar instead of change "for" a dollar. The is the place where you stand "on" line instead of stand "in" line. This is a different kind of town, a town where you could not get good bar-b-que (air pollution laws I guess), a place that did not allow garbage disposals (sewer system clog ups, I guess).

New York is a place where many things are transported by bicycle messenger. New York (not sure) is probably the only place where bike messengers take the hand brakes off their bikes. What? Yep.

One day after a staff meeting, I was leaving the NBC building, crossing W. 49th Street. The traffic on this street flows from east to west. I looked east (to my left) and no cars were coming so I started crossing the street…and WHAM!!!

I was blindsided on my right side, knocked silly, as I was looking left for the traffic coming from the east, where it was supposed to come from. I was new in town, what did I know? It was a bicycle messenger, with no brakes, no horn, not looking where he was going, and going the wrong way on a one-way street. But this is New York, the rules are different here. Damn, that hurt.

SNUBBED

At WNBC, we had the standard "cash call contest" that Buzz Bennett was doing in Pittsburg at 13Q radio five years earlier. We would select a name once an hour from those submitted and call the person at home. They had to answer their phone by saying, "WNBC is going to make me rich!" and they would win $50,000. We would record the phone calls and put them on the air with all of their screams of excitement as we continued to egg them on to get even *more* excited.

We are carnival barkers, jokesters, clowns, in a way; professional perpetuators of joy and mirth. We show people how to have a good time because many individuals really do not know how to do it on their own. When we have fun, the audience has fun. The audience does not want to miss out on their portion of the fun, so, they listen every day.

I was working on a Sunday afternoon. I called someone and they won an enormous amount of money. The next day a memo/press release was written by the program director's assistant. It said, someone had a cash call winner Sunday afternoon…blah, blah. *Someone? Someone?* Why didn't you mention my name? I could write some very revealing, vile, accurate words here, but unlike her, I choose to take the high road.

I was an important part of this team. Why was I hired to work in the biggest, most competitive radio market on the *planet* if I were not competitive and could not bring revenue into the company?

Perhaps this was the beginning of my realization of the fact that I was in a very racially polarized town, New York City.

But they don't know me. I am strong, I am smart, I have streets smarts AND I have the ability to see things many people do not, and I know this. I feel this knowledge surpasses "academic" knowledge and learning. I call myself a "bad MF." I don't know if that is, in fact, true but that is how I see myself.

I know my stuff, and I know my stuff works. Don't even begin to say anything about my skin color because I have a track record in "white" rock 'n roll radio, music and culture. This is the most difficult area to succeed in for anyone, especially for a man with a high degree of choclaticity.

Yes, the memo said *someone* had a cash call winner. To this very day I am still upset that they didn't use my name. Why? They used everyone else's name. A good, smart, thinking programming department is always looking for opportunities to promote their people. The very purpose of the memo was to promote, yet this assistant failed to do so and those above her did nothing. They didn't want to promote me, send me on personal appearances or let people know who I was.

Getting ratings is the name of the game. No ratings equal no advertising, equals no money coming in, equals…unemployment line here we come. I know why they didn't use my name. Because Batt Johnson is black! Let's not sugarcoat it.

MAKING TV COMMERCIALS IN SPANISH

After we got the winner on my show, we had to create some new television commercials because the total amount of money we had given away had changed. I shot two commercials speaking in Spanish that we shot in Nashville at an NBC television affiliate. Before we left New York, we translated the text to Spanish.

We figured if we ran into a problem, there would probably not be too many people in the studio in Nashville, Tennessee who could help us with proper Spanish. So, we wrote it out phonetically so I could read the cue cards or teleprompter swiftly and smoothly. To save money we shot the next series of commercials at a Spanish language TV station in New Jersey.

Because I was new to New York, and somewhat naïve. I didn't know that there was a *very* large Afro-Latino culture here. I thought I was going to be an anomaly, something special because I am a black American who knew some Spanish. Well, I was wrong, *very* wrong.

When we arrived at the station, we were escorted to the rear of the building where the production studio was located. As we entered the studio, I noticed some technicians on the other side of the room pointing and laughing.

They kept looking at me so I gathered they were laughing at me. At some point before we started shooting, I asked them what they were laughing at. They said, "Are you the guy on the NBC television commercials?" I said "Yes."

Then one guy said, "I guess we were laughing at your Spanish. You know when you said, 'Gane cincuenta mil dolares.' You put the accent on the second syllable making it, dol-Ares. Instead of the first syllable, dO-lares.

We're Caribbean, we don't speak Spanish like that. The way you said it, it sounded like an old 1950s, black and white Mexican movie. It was just very funny to us. If you're going to do the commercial today in Spanish, we will help you."

I laughed with them and thanked them and told them that I was from San Diego, California, seventeen miles from the Mexican border, that's why. We all laughed again. We shot two more commercials, I had no problems and no one laughed at me. Hahahaha.

When you compare the assistant at NBC not mentioning my name as being the individual who gave away the fifty-thousand-dollar cash call jackpot, to the race riots, murderous massacres, rapes and imprisonment of innocent black people for years, not mentioning my name may seem minor.

WNBC-AM New York (1977)

But to a young African American trying to make it in white rock 'n roll radio, was sometimes painful. The barriers to my success were not my lack of talents and skills. My barriers were the redneck bigots who were in management.

One could say, "why don't I go into black radio where there would be less pressure because of my race." That answer is simple. I didn't come from black radio. I love rock and roll music, I studied it for many years, I know a lot about it, and, I am a rocker. Simple.

STRANDED

The dial position of WNBC radio was 66 on the AM dial so we produced a series of sixty-six cent concerts. Yes, the admission for our listeners was sixty-six cents.

One Friday night we hosted at show with a group called The Babys' & Billy Squires at the Palladium on East 14th Street in Manhattan. John Waite was the lead vocalist and bass player and they had a hit on the radio called, "Missing You" (I ain't missing you at all…since you've been gone, away.)

Billy Squires didn't have a Top-40 hit record but it was a kick-ass band. Bobby Chenard, the drummer was a good friend of mine who lived one block away on East 38th Street with one of my best buds, John Belliveau, who worked with RSO Records and the Bee Gees "Saturday Night Fever." I lived at 244 Madison Avenue at 38th Street.

It was a great concert and I was very excited. We were going to go to dinner after the show. Back in those days we traveled a lot by limousine, rock star style, or so we thought. Upon leaving the show I lost track of the rest of my crew because I stopped to talk to some fans. When I finally made it outside, my boss (who shall remain nameless) took off in the limo and left me stranded on 14th Street in front of the world-famous Palladium.

I was PISSED! Why did he abandon me? . . . Because Batt Johnson is black!

One month later we had another sixty-six-cent concert. They did not abandon me this time. After the show we were going to one of the DJs sister's apartment for ice cream. She lived on Riverside Drive at 111th Street. Many considered the area to be Harlem, which was a heavily black populated part of New York City, but it wasn't Harlem. It is called Morningside Heights. Harlem in the seventies did not have the greatest of reputations.

As we drove up Broadway in our black limo, our program director, a white boy from Mississippi, grew more and more uncomfortable. With every rotation of the tires, the more uncomfortable he became. The higher the numbers got from 14th Street to 111th Street, the more he sank down into the cushions of the back seat. He was almost riding on the floor by the time we reached our destination. It's interesting because he is the son of a Mississippi preacher. Don't they teach God's love and we are all God's creatures, and we are all the same. Yes, but not black people.

Just a few weeks after that I was moved from the 10 PM to 2 AM on-air shift to overnights, 2 AM to 6 AM.

FIRED!

One morning when my shift was over, I noticed the boss' office door was open. I stuck my head in and he said, "Good morning, you're just the person I wanted to talk to. Come in, sit down."

"You know, you haven't been sounding the way I want you to sound. I'm going to have to let you go." (This was the first time I heard any of this. There was no guidance, no instruction, no meetings, no coaching, and no help as to how he wanted me to sound.)

I said, "WHAAAAT??!! Really??!!" I threw up my arms and said, "I'm at the top, the top, I'm at fuckin' NBC!!" Where am I going to go? Obviously, again…I was PISSED! But, in radio they don't need a reason to fire you. It is a very different kind of industry and business. It is not like the kind of business you are probably accustomed to. You do not have to do anything wrong, or bad to get fired in this industry, especially if you don't have a contract.

Y', y' you mean I'm out of here?!

I had a GREAT job in Kansas City on a two-man show with Dan Donovan, a partner whom I loved, and Al Casey, a boss I loved. We had great ratings and were growing. NBC hired me, I quit this fantastic job and they moved me halfway across the country. I worked for one year and three days, then…WHAM!

The guy who fired me also lived on 38th Street near me a few blocks down, but on 3rd Avenue, I was on Madison Avenue. He came in early just to fire me and he was going to go back home. So, we walked home together from Rockefeller Plaza on 6th Avenue between 49th and 50th Streets to 38th and Madison.

This is like sleeping with the enemy, walking home with the guy who just fired me. I was trying to be the bigger man and maintain my cool. This is all a true story. As we were walking down 5th Avenue, I saw a penny on the sidewalk. I stopped, picked it up, raised it to the sky and said, "Thank you, God. You know, this is going to come in handy one day soon." (As I said under my breath, "You f***in' a**hole.)

I feel like a member of the "Me Too" movement, the movement was created to expose the widespread sexual abuse, sexual harassment, and racial injustice by powerful men. The difference is, these women did not ask for the abuse. With sick, twisted logic in a strange way, I *was* asking for racial injustice, bigotry, and maltreatment by taking these jobs where I was the only African American on-air broadcaster at the radio station.

Large, mainly Caucasian staffed corporate institutions are not comfortable if there is more than one individual in the office of African descent. If I were not good at my job, if I could not attract an audience, if I could not maintain an audience, believe me, they would not have hired me.

HOWARD STERN ON NBC

Shortly after I left WNBC they hired Howard Stern. I think he was doing the morning show in the Don Imus time slot. The first few times I heard him I thought, "This guy is a disaster." He is one of the worst sounding DJs I had ever heard, especially in a major market. He didn't have a good sound. He sounded like he didn't belong on the radio. He had a unique sound all his own, nasally and whiney.

His humor was targeted toward sixteen-year old pubescent, adolescent males that I didn't find particularly humorous. But it was no more sophomoric and moronic than what I was doing at 13Q in Pittsburgh five years earlier.

Well, needless to say, Howard went on to be a big star making millions of dollars on the radio. He then wrote a book, "Private Parts" and made a movie out of it. Good for him. I am always very happy for any radio person who finds success in any realm. It is not easy to become successful in radio.

I think Howard then went to K-Rock FM doing the morning show against me on Lite-FM. We were a station for a slightly older audience and I had a group of older ladies who would call me every morning, and we would chat.

One day two of them called me and said the same thing about Howard Stern talking about be on the air. They knew that because their sons listened to Howard.

I had the day off for some reason one day, and I was jogging in Riverside Park listening to Stern. He answered a phone call and a young man with a standard African American accent was on the other end.

He said, "Yo, Howid. I wont ta git inta broooadcastin." Howard said, "Well, first you have to get rid of that accent." The kid said, "WHUT accent??"

Then Howard's side kick, Robin Givens, his female, African American radio counter-part said, "Let's see how we can help this kid out. I got it, he should listen to Batt Johnson!" Stern said, "Yeah, you should listen to Batt Johnson. He is the whitest sounding black man on the radio. Batt Johnson, where did he get a name like that anyway? It must have something to do with his penis size."

This is not hearsay, I heard it with my own two ears. Thanks for the free plug, Howard. It really didn't matter because we absolutely did not share an audience. However, everyone on the radio when I am on, is my enemy.

I know he meant it as a put-down

Sound does not have a color. I am an American citizen who was born and raised in a culture that speaks standard American English. I am not a southerner. I was not born in Alabama, Mississippi, Georgia, Texas, Arkansas, Oklahoma, Florida, North Carolina, South Carolina, Tennessee or any other southern state you care to name.

I am an American who was born in the great northwest in the state of Washington and raised in San Diego, California, no apologies. I speak standard American English, no apologies.

In the African American community, there are many things individuals disagree upon. One of those things is the manner in which some African Americans choose to use our language. It is often referred to as, "talking white," "sounding uppity," or "copping out" if you don't sound like a "brother" (a southerner).

That sounds like the black man is not allowed to speak Standard American English like his or her other American counterparts, without being called an Oreo. You know, an Oreo, chocolate on the outside and vanilla on the inside like the cookie. Back in the day, Oreo is a name that always found its way to me.

There is a term in this country that is used that you don't hear in places like New York. That term is "nigger lover." This is a term that is used by some lower-class Caucasian individuals against other Caucasians who happen to have some African American friends or is in an interracial relationship. This is intended to inflict pain upon the fair-minded individual who has friends of other cultures within our "standard" American culture.

There is another term, "uncle tom," that is used as a derogatory put down by black people against other black people. It is used to describe an African American who is "betraying" their own group, like a snitch, or an African American who is subservient to whites, is "trying to be white," or happens to have white friends.

Actually, this term came from Harriet Beecher Stowe's novel, Uncle Tom's Cabin, written in 1852.

Believe it or believe it, there is still slavery in many countries of the world. These are old statistics but it is all I have. As of 2018, these are the countries with the most slaves: India (8 million), China (3.86 million), Pakistan (3.19 million), North Korea (2.64 million), Nigeria (1.39 million),

Indonesia (1.22 million, Democratic Republic of the Congo (1 million), Russia (794,000) and the Philippines (784 million).

Uncle Tom was a non-violent slave who, in the end, gave his life to protect other slaves who had escaped.

So, in reality, to be called an Uncle Tom, is actually a compliment.

When you analyze the multitude of individuals and cultures that have come to the United States from elsewhere, you will immediately see that we are a massive mixture.

The children of all immigrants born and raised in the United States, speak standard American English: Russians, Chinese, Saudi Arabians, Ecuadorians, Japanese, Cubans, Hungarians, Italians, Haitians, Lithuanians, Spaniards, Turks, Portuguese, Estonians, Germans, French, Argentinians, Egyptians, Finnish, Polish, you name them.

But most African Americans speak a version of English that no other group speaks.

Ebonics was a term I never heard of until the 1990s. The term was coined by African American social psychologist, Dr. Robert Williams in 1973.

Ebonics, or Standard African American speech, African American Vernacular English (AAVE), also known as African American English (AAE), and Black English, is generally considered, by most of our "non" African American society members, as an indicator of a low level of education, a member of the lower socioeconomic strata, less intelligent, and lazy.

An example of this would be a sentence like this:

He be goin' teh da sto. Means, he is going to the store. She steady smilin'. Means she is always smiling. He be done gone. Means he left.

I wonder if Barack Obama would have been elected President of the United States, twice, if he spoke Ebonics, Black English, or Standard African American speech? I can ask this question *and* answer it. The answer is, *heck* no!

Why is it that no other group uses this language the way many African Americans do? Perhaps because no other group of people has had our experience? But we have to consider the fact that many individuals of African descent who were born in England speak like the rest of England. Those of African descent who were born in France, speak like the rest of France.

There is scientific proof that there was an African presence in Central and North America ten to twenty thousand years before the arrival of Christopher Columbus.

Obviously, this was before the arrival of African slaves to these shores. The common story we hear about is that the slaves arrived on U.S. soil in 1619 in Jamestown, Virginia. These were not slaves, they were indentured servants.

Indentured servants were individuals who received no pay for their work but were given shelter, some clothing and food as they worked off their debt for their transportation to these North American shores.

(If you are interested, read Ivan Van Sertima's book, They Came Before Columbus: The African Presence in Ancient America. Random House publishing, 1976.)

We have been here for a long time. Why is there still such strong reluctance within the African American community to speak Standard American English?

Pride is my answer to that question.

Speech is music. Standard African American speech has a cadence, a rhythm, a musicality to it. It sounds very legato, like the sound of a jazz saxophone player. Whereas the sound of standard American speech is more staccato, sharper, curt, and linear.

I believe it is an intentional cultural separation on the part of African Americans. In my opinion, two of the reasons are, self-preservation and ethnic pride.

Howard Stern, you and no one else can shake me from my foundation, for I shall forever maintain my uniqueness!

SWITCHING GEARS

Going from being a top-40/rock 'n roll radio DJ broadcaster to becoming a jazz DJ was easy, I was accepted. Being black, everyone thought I knew a lot about jazz, but I didn't.

True, I was introduced to jazz when I was a child, which means I had an ear for the music. I was introduced to Thelonious Monk, Miles Davis and John Coltrane as a young child. I saw Dave Brubeck and the Dave Brubeck Quartet when I was ten years old at Memorial Junior High School in San Diego where my sisters were students. This is when "Take Five" first came out.

So, you can see that I have a long history with the music, I think I really know the music. But I had to really study hard to get more of the academic side of jazz. When you are a radio broadcaster, you can't just sit and listen to the music like your audience does. You have to talk about it, share information about it, tell stories about it, and share your passion with words. That's why I went to the clubs every night, to hang out with the musicians and get stories to tell the next day on the air. Well, not *all* of the stories, and I was told some incredible tales.

Larry Coryell was a favorite jazz guitarist of mine. The first time I met him was at a club in San Diego called "Funky Quarters" in 1970–'71. They were recording a live album that night. Larry was playing a big, fat, blonde, Gibson L5 acoustic-electric guitar.

I was young, stupid, and in my twenties. At one point in between songs I went up to the bandstand and shouted, "Batt Johnson! Batt Johnson! Has anybody seen Batt Johnson?!" I'm sure the recording engineer loved that. I guess I was trying to get on the record. How stupid? Like the great Nobel Prize winning Irish playwright, George Bernard Shaw (26 July, 1856–2 November 1950) once said, "Youth is wasted on the young." Actually, I thought the famous Borst Belt comedian, Henny Youngman (16 March 1906–24 February 1998), or comedian Rodney Dangerfield (22 November, 1921–October 5, 2004) said it first, but I was wrong.

About ten years later, I saw Coryell again. He told me that someone stole his guitar that night and the next year, Funky Quarters burned down.

Batt Johnson (L), unknown (M), Larry Coryell (R).

Working on the radio everyday was not just a job but a privilege. It gave me access to some of the greatest talent in the world. There was no other outlet for their music in New York, so they *had* to listen to us. They all knew who I was, so when I went to the jazz clubs to hear them play, I would ask them if they would grant me an interview for the book that I was writing, "What Is This Thing Called Jazz?"

Some said, "no," but many said yes. I executed interviews with some of the giants of jazz: Jimmy Heath, Milt Jackson, Elvin Jones, Barney Kessel, Buddy Rich, Chet Baker, Joanne Brackeen, Randy Brecker, Ron Carter, Ray

Charles, Larry Coryell, Herb Ellis, John Abercrombie, Percy Heath, and many, many more.

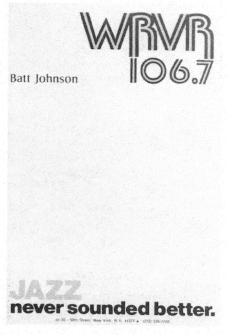

I was proud to be a broadcaster on one of the most listened to jazz radio stations in the world.

I SWITCHED FROM JAZZ RADIO TO COUNTRY

Then when I become a country music broadcaster everyone thought I didn't know anything about country music because I am African American, and I live in New York City. I knew some things but again, I had to really study hard to get more of the academic side of country. Again, I had to talk about it, not just listen to it.

Working in country radio in New York City was a lot of fun. But working as a music radio broadcaster is enormous fun, no matter *what* the format or the city because the job is to create and sell happiness and good times. Forget your problems because you're hanging with the Battman, with a party in his voice!

To give you an idea as to the kind of joy being on the radio can give one, I am including a letter written to me by a very prolific, kind and talented individual.

In case you had difficulties reading the written letter, I typed it out for you.

Dear Bat,

    I want to thank you a thousand times for your kindness in promoting my song on your program because I had nothing but telephone calls from people who heard you say the wonderful words you said about me on your program. I can't tell you how many people, who are fans of yours, who have been calling me now, who heard you mention me on your wonderful program. I can't thank you enough for your kindness.

(Here comes the kicker for me.)

Many thanks. My dear friend **Fred Astaire** and I wrote many songs together, and I'm sure he would have also enjoyed your tribute.

Sincerely,

Gladys

Wow! Are you kidding me?! To get a letter from Fred Astaire's song-writing partner made me feel ten feet tall, as you can imagine. THAT is only one of the reasons working on the radio is so fulfilling. Plus, you get to touch lives in profound ways, often when you don't even know you did.

Viacom, the major media corporation, bought the jazz station, WRVR-FM, and changed the format from jazz to country. People would come from Asia, Europe, and other parts of the world just to record WRVR, and replicate it in their country. It was known well beyond the limited New York border.

One of the original WRVR logos.

DIZ

A GIANT of jazz!

He was born John Birks Gillespie, October 21, 1917 and left us on January 6, 1993.

He was an excellent musician, showman, and scat singer. Because of his wild antics on and off the stage, he earned the nickname, "Dizzy."

But don't let his horn-rimmed glasses, baggy pants of back in the day, bent up to the sky horn, beret on his head, and puffed-out cheeks fool you. Dizzy Gillespie had an extremely high intellect and he brought that intellect to his music.

One of the areas he was an original in was adding layers of harmonic and rhythmic complexity to his music. In the 1940s, Diz and Charlie Parker were at the forefront in the creation of bebop jazz music. In other words, they created bebop.

He influenced musicians far and wide, especially trumpeters. Among them were Miles Davis, Lee Morgan, Chuck Mangione, Arturo Sandoval and Clifford Brown. Dizzy Gillespie and his many contributions will live forever. He was a giant among men.

I shared the stage with the great Dizzy Gillespie only twice. The first time was at a small club in Little Ferry, New Jersey. The band I was working with at the time, "So What", was the opening act for Diz. It took a lot of work to close that deal.

"So What" was fusion. Diz was straight ahead, or traditional jazz.

As I remember, the gig and musical difference, worked. Whew!

The second time I worked with Dizzy Gillespie was at a large theatre in New Jersey. The bill was Dizzy Gillespie, Ramsey Lewis, and special guest artist, Roy Haynes on drums.

We were all downstairs in the dressing room when all of a sudden, the door swung open and hit the wall with a violent, roaring, thud, *POW!*

Dizzy Gillespie and Batt Johnson
WRVR-FM radio, New York, 1979

Dizzy stumbled into the dressing room as if he were stinking drunk, and started to mumble, very loudly, "I want a *man*! I want a *man*!"

Dizzy's manager grabbed him by the arm and said, "Dizzy, stop acting crazy and get upstairs. You're on in three minutes."

Ahh, so *that's* why they call him Dizzy! The forever prankster.

There was a rumor floating around town that WRVR was going to change formats, maybe to country music. One day we received a memo to attend a mandatory meeting on September 8, 1980.

It was to be held next door in the auditorium of the elementary school at 10:00 AM. At about 10:09 or so, the big bosses came walking down the center aisle, they mounted the stage and started the meeting.

They said, "as of 10:00 this morning, WRVR-FM turned to a country format." Yep, from jazz to country at the flick of a switch. As you can imagine, all of the oxygen was instantly sucked out of the room with the collective gasps and inhalations from the staff, and those random deep thuds were the sounds of jaws dropping and hitting the wooden floor.

THE INDUSTRY'S NEWSPAPER

R&R/Friday, March 4, 1983

RADIO & RECORDS

Who is that guy cooking chicken l'orange and biscuits in the Wisk detergent national TV spot? It's New York's Country FM DJ Batt Johnson. The WKHK personality also appears in a Charleston Chew candy commercial and a few movies.

730-1188

Batt Johnson

The meeting was adjourned at about 10:30 AM. When I walked out of the meeting, there was a giant Bekins Van Lines moving truck there with the back doors open.

There were movers carting out the jazz records and bringing in the country. I walked into the control room and the music director, John Brejot was just playing one country song after the other without opening the microphone to speak. My air shift started at 10:00, so I was the first speaking voice on the new station.

After a few minutes of this constant segueing of music, from one song to the other, it became time for a commercial break. The record ended, I opened the microphone and said something like: "Yes, folks, you guessed

right. The format has changed. We are now all country WKHK-KICK-FM."
I heard another loud gasp of air coming from the entire New York jazz radio
listening community.

No, those are not my cigarettes on the console.

Like all radio stations, we had a bank of about ten telephones, all of
which were lit up. Green froth and nauseous, toxic, venom poured out from
the phone lines. New York was PISSED! It was about a few weeks before I
answered the phones and about ten years before I went to another jazz club.

I just didn't want to get harassed or asked a bunch of questions because
that was a major blow to the New York jazz community, culture and world
jazz culture.

Batt Johnson (R) with Lawrence Hilton Jacobs (L) who played Freddie "Boom Boom"
Washington on the hit TV show "Welcome Back Kotter" starring John Travolta.

In a staff meeting one day for the new country format, I told Bill Figenshu, the national program director for all the Viacom radio stations nationwide, "Fig, I'm going to be the BEST damn black country DJ you EVER heard!" I meant it and I worked to achieve it. I bought a lot of country music artist books and really researched the genre.

Be diligent as long as you live, always doing more than is commanded of you.
Sacred Wisdom of Ancient Egypt

I didn't need to buy many CDs because the music was already in my inner ear. The other broadcasters on the station were rejecting the format change. Many of them thought that country music was the music of the Klu Klux Klan. I call country music, black blues with a twang! Country music couldn't be any blacker. Just listen to it!! If you can't hear the blackness that is in country, then you can't hear or understand music.

One of our first staff meetings was a lunch meeting at the new studio, it was also an opportunity for us all to meet our new program director and see one another in a different light, as country music radio DJs.

I arrived at the studio, on time, of course, and there were two others there ahead of me. We were chatting and enjoying each other, as we always did, because we loved one another.

The new boss, D.H. came in. We greet him, and continue chatting. He joined the conversation. Then he said, "we should dive into some of this delicious food we ordered for you guys." (Some cheap, dried up sandwiches, potato chips and sodas.) He asked me what kind of sandwich I wanted. I responded. Then he offered me a Coke. I said, "No thank you." He then said, "What's the matter, don't you people drink Coke?"

From that racist moment on, I knew it was going to be a bumpy ride with this guy. But I had to hang in because this was an important job to have. The first black man to become a country music radio broadcaster in New York City!

I felt that having and succeeding in this job was important for me, for New York, for the world, and for future generations of black and white performers in all genres of performance.

I did it to teach them a lesson, I did it to remind myself of my inner strength and ability. I did it all the way to the end of the country format when Viacom realized it was not garnering the kind of revenue to which it was accustomed.

So, they changed the format again. This time to WLTW, LITE-FM. I must admit, I felt lucky that they didn't fire me because I was part of the previous jazz radio station. They were very diplomatic in their decision-making process. They allowed the DJs to make their own decision as to whether they wanted to be part of the new country music team and format.

Many of the broadcasters simply stopped performing They stopped putting their heart and soul into every word they spoke on the air. As a professional, one can NEVER do that because you NEVER know who is listening. Your potential next million-dollar job offer could be listening right now.

I wanted to stay, I wanted to be part of something novel, something unusual, and possibly something exciting and I showed that with my actions and daily performances. I started reading books about country music, its star singers, musicians, songwriters, producers, filmmakers, and legends, and displayed that knowledge on the air as if to say, "Yes, I'm black, and I know my shit."

I think the National Program Director, Bill Figenshu was supporting me behind closed corporate doors. Perhaps they realized that sometimes it is not about the color of my skin but rather the color of the green that I can help bring into the coffers of the radio station and the corporation.

I hosted a few country music shows and events. I am CERTAIN people were surprised to see ME walk out on stage of Country Music Hall of Fame, Ernest Tubb's show on Long Island. Believe me, it was equally strange to have people come up to me with Long Island accents telling me what a great job I did. Excuse me? You're supposed to have an Alabama, Mississippi, Georgia, Texas accent, no? I was as confused by them as they were by me. They heard me on the radio every day, but they never saw me before. *Surprise!*

Batt Johnson and country music legend, Ernest Tubb, the Texas Troubadour. His biggest hit was "Walking the Floor Over You". (I wonder if he is calling me the "N" word in his head here. No, I was just kidding. Just trying to make you laugh.)

I met Charlie Pride, the most successful black, country vocalist ever, also Willie Nelson and many others. I interviewed Rosanne Cash (a very sweet woman), Bobby Bare, Charlie Daniels. I always brought my guitar to my interviews so they could play live on the air. I knew they wouldn't bring theirs. I was always thinking ahead. Playing chess taught me that. Country radio was fun.

KICK 106 FM
WKHK
COUNTRY MUSIC IN STEREO

Personalities

41-30 58th Street New York, NY 11377 (212) 335-1700

Batt Johnson

Batt's charm has won him an avid following among WKHK listeners. One of WKHK's most popular air personalities, Batt's enthusiasm is especially evident before a live audience.

He can generate excitement with any crowd. Batt's radio experience includes some of the nation's top radio stations in such markets as Los Angeles, San Diego, Phoenix, Pittsburgh, Kansas City, and WNBC in New York. Batt enjoys writing and traveling.

Before Lisa and I went to Africa, I bought several books on country music and the musicians because I was going to be on the air playing country music when I returned to New York from Africa. The format had changed from jazz to country.

One day while still in Abidjan, West Africa in the Ivory Coast, we were at a bus stop going back to our hotel. I said to Lisa, "I'll bet you a thousand dollars that at this very moment, right here, right now, that I am the only person on the entire continent of Africa who is reading a Dolly Parton country music book." We laughed about that for many years.

I already had country music in my inner ear because my dad, being from Texas, used to sing country songs all the time. In fact, "My Bucket's Got a Hole in it" by Hank Williams, Sr. was one of his favorites.

Wellllll, my bucket's got a hoooole in it.
Yeah, a great big hoooole in it.

Well, my bucket's got a hoooole in iiiit.
It don't WORK no more.

BATT JOHNSON

I worked in many of the major broadcasting markets; San Diego, Los Angeles, Phoenix, Pittsburgh, Miami, Kansas City, Missouri and New York. Being a professional broadcaster is like being a professional athlete. First, you are in city "X" playing for this team, then you go to city "Y" to play for that team, then… It is actually how you develop your skills.

WLTW-LITE-FM, NEW YORK

Neither the program director or the general manager of WLTW, LITE-FM ever promoted my television success. I was the morning man, the individual on during morning drive time. Mornings and afternoons are the most important time slots because those time periods have the largest available listening audiences. As in Los Angeles, the New York metropolitan, commuter audience is large and important. They missed many promotional opportunities with me. They didn't care just as long as I wasn't publicized. Why? Because Batt Johnson is black.

I was one of, if not the most visible radio DJ in America. I say that because Jay Thomas was popular and visible. He made regular appearances on the hit TV show, Murphy Brown starring Candice Bergen, Cheers starring Ted Danson and Shelly Long and The David Letterman Show. But my TV commercials were on every day, several times a day, all day, sometimes several times an hour for many years. A smart manager would have turned my visibility into revenue somehow. That's their job. Well, they were not interested.

This was this general manager's first time as a general manager. He was one of those who came from sales and inherited a staff of creative, smart, highly experienced people who do not deal with sales and marketing at all. The DJ's job is total audience accrual and maintenance, in other words, getting the audience and keeping the audience. The sales department's job is to sell airtime to create revenue so we can eat and pay our rent and mortgages.

The world saw me on television, they knew that I am black. A smart leader would tie that back to the radio station, somehow. Figure it out, it ain't brain surgery. You're a leader, right? You have smart, successful people on your team. You should promote them, recognize them, use them to power you to your next level of success.

Our leader at the time did not understand this. This kind of leadership is a model of the Donald Trump style of "leadership," meaning, "no one is more important than I am."

How did I get those jobs if I was not well liked? That's what ratings are. It is kind of like a popularity contest. Why do I say this? Because we are a capitalist, money grubbing, money hungry society; as an African American, a man of color in a world of none, I am scrutinized far more closely than my "white" teammates.

BELIEVE me, if I did not carry my weight over all of those years, I would not have had a career in "white radio." If I were ever hired, I would have been the first to be fired. So, I am going to blow my own horn here for a moment. I was often a better DJ than many of the other staff members at many of the seventeen radio stations I worked for across the country. This is why I say that it is difficult to write your life story without sounding like you are bragging.

I LOVE IT HERE, BUT I QUIT!

When I left LITE-FM I went to WBLS-FM, a legendary radio station and a pillar in the African American community in New York City. It was a black owned and operated radio facility. Some of the original owners were Percy

Sutton and the Sutton family one-time Mayor, David Dinkins, singer Roberta Flack and others as investors.

$4.95 (U.S.), $5.95 (CAN.), £3.95 (U.K.) NEWSPAPER

189-1 **100 YEARS** 1994

THE INTERNATIONAL NEWSWEEKLY OF MUSIC, VIDEO AND HOME ENTERTAINMENT

Radio

PEOPLE: WBLS GOES BATTY

Recently hired **WBLS** New York morning host **Michel Wright**, formerly morning co-host at **WPGC-FM** Washington, D.C., has been paired with new co-host **Batt Johnson**. Johnson, who most recently was attending graduate school, previously hosted mornings at crosstown **WLTW**. WPGC-FM OM **Jay Stevens** is looking for a replacement for Wright and wants T&Rs.

Quincy McCoy, whom I had known for over twenty-five years offered me the morning slot with a female partner. These were some good times. Because of the stature of the radio station in the black community, *everyone* and *anyone* who was *anyone* had to come visit our facility.

As a result, I interviewed some amazing people like NBA coach Doc Rivers when he was a player as a New York Knick. Our sports director, Larry Hardesty, made Doc our official on-the-road correspondent and he would report live during our morning show after many of his road games. When he was in town he would come into the studio with us. He was always fun, insightful, kind and giving.

Gladys Knight was probably the most radiant interview we conducted. What an unassuming, gracious sweetheart of a woman.

Roberta Flack gave us some of her precious time in between concert tours for an interview. Master African American producer, arranger, writer, and guitarist, Nile Rogers came by one day, and during the interview he told us how Mick Jagger and the Rolling Stones begged him to produce an album with them.

Rock and Roll Hall of Famer, Daryl Hall spent time with us in the studio one winter morning. Martha Reeves, lead singer of Martha Reeves and the Vandelas had a reputation of being a difficult personality and interview. We were preparing for a battle but she was a sweetheart, with a lot of great stories about coming up in the music business.

Barry White was one of the more memorable interviews.

We got a call from the front desk alerting us of the arrival of Barry. I waited a minute or so, then went to the studio door to greet him. I opened the door and BAM! There he was, all six feet four inches, three-hundred pounds of the "Walrus of Love." Yes, he was a big man. I escorted him into the studio, then we announced on the air that he was in the studio with us.

The phones instantly started ringing. Almost every single one of the callers was a woman and almost every single call was the same:

Click!

Barry White: Hello. (With his big, thunderous voice that shook the console and made the CD skip.)

Caller: Oh, Barry White! Barry White! I can't believe I'm talking to Barry White! Barry White, I love you so much. I love your music so much. Oh, Barry White, Barry White, I can't believe I'm talking to Barry White!

Barry White: Yeah, baby, yeeeah. (In that unmistakable, ultra-deep, double-barrel, velvety, smooth, trademark fog horn voice.)

Next caller: Oh, Barry White! Barry White! I can't believe I'm talking to Barry White! Barry White, I love you so much. I love your music so much. Oh, Barry White, Barry White, I can't believe I'm talking to Barry White!

Barry White: Yeah, baby, yeeeah.

Next caller: Oh, Barry White! Barry White! I can't believe I'm talking to Barry White! Barry White, I love you so much. I love your music so much. Oh, Barry White, Barry White, I can't believe I'm talking to Barry White!

True story. *Every, single call* was almost *exactly* the same word-for-word from Barry White and the amorous listeners. Tom Jones used to get panties thrown on stage to him. I wonder what Barry White got?

Being a radio broadcaster is a fantastic job. Many people know who you are, you get free event tickets, free clothes sometimes, make paid personal appearances, get free drinks, free dinners, free music, famous musicians want to hang out with you so you will play their record and say something nice about them into the ears of a hundred thousand people. When you develop a following, politicians want to connect with you and do business with you, which can be dangerous, and many other perks exists.

Being a morning radio DJ in a city the size of New York is a privilege. Having an opportunity to wake up the city and make its people aware of what will be happening that day is a major privilege *very* few people get to experience.

Batt Johnson (L), Michel Wright (M), Governor Mario Cuomo (R) at a Midnight Basketball promotion. This program was designed to keep kids off the street at night. Wait a minute! They have to go to and from the game, right?

A chat with Governor Mario Cuomo after the Midnight Basketball promotion presentation for WBLS radio. He was surprised that I knew his law school professor, His Honor, Judge Re.

Being on the radio comes with a lot of unacknowledged, unrecognized stress. We were never made aware of the stress related negatives of such a job.

Although we only work three or four hours a day, those hours are extremely intense.

First, it is live. There is no delay or safety net.

Second, *everyone* hears what you say, EVERYONE, including people in at least three or four neighboring states, or more.

When I was working at NBC, which was a clear channel AM radio station, which means that no other station is broadcasting on that frequency. At night, I had friends in Phoenix, Arizona listening to me when I was in New York.

Another stress inducing fact is that there is also a continuously running tape that records the entire broadcast day, that is listening to you TOO.

Third, the program director, my most immediate boss, has a tape recorder in his or her office that is activated every time the on-air broadcaster opens the microphone to speak. They are listening to everything! There are few other jobs, that I can think of, where your boss is listening to everything you say and do for four hours straight.

For four hours a day, five or six days a week, you are in charge of a fifty to one-hundred-million-dollar piece of electronic, communication machinery. Stressful.

My on-air partner and I had a rather rocky relationship and sometimes it showed on the air. People would always ask me, "Do you two get along with each other?" David Hinkley from the New York Daily News asked me in an interview if we got along. I lied and said, "Oh, yes, we're friends. I pick her up for work every morning at 4:30 and we come in together."

One night, my partner and I had a public appearance to host a show with Queen Latifah at the World-Famous Apollo Theatre in Harlem. We were all chatting back stage and Queen Latifah went to her dressing room, and I was still talking with the musicians and others there.

A few minutes later I hear the crowd roaring, so I went to the front of the theatre to see what was going on.

My partner had gone to start the show without me! She decided to make a solo appearance, even though my name was on the bill too. I was confused, upset, and angry. We were a team! Why would she do something like that? I don't remember the reasoning behind such actions but the professional relationship was not going well.

David Hinkley wrote a very nice piece about us and included a very large, half a page photograph. One of the reasons people would ask if we got along is because she would constantly cut me off on the air, mid-sentence, when I was in the process of making a point…any point. This was live radio, no delay, no editing. She would interrupt me as if I weren't even there. Sounds like she was in competition with me, not realizing that if I won, she won and vice versa.

It would happen every day. What the____? One day, our boss called us into a private meeting and said, "this has to stop." The next day, the same thing occurred. This went on for another month or so until I arrived at my wits end.

Twice an hour, the news director and sports director would come into our studio to do their live, combined broadcast. We also had a control board operator who functioned as our hands to play the commercials and the records/CDs for us.

One day, my partner interrupted me one too many times. At the end of the news and sportscast, I asked them to hold on for one moment before leaving the studio because I had an announcement to make.

It was 5:50 AM. I grabbed my headphones and starting winding up the cord as I said, "I have had a wonderful time at this station working with all of you over the past year or so, but I am afraid that as of this moment, I am officially resigning my position at this radio station." I was angry, but I very calmly placed my headphones into my backpack, got my jacket and very calmly walked out the door.

I agree, this was not a very professional move on my part. As I was walking out of a very lucrative six figure job in the largest, most competitive commercial radio market in the world. I was thinking that my integrity, sanity, peace of mind and professional tranquility were far more important to me than the money at that time. I had two other jobs. I was still acting in television commercials and corporate films and doing my television home shopping job. I was tired, bordering on being burned out, and I didn't want to do something I would *really* regret. But I couldn't take it any longer. Bye!

Sometimes our differences would tag along with us on personal appearances and we would clash in public, on stage. I had never experienced this kind of resistance and unprofessionalism before. I guess this was the way she was accustomed to operating.

I was getting up at 2:43 in the morning, the show started at 5:30. I would read the New York Times, New York Daily News, New York Newsday and the New York Post every day before hitting the air. The show ended at 10:00 AM. I would then do my acting and television life. I would audition for TV commercials, movies, plays, modeling and hand modeling jobs or go to Queens, another part of New York City and do my television home shopping job. I was doing very well financially, but I was *tired*.

As you can imaging, all that day my phone at home was ringing with my bosses and the newspapers on the other end. I never told the newspapers that I quit and walked off of my job in a rather unceremonious fashion. Now, the truth is out.

That was a heck of a day. I also had an appointment to see my doctor for a colonoscopy that day. As I was lying on the examining table with my medical gown open in the back, the nurse said, "Are you Batt Johnson?" I said, "yes." She said, "The Batt Johnson from the radio? I was listening to you this morning." Then she stuck a plastic tube up my behind to shoot air into my colon to expand it so the doctor's camera with a light on the end could see all of the nooks, crannies and creases. I was thinking, yes, Marsha, you now know what I look like, what I sound like and what my butt looks like, inside *and* out.

CHAPTER 16

Home Shopping Host at Q2 Television

Between 1986 and 1999 I was very busy. I was working on the radio six days a week, getting up at 2:43 every morning, starting the show at 5:30 AM and going until 9:00 AM. Then I would audition for or perform in, television commercials, corporate films, an occasional modeling job or hand modeling job, and working as a home shopping host of Q2 Television, a sister station to the mammoth QVC Television Network. Michael Alan Naso was my television agent who is responsible for helping me get four television jobs, he also happened to be an attorney. In addition to the home shopping host job at Q2 Television that he helped me procure, he also helped me book a PBS-TV show called Only One New York as a host, Campus America Television as a newscaster, and VH-1 (MTV Networks) as a VJ (video jock host).

Q2 was LIVE TV! No delays, no recording, no retakes, no take twos. Live TV, you get ONE shot to make it perfect.

One day I was selling a motion detector light bulb kind of device and taking an occasional phone call on the air. A young man called and said that he had purchased two of these devices. One for his mother and one for his grandmother.

One Christmas Eve he was spending the night at his grandmother's house. It was a regular Christmas Eve, great dinner, family stories, the crackling sounds of logs in the fireplace. The smell of the Christmas tree in the room, ham, turkey and gravy.

He was telling such a warm, family story but he had a slight southern accent so my "redneck radar" was up somewhat. He went on to say that his family went to bed early on this particular night. As he was dozing off to sleep he heard rustling in the bushes outside his window. He peeked through the curtain but saw nothing.

He then said, "I went to the front door and peeked through the peep hole. At that moment your wonderful motion detector light came on and guess what happened…I saw a nigger standing there." The caller then quickly hung up.

Don't forget, this is live television with no delay system in place. I then said to the television audience, "See, I told you this was a good product. It detects motion and reacts immediately. I'm happy you are enjoying it, sir. Thanks for calling, enjoy your day."

When my shift was over, friends, colleagues and staff were consoling me, telling me how sorry they were that this happened to me. All the while I was thinking, that guy was obviously a misinformed, bigoted ass, and a coward. There was no reason to get angry with him for he was simply a product of this American culture, as am I. I just feel sorry for him and at the same time, I am SO happy I am not him.

About six months after that on-air incident occurred there was a similar event. Notice, nothing like this had EVER happened to me as a professional radio broadcaster. Perhaps it is because the villainous racists could not see me.

Who knows? I went out to public appearances in every city I worked radio in. They saw me. They knew I was black. Why didn't those situations occur earlier?

One Saturday afternoon at Q2 Television in Queens, New York in the famous Silver Cup Studios, I was covering a shift for someone who had gotten sick. One of the products I was selling that day was a combination car washing and polishing product. So, as I was going through my sell, I was receiving many live on-air phone calls. All of the individuals were very nice people. Then I get a call from a guy who said, "That product looks very nice. In fact, I have something very similar that I use on my wife's car but I don't really need that, I'll just have the nigger wash the car."

Here we go again. These people think they are hurting my feelings but they aren't even penetrating the surface. They are simply making themselves and their mothers who "trained" them look ignorant.

Working at Q2 was a lot of fun and there were some really wonderful people there. Gary Ray, who is still a friend today, was someone everyone loved. He has the kind of personality that forces you love him.

One day I was doing an exercise show selling treadmills, exercise bikes or something, so, I was dressed in workout clothes. Gary was in the process of starting his electronics show right after my exercise show. The studio was a very large room so the stylists and producers could prepare for many shows at once, thereby creating a continuous, harmonious flow from one type of show or product to the next.

I finished my segment and stood right next to the camera that Gary Ray was going to present to. The floor director started counting down…3, 2, 1. At the count of #1, I turned around, pulled down my sweat pants and started slapping my ass with both hands as fast and as loudly as I could.

It was LOUD! Plap! Plap! Plap! Plap! Plap! Plap! Plap! Plap! Of course, Gary starting laughing uncontrollably and no one in the TV audience knew why. The only thing he could do was say, "That Batt Johnson is such a character!" The whole room started laughing. Don't forget this is all on live television with no delay system. What a way to start a show.

You have to understand that Gary Ray is an individual who possess such profound people skills, magnetism, and professionalism, that I knew he could handle whatever I threw at him. That is why I threw my naked ass at him.

I guess I was feeling my oats because earlier that day I met Cindy Crawford as I was finishing another show. I walked to the freight elevator, pushed the button and in seconds, it arrived. The doors opened and I stepped in. Inside there was only one person. I stepped in and standing right before me was Cindy Crawford, mole on the top of her lip and all. She was one of the biggest supermodels of our time in the '80s & 90s.

She smiled, extended your hand and said, "Hi, I'm Cindy." I said, "Hi, I'm Batt. You're lucky I just finished my show. I would have grabbed you and dragged you into the studio and had you help me sell some metal model cars on live TV. I am a television home shopping host here at Q2 Television." She said, "I would have loved to help you but I'm under contract and that is forbidden."

She was incredibly nice. Is that the reason I slapped my ass in front of Gary Ray as he was going on the air live? I don't know but her relaxed, cool vibe, gave me energy.

CHAPTER 17

My Acting Life!

There is a big difference between how individuals of African descent were perceived and utilized in the media in 1952, and 2022. We take it for granted now in 2022 because we see so many chocolate faces on our TV screens. But when I was starting my acting career, there were few. The road was not paved with gold bricks just waiting for me to walk on them. I had to get clever, creative, and cognizant.

ACTING SCHOOL GRADUATION NIGHT-DONALD SUTHERLAND

I remember the night I graduated from acting school at the Weist-Barron School of Television in 1981 in New York City. After the event, Lisa (you know, my ex-wife) and I went to a restaurant called Saloon to celebrate. It was across the street from Lincoln Center, where, every season, for many years, we went for dinner before going to the ballet.

On this evening, when we arrived, we were walked to our table. We sat down, and then I remembered that I had to call one of the agents who had liked me that night at the graduation, which, by the way, was also an actor's showcase.

I excused myself from the table and went downstairs to place the call. Upon my arrival at the bank of telephones, I realized that I did not have any change.

That's surprising because in those days, actors walked around New York with a pocketful of quarters and subway tokens. These were the days before cell phones, you understand. I had changed my clothes and put all my change in a coffee can which was located in the kitchen. This is something I did every day, which is why I didn't have any change with me. I went back upstairs to get a quarter out of my secret stash of money in my briefcase.

I went back downstairs, put the quarter in the phone, got the number, that was on a piece of scratch paper, out of my pocket, and dialed the agent. As the phone was ringing, I happened to glance back at the staircase. I saw a pair of neatly shined men's dress shoes descending. Then the pant legs appeared, and the legs kept going and going, then the waist, then the looong chest, then the neck. At the very top of the neck was the head and face of 6'4" Donald Sutherland, movie star. Holy cow!

He walked past me and into the men's room. I quickly hung up the phone before the answering machine came on. (Yes, we also had answering machines with the regular cassette tape or the small, micro cassette tape then too.)

So, I slammed the receiver down and entered the men's room. I just "happened" to end up at the urinal right next to his. It was just the two of us there. As I was dripping a few forced droplets of liquid from my body, because I really didn't have to go, I said, "I would shake your hand, but I'm a little busy right now." He laughed and said, "Oh, that's ok." I thought, "Oh, he has a sense of humor, gooood."

There is an unspoken code within the heterosexual male community that says, you never speak to another man in the men's room when he has his business in his hand.

Then I put the big promotional push on and the real reason for going into the men's room. I said, my name is Batt Johnson and I just graduated from acting school at the Weist-Barron School of Television an hour and a half ago." He said something banal like, "Oh, how wonderful," "Congratulations" or something equally socially expected, however, anything that was said at this awkward moment that I created, would be just that, awkward.

He finished, washed, and went back upstairs.

A few seconds later I did the same and returned to my table and told Lisa what just happened. Of course, she didn't believe me. I reached back into my briefcase, pulled out a headshot, and walked over to his table, placed it in front of him, and said something like, "You just never know . . . enjoy your evening."

He was probably thinking, "What an arrogant little shit! He will either make it as an actor, or wash dishes for the rest of his life because no one could stand his extremely high self-esteem."

I used that evening as a sign that I was going to be successful as an actor, and I worked VERY hard to make that sign become a reality. For the most part, I feel I made that happen, even though I never appeared in any major movies or major television shows as a principle performer . . . but I did okay.

I continued to get acting jobs over a period of more than twenty-five years. Not bad, not bad for a skinny little kid from San Diego . . .

WHAT ARE YOU DOING HERE?!

On a cold, rainy morning right before the New Year, I went on an TV commercial audition for UPS at Grey Advertising at 777 Third Avenue in New York.

I arrived early. I opened the door and saw ten or twelve tall, young, thin, blonde haired, blue eyed females in the room. I signed in and took a seat. About two minutes had passed when I noticed one of the young women staring at me. What's *this* all about? Another five minutes went by. Then she got over and sat next to me.

We say hello. She then said, "What are YOU doing here?"

I thought...WHAT?

Yes, I was somewhat insulted but I had been around for too long to let something like that rattle me. In this situation, "I" am the superior being here, NOT her. She probably had little, to no talent, no knowledge of the business and no experience. She was only one of many ill-informed "princesses" who thinks that having blonde hair will get her to everywhere she wants to go. Paris Hilton is a symptom and a result.

I worked as an on-camera television commercial actor and voice actor for over twenty-five years. As an actor, it was not unusual for me to walk into a casting lobby and be the only one who looked like me. That was never an issue. I was used to it. I am an American. I am quite used to be the only individual in the room who looks like me.

When one hasn't been in the business very long, certain bits of information may not have quite made its way to them. The agent sends you because they think you can book the job. This young woman had no idea of all of the characters in the commercial. She was assuming we were for the same part, which DOES sometimes happen. Sometimes the director and the client are not sure which way they want to go until they see and hear you read the script.

Well, as it turned out, I did get the job. It was for a UPS shipping clerk. I did not see the airhead on the set. I can assume that she did NOT get the job. If she did, she was shooting on a different day.

Sometimes the old-timers would attempt to intimidate you in the lobby while you are studying your script. Once, I overheard two old friends chatting in the waiting room lobby for a movie audition.

Man #1. Hey, Jim! How are you?
Man #2. Ah, not bad, not bad.

Man #1. I have a darn headache.
Man #2. Too much booze last night, huh?

Man #1. Yeah, you know it. I went out to dinner with Tom Cruise last night. I didn't even know he was in town. He surprised me. He usually gives me a heads up when he's coming in.

I believe this whole thing was fabricated to try to intimidate me and to make me think, "Gee, if this guy knows Tom Cruise, he MUST be a good actor. I don't stand a chance at getting this job!"

They don't know that I thrive on competition. And no, I did not get that job but I did a good job with the audition.

OH, NO. NOT AGAIN!

I once went in on a television commercial casting call for the Maryland State Lottery. The roll was for a "wacky doctor."

When I arrived, I opened the door and saw about six or seven, sixty-five plus year old Caucasian men, many of whom had white beards, all had white hair.

I walked in, black guy, black hair, no beard. I signed in, then I sat down. The gentleman next to me had the *audacity* to say, "What are YOU doing here?" I chuckled and immediately responded, "I'm here to take your job. What are YOU doing here? You should have stayed home." He laughed out loud and said, "Ha, that's a good one."

What he didn't know or understand was who he was dealing with. I considered myself a media warrior. I had broken down barriers. I was a Buzz Bennett trained media gang member. Trained to fight to win.

These are some of my accomplishments that give me courage and an ultra-sense of self-confidence in a vast sea of color barriers. I guess what I am saying is, "Don't mess with me. I know my stuff. Hire me and I will show you."

THEATER

Find Your Way Home	Weston	Actors Playhouse
Deep Are the Roots	Brett	Actors Playhouse
The Zoo Story	Jerry	Actors Playhouse
A Moon for the Misbegotten	Hogan	Prince Theater
Del Tingo al Tango	Bouncer/Dancer	Wings Theater
Tango du Jour	Director	Poet's Den Theater
The Tango Zone (several seasons)	Host/Actor	Poet's Den Theater
Tango Floor-Gender Wars	Writer/Director	You Should be Dancing Studios

FILM

Game Day	Sportscaster	Steve Klein, Dir.	Independent feature
The Killing Hour	The janitor	Armand Mastroiani, Dir	Independent feature
The Youngest Guns	Lecturer	Ben Mittleman, Dir.	NBA documentary
An Angel for	The Angel	Ricardo Elizondo Dir.	Independent
Your Solitude			tango short
New York Tango			Documentary

TELEVISION

The Gastineau Girls	E! Entertainment TV
One Life to Live	ABC-TV
Love, Sidney	NBC-TV
The Other Woman	CBS-TV Movie

TELEVISION HOST

Q2 Television	national host	QVC Networks
VH-1	national VJ music host	MTV Networks
Only One New York	co-host, anchor	WNYC-TV PBS
Campus America	co-host, anchor	NCTV Network
Infomercial	national and international host	Synchronal Corp.

COMMERCIALS

Reel available: NY Film & Video Award Winner, Mic Award Winner

CORPORATE FILM

Prudential Insurance, IBM, Sony, American Express (**Int'l Film & TV Festival Award Winner**), Mastercard, NYNEX, Republic National Bank, Citibank, Chase Manhattan Bank, Merrill Lynch, Prudential Securities,

Price Waterhouse, Paine-Weber, Computer Associates, AT&T, Gulfstream Aeronautical (**Int'l Film & TV Festival Award Winner**), Continental Airlines, Xerox, Hoffman-LaRoche, American Cyanamid, Exxon, Bristol Meyers-Squibb, Merck & Co; Parke-Davis, Lucent Technologies, Oppenheimer Funds, GE Capital, and more.

EDUCATION - TRAINING

Actors Playhouse: with Ken Cooke
HB Studios: with Edward Morehouse
Weist-Barron School of Television: Commercials
Reed, Sweeny, Reed - The Teachers: Commercials
Bill Wade School of Radio & Television Broadcasting: First Class FCC License
BA Social Theory/Media Studies-Empire State College
MA Communication Arts-The New York Institute of Technology, New York University

Adjunct Professor and Instructor at:
Cornell University, the Weist-Barron School of Television, New York University, the New York Institute of Technology and Mercy College

ON-CAMERA TV COMMERCIALS: A PARTIAL LIST

Pepsi
Norelco
Wisk
Charles Schwab
McDonalds
Sears
Kodak
Papa John's Pizza
Burger King
Puffs Tissues
NYNEX
Eastern Airlines

Wendy's

TJ Maxx

Today's Man

The Ad Council

ABC-TV

Charleston Chew Candy

Fed Ex

Cottonelle Tissue

Hot Bites Chicken

JC Penny

New York Daily News

MCI

Bulova Watches

RADIO HOST/DJ

WQEW-AM, New York: American Popular Standards (Big bands)

SONY WORLDWIDE RADIO NETWORK, New York: Contemporary Jazz

WBLS-FM, New York: Urban Contemporary

WQCD-FM, New York: Contemporary Jazz (CD 101.9)

WLTW-FM, New York: Adult Contemporary (Lite FM)

WKHK-FM, New York: Country (Kick FM)

WRVR-FM, New York: Jazz

WNBC-AM, New York: Pop/Rock

KCMO-AM, Kansas City, MO: Pop/Rock, research director

WHYI-FM, Miami, FL: Pop/Rock

KGFJ-AM, LA, CA: Urban Contemporary program director, research director

WKTQ-AM, 13Q, Pittsburgh, PA: Pop/Rock, program research director

KRIZ-AM, Phoenix, AZ: Pop Rock, music director, research director

KUPD-AM/FM, Phoenix, AZ: Pop/Rock

KCBQ-AM, San Diego, CA: Pop/Rock, asst. production dir., public service dir.

KPRI-FM, (KGB-FM) San Diego, CA: Rock

KBKB-FM, San Diego, CA: Pop/Rock DJ, newscaster

"YOU'RE TOO DARK TO WEAR THAT WINDBREAKER ON CAMERA"?

Whaaaaat? Those were not the words I was expecting to hear while going into the audition for that Maryland State Lottery TV commercial.

For the audition I didn't have a lab coat or stethoscope but I did have another idea, as I usually do. I wore a dark blue windbreaker, and slacks. My windbreaker was made of a crinkling, crackling kind of material. At the proper moment with quick, jerking movements, I was going to snatch it off and the windbreaker would make a lot of noise on their microphones, thereby adding an additional element of excitement for the "wacky doctor."

The next day my agent called me and said I got the job, even without a callback. This Maryland State Lottery commercial was later picked by the states of Arizona and New York from which I received additional fees for each market, and it was nominated for a Clio Award.

That's what the old bigot gets for insulting me at the audition. As they say, living well is the best revenge.

The commercial was shot overnight in a Baltimore, Maryland hospital. The director was Allan Charles of Charles Street Films, who was ultimately responsible for hiring me on this job and a few others. Also, in the commercial was his son, Josh Charles who was about ten years old or so at the time. Josh went on to do great things.

His film debut was in John Waters' *Hair Spray*, then with Robin Williams and Ethan Hawke in the Academy Award-winning, *Dead Poets Society* and many more films. On television he played sports anchor Dan Rydell in Aaron Sorkin's Emmy Award-winning *Sports Night*, and the CBS drama *The Good Wife*.

I was still quite young, in my thirties but I was a seasoned pro and quite used to bigots, even when they don't say anything. Over time you develop another sense. The bigot sensory sense.

I had been in many radio and television ratings wars and television commercial, voiceover, modeling, hand modeling, movie and theatre

279

auditions, and jobs. I was a talking teddy bear, a talking world globe, I played Louie Armstrong singing Argentine tango songs in Spanish (https://www. youtube.com/watch?v=P2jwtsD-2u4). This, you *must* see. I am certain you have never seen anything like it before.

The amazingly talented and highly intelligent, Luis Bianchi filmed me in front of a green screen, then inserted me inside of an old 1930s or 40s black & white Argentinian movie. Pure craftsmanship. This is a video where the story cannot be told in still photos in a book. You must experience the video, in its entirety. Go to YouTube.com and search Batt Johnson-Louie Armstrong tango.

As an actor, my philosophy is: "My all is for rent." That is why I also performed as a model and a hand model. Voice-overs and cartoon/character voices are also a lot of fun, that is if you can get them.

There was a new animated series being produced in New York in 1985, called Thunder Cats. All of the characters were superhero cats and there were two human characters, a young warrior boy, and a girl, as I remember. I loved the audition for this job.

There was a table with all of the characters on large two feet by three feet (I'm guessing) laminated cards. Each character was in color. The actors had to find their character, study it, and then create a voice for it.

My character was "Panthro the Powerful." He was a black panther/human with muscles up the wazoo, blue skin, a wide nose, pointed ears, studded suspenders, I think in the original drawing he had a black cape, and

Batman-type boots that came up to just below his knees. Actually, he looked like a mean, blue/black Batman.

So, I created a deep, dark, James Earl Jones/Darth Vader kind of voice for him. They liked it, and they hired me.

We were in the studio recording the first episode. We had been working for a few hours, then the director called me into the control room and said he wanted me to use a voice closer to my real voice. We had sixty-five episodes to record and he wasn't sure if I could sustain the use of this voice I had created for that period of time.

The next day, I received a call from my agent. She said they were no longer going to use me for the project. Instead, they hired Earl Hyman, the guy who played Bill Cosby's father, Russell Huxtable, on the hit NBC-TV sitcom, The Cosby Show. This role earned him an Emmy Award nomination in 1986.

I later discovered that my natural voice was too close to the superhero boy's voice. So, to avoid any confusion, they replaced me. That is polite, politically correct speak for, they *fired me.*

I was shocked and a little angry that my agent did not fight for me and stick up for me, at least I don't think she did. At one thousand dollars per episode, I saw that $65,000 vanish from my hand like Houdini's most grand performance. Whisss!!

About twenty years later I was on the subway going home from a dinner engagement. The subway car was filled with half-drunken Columbia University students who were coming home from Greenwich Village. This is a historic part of New York City with many bars, clubs, shops, and restaurants. The place where Bob Dylan, Joni Mitchell, Joan Baez and many others, took off their training wheels and grew their professional musical wings.

Seated next to me on my left were two young men talking about their youth, the video games they used to play, and the television shows they used to watch. Then they started talking about Bugs Bunny, Porky Pig, and Popeye.

One of the young men remembered one of his favorite animated shows that had all superhero cats, but he couldn't remember the name of the show. His friend used to watch it too, but neither could remember the name of the show.

I was listening to the whole conversation. Obviously, I knew *exactly* what they were talking about, so I chimed in and said, "Thunder Cats".

There was a pause, as my answer took a moment to swim through their somewhat thick alcoholic haze. The young man seated two seats down from me said, "How did you know that?" I said, "Well, because I played the first Panthro the Powerful on the Thunder Cats series."

Everything amplified and escalated tenfold. They started freaking out, screaming,

"NO WAY! NO WAY! NO, FREAKIN' WAAAAY!!! DUUUUDE! REALLY???? DUUUUUDE!!!!

NOOOOOOO! I'M ON THE FREAKN' SUBWAY IN NEW YORK FREAKIN' CITY WITH FREAKIN' PANTHRO THE FREAKIN' **POWERFUL!!!**"

Everyone in our car started looking at us as if to say, what the heck is going on here? Then I recited a line from the show in the character's voice and they COMPLETELY freaked out and got louder!!! They all wanted to shake my hand, kiss my shoes, get my autograph, and take me home to meet their mothers.

Hahaha, that moment alone was worth missing out on that $65,000, and the show ran from 1985 to 1989. I could have bought Manhattan with all of that money.

Michael took a break from shooting the TV show, Law & Order, to shoot this film they later called "Q".

The original title of the film was "Serpent," then "Quetzalcoatl." They finally settled on "Q". This is the first movie I worked on. It starred Michael Moriarty, Candy Clark, David Carradine and Richard Roundtree.

"RING AROUND THE COLLAR."

The biggest, longest-running television commercial I ever filmed was for Wisk laundry detergent when I was the husband with "ring around the collar." (https://www.youtube.com/watch?v=IfvyJipPk6Y)

This commercial ran for over three years and several, several times a day. In fact, it ran so often that even "I" was tired of seeing it but I wasn't tired of going to my mailbox to pull out those fat residual checks. Some were so big, I don't know how the mail carrier got them into the mailbox.

One day I was walking east on 57th Street in Manhattan and a woman was walking toward me with a little girl about five years old. The woman said, "LOOK! There's the Wisk man with ring around the collar."

She stopped me and told he how much she loved the commercial and they were on vacation from Kansas City, Missouri. I told her that I lived in

Kansas City before I moved to New York and that I was on KCMO Radio there. She said, "I listen to that station all the time.

My first major highway billboard

What's your name?" I said, "Batt Johnson." She let out yelp as if she had just been stung by a bee. "I used to listen to you and Dan Donovan every... darn...day! You guys were funny. I can't believe you are the Wisk man and I ran into you in the middle of New York City!"

"I thought there was something familiar about your voice on that TV commercial. This is so exciting." She then handed me her shopping bag and asked me to autograph it for her. I did, we exchanged pleasant words and departed.

The Wisk commercial was also the most recognized television commercial in the history of Lever Brothers, an English company founded in 1885. They are famous in the United States for making soap. They never had African Americans in any of their TV commercials in their more than one-hundred-year history.

The advertising agency, or independent firm, conducts telephone out-call research when a new product is released, or a new commercial is aired.

They ask such questions as: Did you view any television program in the past twenty-four hours?

What programs did you view?

Did you see any commercials?

What commercials did you see?

Do you remember anything about the commercials?

The ratings for this commercial were sky high.

The woman who played my wife in the commercial was Marion Ramsey. Marion is a great spirit and a great actress. After she performed in the commercial with me, she moved to Los Angeles.

She was immediately cast in the play, "Little Shop of Horrors." One night a producer was in the audience. The next day he contacted her agent because he was working on a new project. She was cast as high, squeaky voiced Officer Hooks in the wildly successful comedic film series, "Police Academy" of the 1980s.

That radical bump up in income caused the IRS to come a knockin' at her door.

They wanted to know how she went from a twenty-five or thirty thousand dollar a year income to hundreds of thousands, if not millions. (I'm not exactly sure as to how much, but you get my point).

Good for her. She earned it, she deserved every dime of it. She is a hard-working professional and she is a star!!!

I could always tell when one, or more of my commercials were running because people would look at me when I'm walking down the street. Can you imagine what life is like for someone who is really famous?

Some people can't even go out to dinner without being mobbed. The public thinks they know you because you are in their living room every day. It can be frightening.

I was on the subway one day and it was somewhat crowded. A guy was standing in front of the doors across from where I was seated. He kept looking at me and smiling. Of course, I thought he was gay and was hitting on me. At one point I looked up and our eyes met.

He raised his head and eyes with a sharp upward motion a couple of times. I turned around and there I was. I was sitting in front of a photograph of myself in a print ad for Ron-Rico Rum. I had on a red, yellow, and orange Hawaiian type shirt in the ad. We both laughed and I got up and moved to another seat. That was a very humorous event. I laughed about that moment for years.

AMERICAN PASSION-THE PLAY

In all of my years of working as an actor and a broadcaster, there was only one audition that was truly honest about the color of my skin not being an issue.

A new play was being produced on off Broadway to eventually go to Broadway. It was called American Passion. It was about a local DJ that the high school kids all listened to everyday.

One of his mysterious qualities was that he often knew, and would talk about some of the secrets of his listeners on the radio but would not always use their names. The kids were baffled as to how he knew such things.

Was someone calling him and telling him their secrets? Was one of the kids really the DJ? Was he psychic? Was he a spirit?

The audition was set-up to replace the individual who had the job, a prominent New York City radio DJ named Roscoe, whom I knew. I later found out that he was experiencing some health issues and could not guarantee that he could perform the entire run of the play, however long that would be.

The audition was set up in such a fashion that when I walked in, there were giant pieces of wood set up to create a wall so the casting directors could not see the actors as they auditioned. They could only hear our voices.

Well, I auditioned, I loved the audition because it gave me a chance to show my stuff…of which I was very proud. Not cocky, just confident and proud. But I always feel that on every audition. The audition is an opportunity for me to show my stuff! I always walk into the audition room like I own the room and everything in it.

A week or two later…guess what? I got the job! Yip-EEEE!

There was no callback. We went straight to the Joyce Theatre for a run-through of the play with the voice of the originally casted DJ.

We were seated a few rows back from the stage. Immediately to my left, in the next seat was "The Great Norman Lear," complete with his trademark fisherman's hat.

Holy crap! I am sitting next to Norman Lear. Norman Lear. Norman damn Lear! I was thinking, does this mean he likes me, thinks I am talented… WHAT??? I am sitting next to the guy who created such hit TV shows as: All in the Family, The Jeffersons, Sanford and Son, Good Times, Maude, Mary Hartman-Mary Hartman, and One Day at a Time. Are you kidding me?

I was thinking does this mean that I am the guy? I got the job? I really have this job!

I'm going to be on BROADWAY!!

Maybe he will create another great television show and cast me in it. The only thing he said to me during the entire run-through of the show was, "Well, Batt, what do you think?"

Holy cow, he knows my name! I said, "I think I could do a great job with this material." He said, "Yeah, I think so too."

Oh, my! Not only does he know my name, he thinks I'm talented!!!

Well, I was getting a little ahead of myself because the next day, the show was cancelled. I was thiiiiis close to being on Broadway. DARN IT!!

AUDITIONING FOR WOODY ALLEN

The only other time I auditioned for something when the casting directors, producers and the director, in this case, Woody Allen, were behind the wall was around 1981 or '82.

When Woody was working on a new movie, he did not have titles for them. He would give a working title according to the season he is working on it. He would just call them the "spring project" or the "summer project."

This was the "fall project." He was looking for unusual types with unusual skills. I didn't know how unusual I was or what unusual skill I had for "this" movie roll. At the time, I was working at WKHK, KICK-FM radio which was a country music station in New York City, and I was an on-air DJ there, I hadn't been acting for very long.

When it was my turn to audition, the casting director said, "Sing us a song." I thought, sing you a song? I came with a monologue. I wasn't expecting to be asked to sing. Geez, I can't sing. Sing? Sing?! What am I going to sing? So, I broke out into a loud, country singer's voice singing Hoyt Axton's "Wild Bull Rider," in a country, southern accent.

Hoyt Axton was pretty famous but his mother, Mae Axton was more famous. She co-wrote the Elvis Presley hit, "Heartbreak Hotel," and also introduced Elvis to Colonel Tom Parker, who went on to manage Elvis for many years. The famous Colonel Tom Parker quote is: "I finally found me a white boy who sings like a colored boy."

So, without skipping a beat, I started singing. Well, I'm a wild bull rider and I love the rodeo…

Why did I do that? What was I thinking? Woody Allen liked Dixieland jazz and Gypsy jazz. He played his clarinet every Monday night at Joe's Pub, and he wasn't playing country. What was I thinking? Actually, I wasn't thinking, I was reacting and I had an immediate response for them.

A professional is always ready. Many years later, as an acting teacher, I would often tell my students that, *"Whenever an opportunity presents itself for you to show your stuff, show your stuff!!"* We are actors. We are not like other people.

Nope, I didn't get a callback for *that* movie job.

The movie turned out to be "Broadway Danny Rose," a black-and-white comedy about an agent who isn't too successful and ends up in a love triangle involving the mob. Lots of weird looking characters in this movie. But, of course, I loved it for its strangeness and because I was a huge Woody Allen fan. At one point in my life, I had seen all of his movies and read every book written about, and, or by him. I still have them in my library.

AUDITIONING FOR PENNY MARSHALL

It was just a regular day, a regular day filled with about five or six auditions, a combination of on-camera, voiceover and modeling go-sees. That is what they call modeling auditions, go-sees. You go, hand them your headshot or comp card, they take a picture, or two of you, snap, snap, you go home. But there may be several, several individuals in front of you, so you may not leave so quickly.

This audition was for a movie about a giant meteor hitting earth, or something like that. I don't remember who the stars were but they were someone I would have liked to have worked with.

I read for the undercover FBI agent roll. I walked in with my sunglasses, flashed my FBI ID that I made the night before and walked to the mark in front of the camera.

When an actor walks into the room to audition with props, it screams amateur. I knew that, but I did it anyway (stupid). As I was walking toward the camera, I glanced to the left of the camera, and seated on the dark brown leather couch was Penny Marshall.

I thought, "Holy shit, that's Lavern and Shirley." I didn't know which character she played because I didn't watch the show that much, but that was her, complete with overbite and all.

She was the director of this film project. She walked over to me, extended her hand to shake mine and said, "Hi, I'm Penny. We're looking for someone with a very specific kind of voice for this roll. I understand you have had a long radio career, so I wanted to see what you had to offer."

Ok, I did my lines, two takes. Said, "Thank you" and left. Nope, I didn't hear from them. There's another job I didn't get, but that is the life of an actor. You can't get *every* roll you audition for.

A few years later I was in Los Angeles doing media training for the NBA. This trip was to work with three players of the Los Angeles Clippers basketball team. Part of my session with the players was filmed for the documentary, The Youngest Guns, which may be seen on my website, www. tangointoxication.com.

As I approached the locker room door, there was Penny Marshall standing with many sports reporters, lights and cameras. I knew she was a big basketball fan.

I said hello to her. I could tell by the way she looked at me and responded that she didn't remember me. Maybe it was because we were in LA and she didn't know me from there. Maybe it was because I had on a suit. Maybe it was because I gave a horrible audition as the undercover FBI agent and she wanted to forget it…AND me.

I showed my ID, my real NBA ID, not my fake FBI ID, and walked into the Clippers dressing to say hello to Doc Rivers who was the head coach at that time. Remember, we had worked together on the radio at WBLS-FM in New York. By the time I got into the locker room Doc had left. I think he was pretty upset because the Dallas Mavericks had beaten them pretty badly that night.

So, I walked over to the Mavericks locker room to say hello to Dirk Nowitsky (Just recently admitted into the NBA Hall of Fame in 2023). I had worked with him a few months earlier in Dallas.

I walked into the locker room and I was chatting with some of the players when Dirk stepped out of the shower room. He sees me, his eyes got as big as saucers and he give me a big, half-wet hug and exclaims, "What are *you* doing here?" I said, "I'm here to work with three of the Clippers players but I must admit, Dirk, I've never been hugged by a seven-foot tall, half naked German man before." The whole room exploded with laughter.

NBA MEDIA TRAINING

Deep down inside I always wanted to work with professional athletes in public speaking. Within the American society, it is generally believed that athletes are dumb and African Americans can't speak English. Both of these stereotypes anger me to no end. That is one of the reasons I wanted to work with professional athletes to hone their verbal skills.

Lisa, my ex-wife, was the President of the New York Chapter of the National Speakers Association. Every summer they had their annual banquet that I attended a few times. I noticed that many of these "professional speakers" were, in my opinion, not very good presenters.

I told Lisa that I could really help them. She said I should put together a program and pitch it to the organization. At the time my standard line was, "I don't want to teach, I want to do. I am a doer, I am a performer." She attempted to encourage me many times to pursue this work.

One day she asked me if I would critique one of her colleague's new videos. I agreed. While I was on the phone giving her colleague feedback, Lisa was listening. Afterward, she came to me and said that I had a special gift of analysis, critique and feedback and I should really consider investigating this further.

I gave in and said that I would investigate it. I did a lot of research on media training, coaching, and teaching public speaking. I bought and read many books, watched videos and press conferences. Finally, I was ready to write my first book, *Powerful Principles for Presenters: Tips for Public Speakers Using Proven Communication Techniques from Commercials, Television, and Film Professionals.*

I eventually did media training with many lawyers, architects, business executives, the United States Air Force, the United States Tennis Association, and with some of the Stars and All-Stars of the National Basketball Association.

I worked with the Sacramento Kings, LA Clippers, Dallas Mavericks, Phoenix Suns, Boston Celtics, and twenty years of rookies every summer during the NBA draft.

This is the textbook I used as a professor at the New York Institute of Technology, New York University, and in my media training work with professional NBA basketball players.

In one of my media training sessions at a hotel in Times Square in New York, one player said to me, "I make almost a million dollars a year. I don't need this stuff."

I said, "Well, what if you are in a regular, every day practice session, and you go up for a rebound, and come down on the foot of a teammate and you break your foot, your ankle, your leg, or all three, and it is a career ending injury! THEN what, Mr. I make almost a million dollars a year?"

One of my jobs is to impress upon these young professional basketball players that there IS life after basketball. They don't know it, but the skills I teach them can lead to the broadcast booth, be it radio, television, movies, or all three.

Did you see Michael Jordan in the live-action/animated sports comedy film, "Space Jam"? It came out in 1996 and was a box office smash grossing over $230 million worldwide, the highest-grossing basketball film ever. But think back, how many basketball films were there? Not to be negative.

This film was directed by Joe Pytka. As an actor, I had the pleasure of working with Joe in a couple of television commercials. One of them was for a product called Brand Jordan, Michael Jordan's private under garment line.

Michael hand-picked a few professional athletes to represent his brand of underwear in a series of television commercials. He selected Boxing Hall of Famer, Roy Jones, Jr, a football player whom I can't remember, (Warren Moon?) and former New York Yankee and Baseball Hall of Fame resident, Derek Jeter. I worked in the Derek Jeter segment of the commercial. Derek Jeter was so kind and professional, and Joe Pytka was a masterful director. Working with Joe was the first time I saw and got to work with a 70mm, high speed camera, but I digress. I do that a lot, don't I?

Many of the skills needed for success in the media, I have taught for many years at The Weist-Barron School of Television, The New York Institute of Technology, Cornell University, New York University, Mercy College, and years with private clients.

Usually the players are receptive to the information but occasionally I would get a knucklehead. My basic duty was to teach them the art of the interview.

I once worked with a player from Germany, Dirk Nowitsky. He was one of the best students/clients I ever had. Probably because he was not an American, and was very interested in how the media worked here. He was so good, and we were having such a good time together, that I completely missed my flight back to New York.

Everything I teach, I teach with a video camera. So, we were working and I asked him some standard basketball questions. Then I quickly switched gears and asked him, "What is your opinion of Adolph Hitler?" He said something like, "Well, he was a smart man, but he was…" At that moment I quickly turned off the camera and said, "In this country you can NEVER say ANYTHING remotely positive about Adolph Hitler. It is too easy to edit or re-edit some of what you said to put you in a bad light.

I told him that simply because he is from Germany, some mean-spirited journalist could ask him an inappropriate question about Hitler. Anything could happen. I told him that he should spend some time creating some "difficult, worst-case scenario" questions for himself. The kind of questions he would never want any journalist to ever ask him, and have prepared answers for them. If a journalist asks you anything about Hitler say something like, "Any-time, any human being, does any-thing to harm the body, mind and spirit of another human being is wrong. It is simply wrong, and they should be severely punished for it."

Now, memorize that line because you are going to be interviewed a lot in your career. I can tell you are going to be a star.

THE MOVIE *GAME DAY*

I auditioned for movie work before, and I even got some jobs but nothing major. I finally received an audition for something I thought could be worthwhile. It was for a movie called *Game Day*. I was to audition for the roll of a television sportscaster. The story was about a drunken, crazed, has-been of an NCAA college basketball coach who is trying to make a comeback. It was starring comedian Richard Lewis as the coach. Richard was known for his many TV appearances and eventually known for his work on the TV series, *Curb Your Enthusiasm*, created by and starring Larry David, the individual who created the hit TV show, *Seinfeld*.

The day before the audition I felt that old familiar rasp in my throat. This meant that I was about to lose my voice, as I did every fall and or winter in New York.

It was a cold, winter morning when I woke up on the day of the audition.

I checked my voice and it was not only raspy, when you could hear it, but it was almost completely gone. DAMN!! This has happened to me before. I decided to go to the audition anyway.

I arrived at the building and rang the bell to gain entry. No one answered. I rang again and waited. No one answered. I rang again. Then I decided to check the address. Darn, I was at the wrong address. My building was a few doors down.

When I arrived, I noticed a note on the door saying the elevator was out of order and was being repaired. So, I had to walk up five flights of stairs. At each step I was thinking what else could go wrong today. I finally arrived on the fifth floor. I entered and in the lobby were two heavy hitters, G. Keith Alexander, a major veteran broadcaster on the New York radio scene and David Alan Grier. David is a Yale School of Drama graduate, who just starred in a Broadway play called, *The First* about the life of baseball legend Jackie Robinson. He was also in the Broadway play, *Dreamgirls*, the hit TV show *In Living* Color, the play and the film, *A Soldier's Story*, and *Boomerang* with Eddie Murphy.

In other words, this guy had fantastic credits. But I did not allow that to intimidate me, even if I didn't have a voice that day.

It was my turn to go in and read for the producer and director, both named Steve. I walked in and said, "I'm sorry, but as you can hear I'm working with a little laryngitis right now. I've been doing this kind of work for years, I could do this work underwater." I started to read, I did a below average job, I finished, got up and put the script on the desk. Then I said, "If you have callbacks I'd appreciate an opportunity to read again." They said, "Sure, we'll call you back." I thought, this is some Hollywood bull crap. They aren't going to call me back. I then turned to leave and they said, "No, keep the script." Hmm, maybe they ARE going to call me back. I picked up the script and left.

About a week later my agent called me for the callback time and day. Both of us were surprised.

I arrived at the callback. The Steves were across the room. I give a hearty, "me, me, me, meeeeee!" They said, "That's better."

Steve, the director sat me down at a picnic table with a bench on either side. He opens the script and randomly thumbs through the pages and lands on a page. He turns the notebook around, so the words faced me, pushed it toward me and said, "Here, read this."

What he didn't know was that I am an EXCELLENT cold reader or as I call it, "an ultra-cold read." I can read anything, perfect the first time, one take, sight unseen. I finish the reading and I feel extremely confident. We stand and I offer him the script. Steve said, "No, no keep it." It is at this moment that I think I could have the job. I shake his hand, go to the other side of the room and shake the other Steve's hand and I left.

One week later my agent called me and said, "You got the job!" The way she said it, made me think that it took her by complete surprise.

We shot my scenes in the gymnasium at Lehman College in the Bronx, New York. It was fun, I knew all of my lines because I had time to memorize them. Memorizing lines is not easy for me, not easy.

I was working with Kenny Albert who is the son of Marv Albert, an internationally known sports broadcaster, one of the best in the business. These days Kenny is broadcasting NFL games, NBA games and other big-time professional sports on television and radio. I am so happy for him.

Several months after the shooting of the film I got a message about the screening in Rockefeller Center. I went with my ex-wife, Lisa. Several minutes into the film I notice you never see me speaking. This is starting to upset me. I am on screen often but you never actually see me speaking, but you hear me a lot.

At the end of the screening, not one of my scenes was shown when you actually SAW me speaking. Everything was in voiceover. I was PISSED! PISSED! PISSED! I was so upset that I was seeing red, everything was red. I was thinking, "how could they do that to me?" DAMN!

What can you do? Suck it up and go on to the next one. THAT is what you do!

It is their movie. They can do whatever they want.

I must admit, since this is an honest reliving of my life, there are certain truths that must come out. I always thought I was just an everyday, regular guy. Sometimes I feel a little naïve. I believe in the impossible. I believe that if one can conceive it, it can happen. So, I go for it…everything.

When I came to New York it seemed as though the color of my skin meant something. It meant something to others. I don't know what I look like until I look in the mirror. Then, I just see a smart, creative, inventive, inquisitive, forward thinking somewhat handsome man. THEY see a black man. I see a man who happens to wear a size 10 shoe.

The life of an actor is a life unlike any other. It is *not* a life where you go into the office five days a week for eight hours a day and take an hour lunch break at noon. Also, we have to *audition* for our jobs, which means there will be looooong dry spells when you don't work at *all*.

That is one of the reasons there are so many actors working in restaurants. It is their back-up job, a steady paycheck, tips, plus those jobs often offer the freedom to leave and go to an audition.

I was lucky in so many ways. I always had my radio job as my steady source of income but I didn't look at my acting income as *extra* money. I believe there is no such thing as *extra* money. Do you know anyone who has any *extra* money? It was just money.

I always wanted to be a one-man multi-arm corporation that received income from a variety of sources. Just like the giant corporations do. I don't know where I got that idea because I don't know anything about business. Lisa was really helpful in that regard.

I have only protested, in the streets, marching, twice in my life. Both times were during Screen Actors Guild strikes. One of the issues on the table was producers did not want to pay actor's residuals for commercial work that was on cable television. That's ridiculous, especially from the perspective of the actor's personal business. I became increasingly upset, actually mad, angry as hell. I thought those greedy bastards had better get their hands out of my pocket. So, the picket line I did hit.

On one cold winter day in front of Young & Rubicam Advertising Agency on Madison Avenue around 40th Street, I was freezing on the picket line. I befriended an actor whom I did not know but I had seen him on television, in movies and at auditions. He told me he had a wife, two children, a mortgage on a home in Connecticut and two cars to pay for. His wife wasn't working and because of the strike, neither was he. I felt bad, so sorry for him and I also felt a bit of guilt.

I was so lucky to have a radio career and I worked as an adjunct professor in four colleges as well.

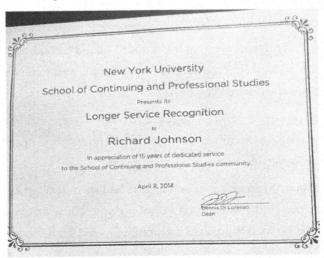

This was the moment I decided to pursue hand modeling also. This is an area of show business that most regular people know nothing about. Actually, there is a whole industry of "parts" modeling, ears, eyes, nose, toes, toenail fungus, fingers, arthritis, psoriasis, baldness, near bald. At least there was when I was in the business. Who do you think models the lip stick, red eye remedies like Visine, earrings, mascara? It is parts models. When I tell people that I have performed as a hand model, they laugh. They think I'm joking.

One weekend day I was whacking weeds in the front yard of my country house with a sickle kind of tool. I started feeling a burning sensation in the web of my right hand between my thumb and index finger. So, I put on some gloves, the only work gloves I had. Well, as it turned out they were the wrong kind of gloves and they dug into my hand more deeply. Before I finished whacking the weeds, the gloves ripped a big swath of skin from my hand. Ouch!

I had a big American Express television commercial hand modeling audition on Monday. My hand was to play an airport immigration officer, checking and stamping passports.

I was upset because it was a big job and I wanted to get it. Lisa said, "Well, maybe the other hand will get the job." That Monday afternoon I went to the audition with brown makeup on my hand. Yes, you guessed it. The other hand *did* get the job.

My work as an actor inspired me to write this book.

It takes more than talent, beauty, and blonde hair to make it in show business.

At one point in my acting career I was the marketing king of New York. I marketed myself more often and more uniquely than, probably, any one.

There are many ways to promote yourself. Actors have put their names and phone numbers on just about everything: Coffee mugs, glasses, coasters, refrigerator magnets, sports drink bottles, pen, pencils, letter openers, rulers, actor business cards, billboards, Frisbees, playing cards, bookmarkers, key chains, notebooks, notepads, mouse pads, calendars, ashtrays and lighters (when people smoked), baseball caps, T-shirts, sweatbands, underwear, bras, pillowcases, paper weights, and so on.

Some even put their audio voiceover reel on their outgoing message on their phones. As you can imaging, some of these methods of advertising yourself are more effective and cost-effective than others.

My main gimmick was the use of postcards. My basic philosophy about marketing is to apply two of the basic principles *of* the advertising industry *on* the advertising industry. Those two principles, as I have defined them for myself, are:

1. Frequency of exposure, or repetition.
2. Stylistic differentiation.

Also, I wanted to have my name, face, and telephone number on agents and casting director's desks as often as possible.

I created my postcards to look like little print ads like you would see in a magazine. Each one was radically different from the one I created before. That way, they would not get tired of looking at the same old ad and *because* it is different, their human nature would force them to look at it.

I marketed myself like McDonalds markets hamburgers, like Ford markets their cars, and like Pepsi markets its drinks.

By that, I mean, I kept changing my ad. You don't see the same ads for major brands today as you did ten, fifteen or twenty years ago. They keep changing them to maintain your attention.

Here are a few examples of what led to my television commercial and acting success. I created all of these postcards. Some of the product names were changed to protect me but I think you can figure out the real names of the products.

This is an ad for OTB (Off-Track Betting).
It started as a TV commercial, then became a print ad in the newspapers, magazines, and a video on the jumbotron at Yankee Stadium in New York City.

A TV commercial for Boulova Watches. I turned the composition up-side down to force agents to turn it right-side up to see my face.

Batt in a Wendy's TV commercial as an 86-year-old doctor.

A TV commercial and a modeling job for Today's Man clothing store.

Dr. Batt in a TV commercial for the Maryland State Lottery

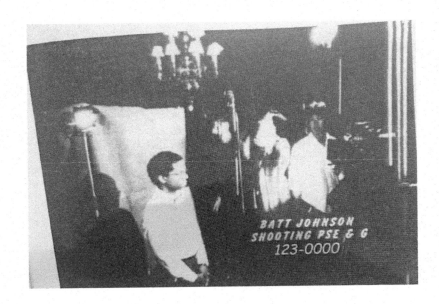

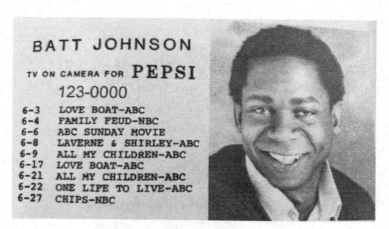

My first national network TV commercial. The information on the left represents the date and what programs the agents could see my commercial

It was directed by Bob Giraldi, known for directing Michael Jackson's "Beat It" video.

*Actually, it was the Sony **Worldwide** Radio Network.*
I couldn't find a globe so I just used the U.S. map outline.

A "comp card," composition card for my modeling work.

This is the "Come On Along" promo for ABC-TV. We were running down the streets of New York with Henry Winkler of Happy Days, Penny Marshall of Laverne & Shirley, Suzanne Sommers of Three's Company, and other big stars on ABC at the time, to promote their shows.

I created a postcard for some voiceovers that I did.
No one was doing that.

A simple card when I went to the William Morris Agency, the largest talent agency in the
world at that time.

I never heard of Charleston Chew candy before I made this TV commercial.

An award-winning corporate film

My first modeling agency, Funny Face.

We were all elements of lousy weather for the new weather man at WJBK-TV Detroit.
You can see the rays of the sun about to appear in the background.
Ice and snow, fog, rain, and yes, I was lightening.

Of all the postcards I created, this one received the most and the best feedback.
This was computer clip art. I colored in the body with a pencil to match my face. Before he was
the color of the paper. Then, just like we did in 3rd grade art, I drew some single line seagulls.

I changed my number, made a postcard about it.
Promote! Promote! Promote!

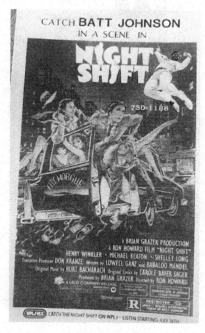

It was fun working in Times Square in this movie with Michael Keaton, Henry Winkler with
Ron Howard directing. Hey, why did you cut my scene?

This biggest, longest running TV commercial I ever performed in.
It was also the highest rated in Lever Brothers' 135-year history.

CHAPTER 18

London-Paris Journal
In Search of Music & Culture

I often keep a daily, detailed journal on many of my international voyages. This one is of my first trip to Europe. I went to England and France doing research to write my jazz book, *What Is This Thing Called Jazz? Insights and Opinions from the Players.*

THE DAY BEFORE MY FIRST TRIP TO EUROPE. SEPTEMBER 15, 1979 1:20 AM

Here I am, the night before I take my first trip to Europe. I am not that excited, maybe because I have no close friends or relatives there. But I do have additional business pressures that may prevent the trip from being boring or mentally relaxing or unstimulating. I have NO idea as to what to expect. I simply want to get interviews for my book. THAT is why I am traveling there.

SEPTEMBER 16, 1979 9:07AM

Whew!! I just sat down on TWA flight #702 to London. What a relief. We almost didn't make it.

We got up at 5:30, showered, ate a bagel, drank some espresso. Then I made Lisa a bathtub terrarium for her plants. We rushed out of the apartment, grabbed a cab and off to Kennedy International Airport we went.

We arrived at the airport and the yo-yo cab driver says, "TWA gate 3, right?" I said, "No, no, #4!" He slammed on his brakes, backed up going the wrong way, then took the other off-ramp to gate #4. We ran inside, checked our bags. Everything was running late. I called my oldest sister, Gloria, in Bremerton, Washington to say good-bye. Then I called my younger sister, Connie, who was living in Oxnard, California.

We landed in London at 8:30 PM. The flight and the landing were smooth. We deplaned, got our bags and took a train from the plane. It was a beautiful, clean, quiet, graffitiless, carpet seated, air conditioned, steadily lit, fast, underground, you may know them as subways, and into London we go. We arrive, get our bags, up onto the lift or the escalator as we Americans call them, and up to street level.

Whoa! What is THIS? I don't recognize the make or model of one, single, vehicle...AND everyone is driving on the wrong side of the street. BE CAREFUL, SOMEONE IS GOING TO GET KILLED! LOOK OUUUUUUT!

We walked and rolled our luggage about four or five blocks to our hotel, past a gas, oops, I mean, a petrol station where petrol was one pound twenty or about $2.60 a litre. Oh, my, I AM in a foreign country that is not Canada, Mexico, Korea or Japan, the other foreign countries I have visited. This is exciting. Everything is new to me.

With my fascination with language and accents, I think I was in the country for about ten minutes when I started picking up the accent. I never heard Cockney while I was in London. Damn it. That is my favorite.

We walk through some quaint, quiet little tree lined streets in Cartwright Gardens. It looks like Gramercy Park. There is a semicircular street with wall to wall hotels. Our hotel is old but very clean. It is a four-floor walk-up with circular light switches that you push as you go up. After a few seconds it automatically turns itself off.

We drop off our bags and go to an Indian restaurant. The food was ok, the wine was ok. Then I had a martini that tasted like it was just vermouth and water, yeuuck! "I'm sorry sir, will you please put some more gin in this?" The little Indian teenager, complete with semi long, black hair, a pony tail and an English accent (Of course he has an English accent, we're in damn, England) said, "More gin?"

We enjoyed a few days of London. You know, taking in the usual tourist sites: The fascinating fortress of Tower Hill along the River Thames, complete with Beefeater guards, Westminster Abbey, St. Paul's Cathedral, Trafalgar Square, Picadilly Circus, Tower Bridge, London Towers, Soho, and many other sites. I only almost got struck by a car two or three times because I was looking the wrong way while crossing the street, they drive on the other side. I got used to it.

One day while walking around site seeing, I saw a poster on a telephone pole advertising the great jazz drummer, Elvin Jones & The Jazz Machine at world famous Ronnie Scott's Jazz Club. PERFECT!! Elvin Jones played with some of the greatest jazz musicians of all time, including with John Coltrane starting in 1960.

That night we went to the club, found Ronnie Scott, introduced myself to him and asked him if I could interview him for the jazz book I was writing. He said, "yes." Great! I'm in.

We sat, had a drink and listened to the rest of the first set. These are all very good musicians. Andy McCloud, the bass player on acoustic upright, played well. He could, however, use a little more amplification. Aree Brown, the reed man on soprano and tenor usually opened the sets with a red-hot, fire breathing solo with the band underneath him. Things usually cooled down from there. Marvin Horn, a quiet subdued personality on stage, had his scales down. He played rather interesting, extended patterns in his solos, but he is very still on stage. Goood music! It was so strange speaking to four black men from New York City and New Jersey in a legendary jazz club in London, England.

The waitresses at Ronnie Scotts were friendly, bar maids were adorable, however, London and Paris are just too darn expensive. Give me New York, or better yet, give me Kansas City, at least for prices.

I interviewed Ronnie Scott and Elvin Jones downstairs in the dressing room. When I went back to my seat, Lisa was steaming mad because I took so long. She clearly did not understand the importance of what I was doing.

THE NEXT DAY, TUESDAY, SEPTEMBER 18, 1979, PARIS

I had an eleven o'clock appointment with Ken Glancy, President of RCA Records. This is my last appointment in London. It went well. Then we rushed to the airport to catch flight # 817 for Paris.

We landed in Paris, Lisa made a phone call to Nancy and Philippe, our friends who would host us, and off to the bus we went. Nancy grew up across the street from Lisa in Pittsburgh. She later moved to Paris to go to art school, or museum curation, art history, or to teach English, I'm not sure. I don't really remember. While there she met a Frenchman (Philippe), they got married and had two wonderful boys.

We arrive at their home after a quick sight-seeing trip through Paris, my first trip there. We unloaded and from the street level, we opened a huge ten-foot tall double wooden door with the nob in the middle of the door. We enter a quaint courtyard to another set of large doors, only these are glass, into a large courtyard with a gigantic tree in the center.

Yep, looks just like the Paris in the movies. There are flats (apartments) on three sides of the courtyard. It is old and beautiful as are many things in all of France. They don't demolish their buildings in most of Europe because they turn fifty years old like they do in America where there is little respect for things old, including people.

The Eiffel Tower is my favorite man-made structure. On my next trip to France I took over a thousand photos of this amazing tower.

We had a lovely dinner at home, a couple of bottles of amazing French (of course) wine and wonderful conversation. Philippe always has to show off his Frenchness. I find them to be proud, nationalistic people. He starts giving me French dinner etiquette lessons.

1. Always keep your hands on the table or at least in plain sight, according to Philippe, "You know the French, they are always pinching or poking the waitress."

2. There is community bread. Always put your bread on the table so everyone can have access. If you put it on your plate that means it is only for you. Bread is a very special commodity in France.

3. When pouring wine, another special French commodity, always pour a small bit into your glass first. The reason is because when you screw the corkscrew into the cork, a bit of cork always goes into the bottle. You pour that into *your* glass first, not your guest's.

4. The woman, your woman, never pours the wine. The man does, always. If the woman does, that means she is drunk, does not know what she is doing or is ill mannered.

5. The man never stands up to pour the wine for others. That means he is reducing himself to a level of that of a servant, removing himself from the rest.

So much for French etiquette, or at least from his generation. I'm most certain things are a little different now, or maybe not.

After all of that, it is time to retire. We have a squabble as to who was going to sleep where. They insisted we sleep in their bed, so we did. No more discussion, I'm tired. I had to get up early because I had an appointment for an interview for my book at Radio France International, the massive, state-run radio station, the ONLY radio station for the whole country of France (at this time, 1979).

MONDAY, 9-24-79 11AM

Radio France International is built facing the Seine River. The building is round like the Capitol Records building in Hollywood or the Guggenheim Museum in New York, round inside and out. In front of the building on the banks of the river is, what I believe is the original Statue of Liberty only it is much smaller, only about twenty feet high or so.

I WENT ON THE RADIO IN PARIS

We enter the building and check in with security. My name is there and we are granted entry. We enter the elevator, go to our floor and meet our contact.

This building is truly amazing. It looks like something at NASA. The architecture inside is round as well. After our interview, we are taken on a brief tour. They have many, many studios. I didn't count them, but every room had brand new equipment in them. For a radio geek, I was really impressed. (This is the exact opposite of what I was to experience the next year at the radio station in Senegal, Dakar, West Africa.)

We entered a studio that was on the air. My contact asked me if I wanted to go on the air with the DJ/host. Of course, I said, yes. He ushered me in, introduced me as a fellow broadcaster from New York City, and said, "Put him on the air." The host waited for the last recorded announcement to almost come to an end, he gave me some headphones and said, in English, "I will just ask you a few basic questions." The announcements ended and I assume he said something like, "We have a special guest today from New York, Mr. Batt Johnson." He asked me some questions in English about my trip and why I was there, of course in a very charming French manner, and before I knew it, it was over. It was brief, but a grand experience to be on international radio in France and other French nations all at the same time. Wow!

Next, we go to my Michael Cuscuna (a wonderful NY based jazz record producer) contact, Gil Gauthrin of Capitol, Emi, Sonnopress Records at #94 Rue Lauriston for an interview. Of course, we're on time, Gil arrives and invites us into his office and we start the interview right away. Gil has a very thick French accent, most of which is indecipherable for me. Good thing Lisa is there with her French savvy to save me when needed. We are having a wonderful interview about jazz in France, his job, jazz record sales in France, label support, concert attendance information, etc.

We were just about to wrap up when a jolly, Santa Claus looking man (without a beard) sticks his head in the door, says something to Gil in almost perfect English, without accent, then closes the door. Gil said, "That is Maurice Collaz. He knows a lot about jazz. You should speak with him too." Gil gave me his number and I later contacted him for an interview. Mr. Collaz has written numerous books on jazz. Now he translates books from French to English and English to French. He also writes for a magazine called "Jazz Hot". As soon as we left the interview with Gil, we raced out to buy a copy. Sure enough, there he was, complete with credits.

CHAPTER 19

Lisa!

I was married only once, and it was to the daughter of a United States Federal Judge. Oh, no! What have I gotten myself into? What did I do? What was I thinking? What is *wrong* with me?

Don't answer any of those questions.

When I was dating Lisa, I had the feeling her father, unwittingly chased men away because they were intimidated by him. Well, I was not, I think he knew that.

Lisa Aldisert is one of the smartest, deepest, most wonderful women I ever met. I loved her, I loved her mind, and I loved her family.

She is the only person I know who graduated from a major university, the University of Pennsylvania, with a BA and an MA, at the same time. She has an MBA from Columbia University, and since our divorce, she has added additional letters to her name, PhD from Columbia University.

She taught at NYU's School of Continuing and Professional Studies, Cornell University and she is a member of the Trustees' Council of Penn Women at the University of Pennsylvania, and serves on the Board of The University's private club, the Penn Club, in New York.

Lisa is an internationally recognized business advisor, trend expert, author of several books and frequently speaks on strategic business topics.

I think speaking is fun for her since she was the President of the New York Chapter of the National Speakers Association for several years.

I know, I know, I'm sounding like her agent. But being an honorable man, I must give up the credit when the credit has been earned.

Being a member of the Aldisert family was a most joyous period in my life, I really enjoyed being in their family. I loved being an Aldisert. Three years of dating, twenty-five years of marriage.

I met Lisa through her brother, Rob. I met Rob through my neighbor, Marty Cicco, who lived two apartment doors down from me.

One day I met Marty at the mailboxes of the apartment building. It was called the New Milburn Hotel. It had four renovated apartments on the ground floor, where Marty and I lived. The hotel was above and housed many Broadway actors and classical musicians who played at the opera, the symphony, and the two ballets at Lincoln Center, all within walking distance.

Marty knew that I was a broadcaster on a jazz radio station. So, one day he knocked on my door to say a more proper hello. I invited him in for a chat. In our conversation he said that he had a friend who was a jazz musician. "Heck man, I am in finance, I don't know anything about music but I would love for you to meet my friend. I think his band is pretty good."

I agreed to meet his friend, Rob, who called me the next day. A couple of days later he came to my apartment. He was wearing a dark brown leather jacket, Kongol kind of cap, a big fuzzy beard and his bass slung over his shoulder. As soon as I opened the door and saw him, I liked him. He instantly became by brother. Over forty-years later, we are still friends.

Rob Aldisert and Batt Johnson hanging at the bar at Jazz at Lincoln Center, NY.

Later that week I met the members of his band, *So What* and attended one of their rehearsals in the band room at Columbia University. They were fantastic! I was very impressed and surprised that they were not further along the road to music success than they were. So, I offered to help them.

I immediately started operating in the capacity of more of a booking agent than a manager. I started looking for opportunities for Rob to play in Greenwich Village. I knew most of the musicians in most of the music clubs, Kenny's Castaways, the Bottom Line, the Village Gate, and the Other (or Bitter) End. But I noticed Rob was not particularly interested in taking this route. I was surprised. I later deduced that he was more interested in a life in the law like his father, than the life of a musician.

After law school, Rob did well. He litigated and tried business, commercial, employment and product liability cases in the federal and state courts of Oregon, California, Washington and some international courts as well.

He also counseled clients in a wide variety of industries including architectural, automotive, pharmaceuticals, medical devices, manufacturing, automotive, recreational products, commercial real estate and technology.

In other words, Rob became a baddass lawyer.

When he was a musician, I worked hard for his band. I got them some free studio time at Vanguard Records recording studio to create a demo to present to record companies to try to get a deal. I had two record labels interested in recording them but the guys didn't want to sign because they were small record companies. I also received a clearance from my radio station to play them on the radio once we got a deal.

On the radio in New York City, for a start!! On the ONLY format that would even BEGIN to talk to them about their music. The band rejected the offer. Huh? I didn't understand...at all.

While at an amateur band competition for a recording contract at Hunter College, I met Lisa Aldisert, my new friend, Rob's sister. Lisa and I eventually became friends, then close friends, then really close friends, then we got married (9-26-1981).

Three years before, when I "met the parents," I thought they liked me. Well, that was until they discovered that I was dating their daughter. Then, I became, something else. I was no longer *just* a friend of Robbie's. They wanted to have Italian grandbabies from their only daughter, I'm sure. I am capable in many areas, but producing Italian babies is not one of them.

Rob was the brother I never had. Many years later I tried to visit him and his family in Portland, Oregon. So many things went wrong. I decided to write something about it. I called the article:

STEPHEN KING MEETS BATT JOHNSON

All I tried to do was go see my family. I had no idea Stephen King knew me. I didn't pay him or give him any indication that I wanted him to write a day in my life for me.

I went to LaGuardia Airport in New York to go to Portland, Oregon to see Rob and his family. There was a storm coming, so they tried to board the plane quickly to take off before the storm arrived. We boarded and taxied to the runway.

Then the winds shifted to a prohibitive tailwind, so we waited for the winds to shift. They didn't. We were then sent to another runway. Oops, more tailwinds, so we waited again.

Air traffic control sent us back to the original runway, where we waited for the winds to shift. I felt like one of the Wright brothers trying to take off on the first flight of man in 1903 at Kitty Hawk, North Carolina. What the heck is going on?

The flight was to leave at 1 PM. At 2:30 it took off, headed for Dallas. When we arrived, there was chaos. People were pushing from the back to get off the plane to make their connection. Fortunately, no fights broke out.

I got off the plane and went to the ticket counter to find out what to do next. The agent was swamped, had a major attitude, and sent me to the wrong counter.

I was then sent to a loooooooong line to get rebooked. You have no idea how long that line was. It looked like the Dallas Cowboys stadium emptied out and everyone stood in this line!

As I stood in line, I called American Airlines on my cell phone for help. My phone battery was getting low, so I decided to get out of this hellishly long line to charge my phone.

I didn't know what else to do. Guess what? The charger outlet wouldn't hold my plug. All of the other stations were occupied, so I had to physically hold the plug in the socket with my hand while I listened to their sleepy elevator music on hold.

They should have many more electrical outlets at the seats than they do, especially since everyone has at least one cell phone these days. This airport doesn't even have horns or beepers on its electric carts for seniors and the disabled.

The driver has to yell, excuse me, look out, move please, coming through. At least Stephen King could have written in some horns for the carts.

I had placed my ticket and boarding pass on top of my luggage when I was in line but when I arrived at the charging station, they weren't there.

I backtracked and found them on the floor, and yes, I almost got hit by one of those passenger carts without a heart or a horn.

I then received a text from American Airlines saying I was automatically booked on another flight. Whew! I'm saved!

Not so fast, Mr. Johnson. I was booked on a flight for July 5th, but this was July 2nd. Three days stuck in the airport? I felt like Tom Hanks in the movie *Terminal*, living at the damn airport!

I called my ex-sister-in-law, Jenny Shea, to tell her that I was going to be delayed. She tried to help by looking up additional flights for me. Bless her heart. I love her for many reasons.

I finally connected with American on the phone. ALL flights were booked. Not. One. Single. Seat was available. I knew I was taking a chance by traveling on a 4th of July weekend, toward the end of COVID, when everyone in the universe wanted to travel, and many families have additional cash from stimulus checks and unemployment.

But I did it anyway because I wanted to see Rob and family in Portland and Ron and family in San Diego.

I reconnected with the airline and they found ONE SINGLE SEAT going back to Newark the next day. I SNATCHED it! I said, "Book it! Book it! Please book it NOW. I'm in dire straits. I don't know why but the devil is chasing me!"

The airline helped me get a hotel room for the night. They sent me an email with all of the information. I called the hotel to confirm the reservation and to ask for directions.

They asked for my reservation number. I gave it to them. They said, "I'm sorry sir, but our reservation numbers are all numbers, not letters." I said, "Are you SURE?" The gentleman on the other end said, "Sir, I've been working here for five years. I know for sure."

I decided to go anyway. I was NOT spending the night in the airport terminal. I caught the Marriott Shuttle to the hotel and I checked in. The room was cold so I turned up the heat. When I woke up the next morning, the room was still cold. I'm TELLING you, NOTHING was going my way!

I hadn't eaten since around ten or eleven that Friday morning. I was hungry. While checking in, I asked where the restaurant was. She said, "It is right there, right around the corner —but it is closed."

WHAT?! Closed! My instinct was to eat at the airport but I ignored my God-given instincts because I wanted to get out of there and not waste any more time.

I went to the bar for a beer. I thought that maybe they had some bar food, peanuts, or something. They had nothing. There were two female flight attendants seated across the bar from me. They overheard part of my conversation and said that I could have the rest of their pizza if I'd like.

Aaaaaaaaaaahhhhhh! The angels sang from on-high. Yes, you are angels, that's why you work in the sky. I accepted it, and the waitress warmed it up for me. I then offered to pay for their drinks AND the three pieces of pizza. We haggled a bit, as is socially expected to happen.

On my way back to my room, I bought a small bag of potato chips and a bag of peanuts, sent out some messages, and went to bed. I am still fuming. I haven't been this angry in many years. I was so angry that I didn't want to speak to ANYONE.

I went to sleep, woke up, and called the front desk to ask what time breakfast was. She said, "From seven to eleven." Ok, is lunch right after that? No, sir, there is no lunch on Saturday but dinner is from four to eight. WHAT? No lunchtime? But Dallas is a major transportation hub. Isn't Marriott missing out on some revenue? Is all of Texas this bad? Holy cow. I couldn't get out of there fast enough.

I showered and went down for breakfast. I ordered, and when it finally came, it was cold. I asked the "waiter" three times for a glass of water, milk, and sugar for my coffee and a spoon to stir it with…three times I asked that guy.

I went back to the Dallas airport and sat two seats down from a woman. I noticed that they hadn't changed the destination sign yet, it said "Ft. Lauderdale".

After a few minutes, the woman asked me if I was going to New York. We struck up a conversation. Then several minutes later there was an announcement of a last-minute building and gate change.

Here we go again, MORE drama. We grabbed our luggage and walked a great distance together to the new gate.

As we chatted, I learned that she lived in Ft. Worth, was Jamaican, a Trump supporter, a conspiracy theorist, and an anti-masker. She said, holding up her mask, "Look at this thing. It's just a piece of cloth, what's this going to do?"

She told me the election was stolen because computers were hacked. She believed that Trump was the greatest president we ever had because he did everything he said he was going to do.

She believed the same thing happened in her "tiny" country of Jamaica and it never recovered (her words).

I became concerned. This is my first encounter with a black-white supremacist.

That sounds like the Dave Chappelle comedy skit about the blind black-white supremacist who hated black people. He didn't know he was black because he was blind.

I have a couple of black Republican friends but they aren't black-white supremacists.

OPTIMISM: SUCCESS IN THE MEDIA AGAINST ALL ODDS

Now, I wanted to get away from this woman FAST before we got into an argument. The plane can't come soon enough.

Finally, the plane arrived. It was from an international location so we had to wait an additional twenty minutes for sanitizing and customs! I just wanted to go HOME!!

(I think this is Karma for living a good life.)

I arrived at Newark airport, waited for almost an hour for the bus that I paid $10.00 for and it never came. I bit the final bullet and paid $100.00 for the final, final leg home.

I MADE IT! What a nightmare!!! I don't want to be in any more Stephen King movies.

Stephen, if you call my agent looking for talent, PLEASE don't ask for me. I am not available no matter how much you are willing to pay me!

Lisa and I had some great times in our marriage, we travelled to many countries: Portugal, Belgium, Mexico, Germany, Greece, Jamaica, Switzerland, Cote D'Ivoire (Ivory Coast) West Africa, Italy, Spain, Morocco in North Africa (a couple of times), Turkey, England, Senegal, W. Africa, Canada, Amsterdam, Norway, Bahamas, Madeira, France (several times), Brazil, and Hawaii, (I know Hawaii is the U.S. but it seemed like another country).

Obviously, some of those countries were more interesting than others. Some were interesting because of their architecture, like France, others for their culture, like Morocco & West Africa, and others for their people, like Spain.

GERMANY

When we went to Germany, we arrived, we got our rental car, as we always did, and started driving. We drove over 2,000 miles throughout Western Germany. We arrived in Cologne, W. Germany and went to the Cologne

337

Cathedral. It was declared a World Heritage Site in 1966 and is the largest Gothic church in Northern Europe, construction began in 1248.

After touring it, we stopped into a nearby pub for a drink. The bar was fairly long and only had two or three people sitting there. We sat, ordered drinks, then the one drunk at the end of the bar started calling me. "Hey, Zhonny! Hey, Zhonny! Come over here and have a zhrink with me, you son offffff aaaaah. Hey Zhonny!"

I said to Lisa, "I think we had better get out of here before I have to kick an old drunk German's ass." Sounded like he was still living with some experiences from WWII, and they don't see many people who look like me around here very often.

I let it slide but when we went to Norway on a different trip…that was, well, a different trip.

NORWAY

We arrived in Oslo and found our hotel, took a nap, woke up and went to dinner. The next day we got our rental car to drive up north to see the fantastic fjords of Norway. A fjord is a large, beautiful salt water inlet from the sea with high rising mountains on either side.

The Hardanger Fjord was my objective for that day. There are fjords all over the world including in Washington State. But in my mind the most beautiful are in Norway. I guess that's because of my mental imagery of the Vikings and all.

But first, a visit to the Viking Museum. A professor in 1913 founded the Viking Museum in Oslo. In it I saw two Viking burial ships, they were smaller than I expected, but the bottoms were beautifully designed for one thing, cutting through the water. They looked like the design of a shark, sleek, hydrodynamic, beautiful.

Also, in this museum was Norwegian ethnologist and adventurer, Thor Heyerdahl's hand-built raft called Kon-Tiki in which he sailed eight-thousand km across the Pacific Ocean to prove a theory.

Before we decided to take this trip to Norway, we checked our world weather atlas. It said that in September and October there is a gulf stream that blows across Norway and it doesn't get very cold, maybe in the fifties and sixties.

As we were driving north there were ten to twelve-foot snow drifts that the plows had made. We drove through tunnels that were drilled through the mountains. When we came out the other side, the landscape became more and more eerie, like a frozen moonscape that had never been inhabited... by ANYTHING.

Every now and then I would see a parked car on the side of the cold, barren, desolate highway. I thought, those poor souls, their car stalled but, where are they? Then I saw two cars parked. Then three! Oh, my, how sad. The air must be thin at this altitude and the carburetors can't get enough air and the cars are stalling out. I hope that doesn't happen to us. This was before the age of cell phones and besides which, we can't speak Norwegian, although in Oslo some spoke almost perfect, standard American English without accent.

I drove a little farther up the highway and saw another parked car. There was a dip in the snow drift so I slowed down and looked over the snow drift. I saw a man and a woman sitting in *lawn chairs* in *bathing suits* sunning themselves with aluminum foil under their chins. WHAAAAT? In THIS weather? Yep. Later on, I saw another one, and another one. I guess this is a thing in Norway.

Five minutes later it started to snow. Then it started coming down heavy to the point of being dangerous. We looked for an exit for a town to perhaps get a hotel until the storm blew over.

We found one. The snow was now above our ankles as we walked around this tiny town looking for some food. We finally found a restaurant and the guy was cleaning the grill to close down and go home while he could. With a combination of French and English, we talked him into preparing some food for us. Whew!

We ate and returned to our hotel. Then next morning the snow was about mid-thigh on me and higher on Lisa. As it turned out, this was the worst winter they had had in the previous one-hundred plus years. Some gulf-stream.

We stayed in this tiny town for a day or two then continued on our adventure seeing the beautiful fjords, mountains, greenery and scenery.

It was time to go back to Oslo. When we arrived, we saw a sign for a jazz club. Great, let's go listen to some music, get some food and some drinks and call it a wonderful day.

As luck would have it, it was not jazz club at all, but a second-rate rock club and the wine was horrible.

As we were standing in the coat-check line to get our garments to leave, I felt a sharp sting on my right ear. I soothed it thinking no one knows me here. Who the heck could that be? Only someone who knew me would do something like that. Then I felt it again. Wow, that hurt! I turned around and there was some guy with his two thumbs in his ears, wiggling his fingers and sticking out his tongue at me. You know, like a kid in elementary school.

I instantly became enraged, I was seething, I wanted to KILL! I took both of my hands and SLAMMED them on his chest as hard as I could. I then grabbed his shirt and JAMMED it up into his chin as I yelled at the top of my lungs, M***ER F***ER! WHO DO YOU THINK YOU'RE F***IN' WITH? I WILL F*** YOU UP!!! YOU DON'T KNOW WHO YOU'RE F***IN' WITH!!!

The poor guy's eyes were as big as truck tires as he threw his hands in the air, mouth agape. At this moment the manager or owner came over and said he saw the whole thing. He shoved the guy aside speaking in a curt, guttural tone that sounded intimidating, even in Norwegian.

The manager apologized and made the idiot apologize to both of us. He then asked us if we would come back. We said we would, (but not with that music or that horrible wine).

I guess the guy had too much to drink and thought I wasn't real, maybe he thought I was a toy or something. I'll bet he won't do THAT again…to ANYONE of ANY color.

ITALY

This next story comes with a disclaimer! I love Italy and her people. So, if you happen to be Italian and a friend of mine, I have no hard feelings. I am simply telling my story. Whew! Now that that is out of the way…

I knew I had to be on my New York alert system before going to Italy because of an incident that happened to a friend of Lisa's. She was walking down the street in Rome and two guys came by on a motorcycle and snatched her purse. She didn't let go and was dragged through the streets of Rome.

I was aware, but not quite aware enough. I had been to Europe a few times but this would be my first trip to Italy. I was driving from France to Italy and came to a hi-way tollbooth. I pulled up to the clerk and handed him a bill of a certain denomination (Lire before Euros). He handed me my change and I handed it to Lisa and I pulled off. She started counting the change, then she let out a yelp. "That jerk ripped us off!" There was nothing I could do, we were barreling down the hi-way.

One day in Rome, we went to a restaurant near the Trevi Fountain, a high tourist area. We ordered, the food came, it wasn't up to the high Italian standards we were accustomed to, but we ate it. We got the check, and by this time, we are on high, high rip-off alert.

Lisa analyzed the check, and yep, you guessed, it. It was wrong. I called the waiter over and showed him the error in my half Spanish, half Italian, half English. He said, "Oooohh, mi scusi! Mi scusi!" He took the check back to the kitchen area and returned with the "corrected" check, apologizing. Then he left.

Of course, we checked it before showing the money. IT WAS WRONG AGAIN!!

I was mildly perturbed before, now I am bordering on flaming!

I waited for him to reappear and I summoned him once again. Of course, by then I was thinking, "Does he think that I am so excited about being in Italy that whatever they say goes? Or, does he think that because I am black I don't know how to count? Or because I'm an American I don't know any better." Well, if that was his thinking he was wrong on all fronts.

He reappeared, kind of gave us a little attitude, as if it was our fault, and took the check back again. He brought it back, we checked it, paid it and got the hell out of there.

If there was any way I could have stiffed him on the tip, I would have. In Europe, the tip is built into the price. So, I couldn't withhold funds for his thievery attempts right in front of my face. He had nerve!

Later that week on a beautiful, bright, sunny day we were walking on a bridge crossing the Tiber River, going to a museum.

Several feet ahead of us I saw a small child come out of a small street. It looked like an alley but it was a street. Immediately following was a woman dressed in all white with her head covered and two or three other children.

In my mind's eye I immediately saw Diane Sawyer from the show 60 Minutes on CBS-TV. A few weeks before I saw her do a story about the thieving gypsy children of Europe, so I was ready.

I told Lisa to hold on to her purse. She said, "What?" I said, "Just hold on to your purse!" I had a feeling we were going into battle.

By this time, we were only a few feet from the gypsies. My eagle-like New York eye saw a newspaper in her hand with smudged ink. I thought she had been sleeping in the street and she was using the newspaper as a blanket or a pillow, not for reading the news of the day.

As we approached, she started a very fake cry (she needed to take some acting lessons from me, I would have given her a discount). With this fake crying act, she started stroking my arm and placed the blurred newspaper over my pocket.

With lightning speed, and rough precision, the little children tried to put their dirty little hands into my pockets.

They picked the wrong tourist that day. I started cursing at full volume and kicking and swinging at full velocity like I was in the ring with Muhammad Ali.

If I connected with one of those right hooks, I would have really hurt one of those little hoodlums. I don't remember if they were attacking Lisa.

I don't think they knew how lucky they were because I was loaded for bear with blood in my eyes.

The same thing happened to Lisa's brother, Greg, who is about 6' 1". The difference with his attack is that they used a rope to fuse his arms to his body to rifle his pockets. I don't remember if they got any money from him.

A few years later we decided to try Italy again. We landed at Fiumicino Airport and took a taxi into the city.

When we arrived at our hotel, I gave the driver a bill big enough to cover the fare and get change.

I think you know what is coming next. I won't use lira because I don't remember the exchange rates from all those years ago so I will use dollars in this example.

Let's say the fare was $30.00 and I gave him a $100.00 bill. I get $70.00 change coming, right? The driver claimed that I gave him a $50.00, so he tried to give me only $20.00 change.

We argued for several minutes as I kept an eye out for the police, who would probably be on the side of the taxi driver. I had no proof plus my Italian was nonexistent. Lisa had some language skill but I'm not sure she could sufficiently present our case to the police under such anger, duress, and transatlantic flight fatigue.

I decided that that trip to Italy would be my last...and it was.

Back in New York, because of Lisa's background as a commercial banker, she was far more financially literate than I was. One day she said, "If we are going to create any wealth, we have to pioneer farther north in the city." She was speaking of north of 96th Street. In my mind, that was the bad part of town. But, I put on my brave little boy armor and walked from our apartment on 70th & Columbus to north of 96th. I was not happy.

For some unknown reason, I have a knack for real estate. I can magically find properties. Perhaps it is the voice of my 8th grade educated father in the back of my head. "Son, sit down. Do you want to know the key to business?" I was thinking, no, I don't care anything about business. I want to go out and play basketball with my friends. He then said, "The key to business is to buy low and sell high." Wow! Profound. I "think" I still hear my dad's voice.

So, I took her advice, armed with my dad's wisdom, I started looking for investment properties. I found an undervalued co-op (cooperative apartment where you own shares in the building's corporation) on Riverside Drive. We bought it.

Then later we decided to buy a house in the country in Tobyhanna, Pennsylvania to get away to, and perhaps for rental property for an investment as well later. We found a cute two-bedroom, one bath house on a quarter of an acre of land with a very wooded backyard.

They were in the process of building a man-made lake behind our house, then I could stand at the kitchen sink, wash dishes and look at the water. Relaxing, right?

Well, they never finished the lake and I got anxious. I wanted to be on the lake. I wanted to be able to wake up, jump in my boat and go fishing at five o'clock in the morning when they are biting.

So, we sold the Tobyhanna property and bought a large three-bedroom, two bath, two-story house, on a lake with a dock, a rowboat, and a canoe in Dingman's Ferry Pennsylvania. THAT is what I wanted! The house had a large screened-in porch with outdoor reclining rocking chairs.

During the summer months we would invite friends to come out. Then Lisa and I would take bets as to when the soft, warm, gentle breeze through the trees and the rocking furniture would put them to sleep. That was a fun game.

In addition to Rob, Lisa has a younger brother named Greg. Like Rob, Greg became an attorney. They all grew up listening to stories of the law on their dad's knee.

Their dad was one of the first Federal Judges of Italian descent in our nation's history. It was a big deal. Back then Italians had to fight for their rights too. In fact, he once told me a story about when he was a child, the Ku Klux Klan burned a cross on their lawn because they were Italian. I wonder when Italians became "acceptable white Americans?"

He was nominated by President Lyndon Baines Johnson and confirmed by the U.S. Senate in 1968, and later became the Chief Judge of the 3rd Circuit Court of Appeals, a ceremony I had the privilege of attending.

I have never said this to anyone, but their father, Ruggero J. Aldisert (we called him Rugi), was like a father figure to me. I admired him immensely. He was kind, witty, loving and insightful. He loved a good joke, Twizzlers, pasta al dente, and had the best eyebrows to ever grow out of the face a human.

He joined the U.S. Marines during World War II, and spent a lot of time in an artillery battalion on Johnston Island and the Marshall Islands in the Pacific. We had the military in common, in addition to both of us loving his children. He used to tell me stories of the war and his time in a hospital in Seattle, Washington, while recovering from injuries from the war.

He lived in his hometown of Pittsburgh until he took senior status (a form of semiretirement) at age 66 because of a heart condition. He then moved to Santa Barbara, California. When he and his wife, Agatha would come to New York to visit Lisa and Rob, two of their three children, Rugi and I would sometimes go on little walks, just the two of us. We were in midtown a few times. He loved walking around looking at some of the buildings and remembering the old buildings when he was here in 1945.

On one of our walks in New York he told me about his involvement in the "Hurricane" Carter murder case of the 1960s and '70s.

Ruben "Hurricane" Carter was an African American middleweight boxer who was arrested in 1966 and convicted of the murder of three individuals, wrongfully. He was sentenced to life but was later released after spending twenty years in prison.

So, Rugi (Judge Aldisert) wrote in an opinion that the prosecutors withheld information from defense lawyers about the shooting from the key prosecution witness. Judge Aldisert also found that the prosecution failed to meet some technical requirements. "Hurricane" Carter was released from prison in 1985. I think Rugi was proud of this case and wanted to tell me because it involved racism and a black man.

This story gained quite a bit of traction among celebrities. Carter wrote his autobiography, *The Sixteenth Round,* in 1974 while in prison. His story inspired the Bob Dylan song, "Hurricane" in 1975. Carter appeared as himself in Dylan's 1978 movie *Renaldo and Clara.*

Denzel Washington played Carter in the 1999 film, *The Hurricane,* where he was nominated for an Academy Award for Best Actor. I'm certain this put a little sting in the situation when boxer Marvelous Marvin Hagler, actors Samuel L. Jackson and Wesley Snipes didn't get this juicy role.

In *Rolling Thunder Revue: A Bob Dylan Story by Martin Scorsese,* a film that came out in 2019, Dylan talked about his relationship with Carter, who was also interviewed in the film. In 2019 the BBC produced a podcast series called *The Hurricane Tapes.* This was a 13-part series created from forty hours of recorded interviews conducted with Carter by Ken Klonsky. Much of this material was in his 2011 book called, *The Eye of the Hurricane.*

He was proud of his work as a lawyer and a judge. He once told me of his one regret in life, that he didn't become a police officer first. However, he would be the first to tell you that, aside from his family, he is most proud of being a Marine.

The Honorable Ruggero J. Aldisert passed away at the age of 95 on December 28, 2014, only about five months after fully retiring. Even at that age, he had still been playing golf.

Lisa invited me to say goodbye to him because she knew how much I loved him.

He was buried with Honors in Arlington National Cemetery, Washington, D.C. Rugi was a hell of a man.

CHAPTER 20

My Divorce

Divorce is traumatizing, like a death in the family, perhaps worse. No matter if you are happy about the divorce or not.

After signing the divorce papers, I bought some furniture, left it in the store, jumped on a plane and went to Buenos Aires, Argentina to continue studying tango.

I know this may sound somewhat cold to some but my married life was crumbling around me, and had been for some time. We agreed upon the divorce. So, I had to get away. I went to the bottom of the earth, Argentina.

Was it escapism, optimism, enthusiasm, agitation, major sadness, anticipation, elation, or fear and denial? You know, like when you go to a horror movie and something scares the heck out of you, but you laugh?

I wasn't sure of the future of my life with my wife, ex-wife, but I bought the ticket several months in advance and I was *going*.

I didn't realize how traumatized I was about the divorce until I returned to New York from the trip.

I realized that I had forgotten to make appointments, keep some appointments, pay some bills, and several other oversights were made by me simply because I was in a haze of a fog and didn't realize it until I returned home.

By writing these memoirs, I discovered that I have a fairly acute long-term memory. This is how I remember the divorce happening.

I was at an Aldisert family reunion in Carmel California where Lisa and Rob's cousins, Eric and Theresa lived and were hosting their annual family reunion that year. One day we were at a public swimming pool and the kids were splashing about enjoying, as kids will do.

Then I saw Jen, Rob's wife come around to the other side of the pool. She said, "Rob wants to talk to you in the bar." I knew something was fishy with this because if Rob wanted to talk to me, he would simply say, "Hey, let's go talk."

Rob and I went to the bar together. We sat down and he immediately ordered a shot of whiskey before we said anything. I knew something was up. We did some small talk, the shot came, he drank it. Then he said something like, "You know I love you, man. But we have a problem. You're going to have to leave the family."

Or words similar to that. We looked at each other. I was thinking that his father, in conjunction with his brother, had a family meeting about my marriage with their family member and decided that it was time for me to go because apparently, she was unhappy. Unhappy? *She* was unhappy? I did nothing wrong or bad to create turmoil within the family. That is my take on that moment in that Carmel, California bar at the Aldisert family reunion in, I believe, 2006.

A few days later, I believe the date was June 24th, 2006, Lisa and I were back in New York from the family reunion.

I was sitting on the couch watching CNN. Lisa came out of the bedroom and said, "I want to talk to you."

Those words are never good words to hear. If she wanted to talk to me, she would just talk to me, right then and there.

In "wife" talk, this means she has something special to say to you that you probably...do...not...want...to...hear. I said, "ok, let me take a shower first, and I'll be right out."

I took my shower, came back to the couch, and a couple of minutes later she came out and sat on the couch next to me. She then repositioned herself where her whole body was facing me. I mirrored her body language, meaning, "I am ready for whatever you have to say. I am with you. I think I know what this is all about."

We were looking each other in the eye for a few seconds. Then she said, "I think it is time we got a divorce." There was silence. We were looking each other in the eye. A tear rolled out of my right eye and onto my cheek. Then the other eye released a drop of water. We were still looking each other in the eye, no words were spoken for several seconds.

I then nodded, and said, "ok."

Still, silence. After several more seconds of looking each other in the eye, we started to laugh.

I know, I know, it sounds strange, but this is *exactly* as I remember it. I think we were laughing because we both knew this was something that had been coming for a looooong time and the burden, the pain, the unhappiness was FINALLY over.

This was a heavy time in our household. Our marriage was dying and so was our beloved dog, Django.

We had taken him to the vet several times, tests, tests, tests. The diagnosis was always inconclusive. He was listless, sad eyes, not eating. One day he urinated blood on our expensive antique Chinese Art Deco rug. We rushed him to the vet again. A new lab test just came in saying that he had Myeloid Leukemia.

You want to talk about a sad day? While in the vet's office, Lisa held him, the doctor injected him to put Django to final rest. Lisa held him as he drifted off to his final sleep. I am tearing up just writing about this moment.

This was so sad. Django was a Bichon Frisé, Poodle, and Shih tzu. I think he had a thin bloodline because of it, but he was cute a hell. We named him Django after the French born Belgium, gypsy jazz guitarist, Django Reinhardt, one of the greatest in the world in the 1930s and 1940s.

When I walked Django, everyone, eight to eight, woman or lady, cripple, blind, or crazy (I know, not pc) would stop to pet him and ask what he was. The most beautiful women on the upper west side of Manhattan, really incredible women, would stop me. All the while, I am thinking, "Where did these women come from?"

I am *certain* that if I didn't have Django with me, they wouldn't give me the time of day. Even if I were lying in a pool of my own blood, writhing in pain, they would step right over me and keep walking.

Even young men in their teens and early twenties, who were trying to be cool, would peek out of the corner of their eye to take a closer look as we passed one another. Django was a baddass!

I remember reading an article about a community in, I think it was, Holland. There was a popular pet shop which was located across the street from a city park.

The pet shop would *rent* puppies to single men as a way to meet women. Yes, of course it worked. How smart.

Django's death was sad, *so* sad.

Next were legal proceedings. The divorce was adult, amicable, inexpensive and brief. I was shocked! We had a good lawyer. (Want his number?)

Lisa and I are still friends and we speak on the phone occasionally.

CHAPTER 21

My Dance Life

Lisa's birthday is January 17th, twenty-three days after Christmas. This means I had to come up viable gift ideas within close proximity of one another.

I discovered that I had a knack for buying earrings that she loved. But how many earrings can a woman wear?

I remember when we were dating, I bought her an off-white, thin navy-blue pinstripe pants suit. I thought that was the classiest thing.

Well, she never wore it. I learned a lesson.

I was happy to have stumbled upon earrings and scarves but I needed a new gift idea. One afternoon I was walking up Broadway, coming from a day of the radio show and five acting auditions, and I was *tired*.

I happened to walk past the DanceSport Dance Studio that I had walked past a thousand times before during the twenty years I had lived in New York. But this time a light bulb went off. Ping!

I knew she loved dance. We were members of the New York City Ballet for nineteen years at that point. She had even taken some ballet classes. One day she purchased some instructional dance videos for us to learn to dance together. But I rejected the idea. I didn't want to learn to dance. But for some reason, dancing now sounded like a good idea.

I walked up the stairs and bought a gift certificate for a combination of private and group dance lessons for us…and I haven't stopped since.

PAUL PELLICORO'S

DanceSport

New York's Largest Ballroom & Latin Dance Studios
1845 Broadway (60ᵗʰ Street), New York, NY 10023 Tel: (212) 307-1111

RECEIPT #: 1070

Date: 22-Dec-97

PAID BY : BATT JOHNSON GC#553

receipt for GIFT CERTIFICATE

VALUE OF THE GIFT CERTIFICATE:		$75.00
USED CREDIT –		$0.00
PAYMENT: –		$75.00
BALANCE DUE =		$0.00

GIFT EXPIRATION DATE: 23-Dec-98

REGISTRAR: MADDY

TYPE OF PAYMENT: AMEX

GIFT RECIPIENT: LISA ALDISERT   22380

I kept this receipt because I knew I was going to dance for the rest of my life and I would, perhaps one day, want to look back on my very beginning and training as a dancer.

This was December 22, 1997. Well, Covid-19 stopped me and everyone from dancing in 2020, but before that I never stopped dancing.

I started with ballroom dancing. I studied all of the popular partner dances: hustle, swing, west coast swing, jive, jitterbug, lindy hop, samba, rumba, foxtrot, ballroom waltz, Viennese waltz, merengue, cha-cha, bachata, salsa, mambo, all of it. Kizomba hadn't crossed my path yet.

My work days were spent looking at the clock with my tongue hanging out, drooling on my shirt, waiting for 5:30 to occur so I could take my first of a series of four classes that day. I was in dance class from 5:30 until 9:30 PM. Then was time for one of many practice parties, one on three different floors of DanceSport Studios near the corner of Broadway at 60th Street, New York City.

SALSA

I studied salsa and danced it every day and night for many years. To this day, I still thank all of my salsa teachers who taught me how to translate what I was hearing into how it made me feel and want to move: Franklin Ayala, Raul Avila, Andriana Kourdi, Veronica Britez, Mario Diaz, Rosa Collantes (RIP), Brenda Ramos, Alejandra Gochez, Paul Pellicoro, Talia Castro-Pozo, Ron Rosario, Ricky Ricardo, Juan Matos, Gildred Ribot, Jhesus Aponte, Roula Giannopoulou, the Eddie Torres Dance Company, Razmatazz Dance Company, Piel Canela Dance Company, Mariana Parma, Angel Ortiz (RIP), and Kelvin Roche. Rebecca Sweet is another highly influential individual who always, no matter how poorly I was dancing in my student showcase ballroom performances, would always make of point of coming over to me and encouraging me to keep dancing, dance, dance.

If you were a contributor to my love of salsa and dance in general and your name is not here, please, forgive me. Salsa dancing was a very important part of my life, over many years, with many influencers.

I went to most of the salsa clubs in New York. I loved it so much. I couldn't stay out too late because I was married and my wife didn't appreciate the fact that I danced so damn much. Actually, we started dance together and as time went by we took different styles of dance. She enjoyed the international ballroom style and I was falling in love with salsa, cha-cha, swing, samba, and hustle. This was much before my discovery of Argentine tango.

I went to three different locations of the Copacabana club over the years, SOB's, El Flamingo, among many, many others. El Flamingo was on West 20th Street, one block before the West Side Highway, on the north side of the street. A HOT new salsa club.

THERE SHE IS, MISS AMERICA

I remember one night there was an unusual energy in the air. Obviously, you can't tell by looking at people, so you have to start asking questions. "Hey, what's going on?" Things seem a little unusual tonight." I am feeling a different vibe, what's happening?" Finally, someone told me that ex-Miss America, actress, Grammy nominated singer, Vanessa Williams was coming to the club that night to dance. We all remember her as the first African

American woman to be crowned Miss America. She was also on the hit TV show, Ugly Betty and the movie Dance with Me with Chayanne and Eraser with Arnold Schwarzenegger.

I knew she danced salsa but I never saw any video or film of her dancing. I went out on a limb and stayed late. I knew I was going to get grief from my wife, Lisa and I had to get up at 2:43 to do my daily morning radio show on LITE-FM the next day, but I stayed until she came.

Then, BAM! There she is, she arrived and it was not too late. Yes, she had bodyguards but it was not too obvious, insulting or over the top. There was an air of discreet discretion. I saw her come in but obviously I didn't make a fuss, say hello, or even make eye contact.

After a few minutes of changing her shoes, chatting with friends, drinking some water, she took to the floor. She danced one or two songs with different guys, then various guys started cutting in. I'm thinking, this is my opportunity to dance with her without the possibility of being rejected with a big fat, "No thank you!"

This was a very hot salsa club with some of the best dancers in New York. It also had live music very often. One of my main teachers, Franklyn Ayala, was often the DJ there. The floor was heated, there was energy in the air and on the floor. Vanessa was dancing with the various guys who cut in. It was pretty damn exciting.

She danced on the "one". I was not, at that time, very proficient on the one, but I could fake it. On one and on two are musical terms used in the two common styles of salsa dancing. "On one" means that your first step is on the first beat of the music. "On two" means that your first step is on the second beat. Pretty simple, right? Dancing on two is usually confusing to people because the "one" is the first beat you hear.

I was not and I never became a professional salsa dancer but I had enormous confidence in my abilities and knew I could give her a good ride. Also, because of my awareness of jazz makes me a slightly different kind of dancer, in both salsa and tango.

I waited and waited for an ideal, polite, unobtrusive, professional opportunity to jump in. It came, I saw it and jumped in I did.

Whoa, she is taller than I knew! She is only 5'6" but taller in heels, of course. She moves well. I think she is having a good time. I'm *not* trying to impress her. I'm just trying to bring some memorable joy to her life and vivid salsa moments while back in her home state of New York.

It was fun for me. I think she was having a good time. Well, after a short while, they next guy cut in and away she went. When it came time for me to leave, I went to her table. As I approached, her two bodyguard's attention was all on me. I approached, thanked her for the dance and welcomed her to New York. I said good night to her beefy bodyguards and grabbed a taxi for my bed. 2:43 AM comes reeeeeal soon! I had to perform my 5:30 AM morning radio show at 106.7 LITE-FM and figure out a way to unruffle the feathers of Lisa because I stayed out late. Damn!

I really, really love, even to this day, love salsa dance and salsa music. I still do it every day of my life. I just don't do it with a partner. I am constantly doing my footwork, even in the most inappropriate of situations or locations, waiting for the subway, in the subway, in the grocery story, waiting for a bus. That is another way for me to celebrate my life.

TANGO

THEN, one day when I was just walking down the street, minding my own business and then…WwwHAM! I was hit with a bolt of Argentine tango lightening and my life became forever changed. When I fell for tango, I fell hard.

I took group lessons seven days a week, workshops, private lessons one, two, three, four, even five days a week for thirteen years. I was hungry and thirsty for tango. I wanted to be a good tango dancer. I would watch videos every day. There is a Julio Balmaceda video that I would watch three, four, five times a day, for years. I wanted to dance like him in the worst way.

Batt Johnson (L), Julio Balmaceda (RIP).
Julio is translating what his partner, Corina De La Rosa said about the men dancing milonga
like menopausal old ladies.

When I started studying the mechanics of the movements of tango is when I started studying the movements of animals. Many of my teachers would say, "Like a cat, like a cat. You have to walk like a cat." I really didn't understand what they meant. Especially since a cat has four legs.

One Monday night while walking across Canal Street near Chinatown to go to Lafayette Grill to hang out with Tioma Maloratsky, I saw a video store. I knew it was a porn video store but the sign just said video. Maybe, just maybe they had videos from National Geographic or something so I could study how tigers, lions, and panthers walk and move.

I walked in and asked the clerk if they had any animal videos, any cat videos. His eyes got kind of big and he said to ask the guy in the back. They guy in the back said they had none. When I returned to the front, there were two guys laughing their heads off. I knew what it was. I said, "You guys think

I'm looking for videos of people having sex with animals, don't you?" They were laughing so hard, they couldn't answer me. I said, "I assure you I am not. I want to study how lions, tigers, and panthers walk." I knew they were thinking, "suuuure you do, you're a sick man, sir."

MOMENTS FROM AN INTERVIEW WITH ADAM HOOPENGARDNER INTERVIEWING BIPIDDY BOPIDDY BATT JOHNSON.

Adam Hoopengardner is an Argentine tango teacher, performer, organizer of numerous tango events, and is a good friend. He invited me to be in his first rounds of guests on his podcast, "Tango Uncorked" on the Podbean app. It is fun, it is interesting, and people drop in from all over the world to say hello or to just voice their opinion.

Here are some excerpts from our one hour and forty-minute conversation in 2019 before the Pandemic of 2020 subjugated the world.

Adam: So, you only worked as a performer all of your life?

Batt: Yes, and I think I became successful in radio because I am a very active music listener, and I'm extremely serious about it. It gives me so much joy. Music resonates with me more than anything.

Adam: I remember we were having Thanksgiving dinner at Ciko and Ed's home one time. You and Ed were kind of quizzing each other and you were very on top of it. You knew a lot about the most random stuff. Do you study the history of the music as well? And tango as well?

Batt: Yes, in my bedroom, I have a built-in bookshelf that is eight rows high and five slots wide and is about ten feet long and eight or nine feet high and it is all books. Most are music, television and acting books.

Adam: I wanted to ask you, there is something I have always noticed about you...I remember we had lunch one day and we popped into a deli and you just started chatting with the deli guys. My point is where do you get this energy? How is it that you're always so...I don't want to say happy, but what drives your optimism and your love for humanity? It's something very uniquely Batt Johnson.

Batt: How can I say this without sounding corny? It's simple. I love people. We all have something to offer and I want to know what individuals have to offer. Look at that guy over there, look at him, he looks like he has NOTHING going on. But I bet he does. Let's go talk to him and find out.

I love people and they are really interesting. When I talk about this, I often point out some random person and I'll say "See that guy over there?" You could take that guy's life apart and write the most interesting movie you've ever seen.

We are all so incredibly interesting, and I like to dig in there and find out who people are, what makes them tick. That is one of the reasons I was successful on the radio and acting. I understand how people think. Even if I don't know you, I know you!

We are truly, all the same. It doesn't matter if you grew up a Buddhist, in the countryside of Brazil, a snake charmer in the Fjords of Norway, or as a Republican in Arizona...it doesn't matter. We are all the same. In this country, we are so adversely racially focused. There is only one race! People fuel me because they are so interesting and they don't even know it.

Adam: I agree and I was thinking about self-esteem the other day as I was mentally preparing to chat with you in this interview.

You seem to have an abundance of self-esteem. It's not arrogance, it's not cockiness.

But I saw people and I was on the subway observing this. I see all these interesting people around me and I think the one thing that destroys the individual is our own lack of appreciation for the self. Self-esteem. That's sad. I suffer from it and I'm guessing you have moments. I'm assuming you're not 24/7 Bippidy-Boppidy Batt Johnson.

Batt: I didn't even know I was "Bippidy-Boppidy Batt Johnson."

Adam: You are though! We don't see ourselves the way other people see us. And when I observe you I can see that you probably don't go to a milonga if you're not in the headspace.

Batt: It doesn't work that way for me.

Adam: It doesn't work that way, meaning you won't go out? Or you will?

Batt: No, I always want to dance, music transforms me. I have a bizarre switch in my head. When I am in a creative environment, any kind of creative environment, be it a recording studio, television station, an art studio, a rock and roll club, an art gallery, radio station, dance event, a jazz club, a concert, it doesn't matter.

As soon as I enter the space, I am ready. I am ready to create. I am ready to make something happen. Come on! Let's do it…NOW! Let's go!

When I go to the milonga, the music transforms me. I mean, I got into radio because of music. I started dancing because of music. To me, there's no such thing as being in a bad mood at a milonga…well, unless I am having a girlfriend fight.

But when I hear that music when I walk in the door. I'm ready! I'm ready! I want to give some love. I want that music to come into my ears, into my brain, into my chest, into my body and do me. MAKE me feel. Make me want to be a member of the orchestra. Then I will give it to her. It's really simple. I am musical and motivated by music.

Last week I was at your milonga, Tango Café, and a guy walked up to me, an older Latin, well dressed, good looking gentleman, and said to me, "Someday I want to talk to you." and I said "Okay well, Let's talk right now." We walked to another room with less noise. Then he said, "Everybody loves you and you're always so happy and you're always so up. What's your secret?" I said, "Huh? I can point out a couple of people in this room right now who hate me so much they won't even talk, or even LOOK at me! What are you talking about?

He then said, "That's not what I see. Everyone loves you." Hahahahah, that's crazy. I don't really feel that. I just love people. I just want to give a little love.

I think about that a lot more now days because, well, I hate to bring this up, but it's our current administration. The first few months after we got our new individual in the White House, I saw it in the streets. I saw so much anger, so much nastiness and I thought we have to double up on the love. We have to double up to counteract this venom that is coming out of the White House.

Adam: It's true but it's sad, well it's not sad, its society. It's what it should be like when there's hate being accepted and almost advocated in a subtle way. It takes other people to pay it forward in a positive way and try to make up for the negativity.

Batt: We are all we have and I think that part of my attitude comes from my parents. I also spend some time studying yoga, and reading Eastern philosophy books. I spent some time in the world of ultra-positivity.

Adam: I was going to ask you about your peer-groups, kind of a clinical way of putting it. Studies have shown (also a clinical way of putting it) that we tend to be creatures of our environment in terms of who we hang out with. Nurture vs nature. So, you mentioned that your parents had a positive influence on you, but I'm also curious about when you were younger in San Diego and you were in college. Who were you hanging out with and how did they create a positive outlook, or foster this outlook- if it hadn't already been that way when you were younger?

Batt: Looking back on my life, I had a wide variety of friends, I had a lot of Japanese-Americans friends.

Adam: They're polite.

Batt: Well, that's a stereotype. Actually, they made me an honorary Japanese. They used to invite me over to the house. Their parents would cook for me, and love on me. I also had a lot of Mexican friends. Same thing. They would invite me over to their house and cook for me and their mothers would love on me, I had a lot of white friends. Now, where I grew up, we didn't have the Irish neighborhood, and the German neighborhood and the Jewish neighborhood.

They were just white people. In the town where I grew up we had many from the Philippines, we had a lot of Guamanians, because of the US Navy, there were a lot of people from Guam. We had a lot of Mexicans, black people and Japanese. Not many Chinese, but a lot of Japanese. I just learned from those cultures and those people. That's how I really knew that were just people.

Adam: You were shaped by having the different experiences around different people...the diversity.

Batt: One of my best friends, named Danny O'keefe, blonde haired, freckled face, Irish kid. I didn't know he was Irish. He was just Danny O'keefe! Irish, what does that mean? I didn't experience the vast array of black people. You know the black people I knew were Americans.

I didn't know any Africans, Jamaicans, black Puerto Ricans, black Brazilians, Dominicans, or Cubans. I knew Spanish speaking black people, or people of high melanin content existed but I didn't know any. I often say that I have a high degree of "choclaticity." I think those are the things that made me who I am. Hanging out with different kinds of people, I mean really hanging out, investing in them.

Adam: I noticed that. I lived in New York, by the way this month marks my 15th year. We should celebrate. I have noticed, now that I've been here for so long, and meeting people that have grown up here. They have a very different relationship to people than I did growing up in a pretty segregated part of Cleveland, which is like a white suburb.

And you hear things as a kid like "Oh there are those Arabs." Here we are all minorities, even if you're white. Whereas where I grew up not so much so. You are influenced by the talk around you. "Oh, we have two black kids in the school." It's almost like you are being told that they are rare. Really, I didn't live around them.

But you grow up as a kid thinking that "Oh, they are so different from me. But there's only two of them." Instead of growing up around mixed races as a child and understanding that we're all just people. There's a learning curve there, for me, I went through this experience. Like I had to get the hell out of there and travel the world. I also had a desire because I knew at that age, deep down we were all just people, but I had to experience that first. The way I was brought up, and it wasn't like my parents said this or that, it was the society. Just feeling like this is weird. Why do I feel so separated from people based on their language or color? It seems so silly.

Batt: It IS silly. But language, that's another thing. I was exposed to other languages a bit, not like a New Yorker is, but I was exposed to Spanish and Japanese and not French, German, Italian, and other European languages. Spanish was my first foreign language. I grew up 17 miles from the Mexican border. People say, so you know the lyrics to the songs in the milonga don't you? Uh, no, I don't. And even if they were in English, I still wouldn't know. I don't listen to the lyrics when I dance.

Adam: So, you hear it more as a melody, not necessarily as a story as the words are being spoken.

Batt: Yes, but even songs in English, I don't pay attention to the lyrics. I hear music as music and the words as words that are being delivered in a musical way. The words have to be delivered musically or it would sound HORRIBLE! So, music is the basic, necessary foundation for any given composition.

Adam: I don't pay attention to the lyrics literally. I pay attention to the sounds of the lyrics. Otherwise they could just be speaking.

Batt: Yes, I agree. In rock and roll you can't hear the lyrics anyway because it is all distorted and everyone's trying to sound like a black Mississippi cotton picker from 1936. "What did he say? I don't know. Doesn't matter."

Adam: The Rolling Stones named their band after a Muddy Waters song out of respect and adulation. Many of the British musicians from that era studied the music of Chuck Berry, Little Richard, Howlin' Wolf, Lead Belly, Lightening Hopkins, etc.

Batt: Yes, they studied the music of the African American blues, and rhythm and blues musicians, then stole it. If the American musicians would give credit to the African American musicians who created it, I guess we could no longer call it thievery. But most non-African American individuals refuse to give us credit for constantly creating new, different and exciting music forms such as rhythm & blues, better known as r&b, hip-hop, blues, rock and roll, reggae, ska, disco, calypso, spirituals, ragtime, boogie-woogie, gospel, jazz, doo-wop, soul, and others.

CRAZY FOR TANGO

I have studied tango in both North and South America with over one-hundred-seventy-two of the most influential tango dancers, tango teachers and tango performers of our time including Horacio Godoy, Osvaldo Zotto (RIP), Guillermina Quiroga, Gustavo Naveida, Julio Balmaceda (RIP), Carlos Gavito (RIP), Jorge Torres, Lorena Ermocida, and Omar Vega (RIP).

Other major influences include Maria Jose Sosa, Natacha Poberaj, Junior Cervila, Rebecca Shulman, Oliver Kolker, Gabriel Missé, Maria Elena Ybarra and Diego Escobar. I have also performed with well-known visiting professional tango dancers and musicians from Argentina including with the Octavio Brunetti (RIP) Orchestra.

I taught tango in New York City at the Dardo Galletto Studios, Piel Canela Latin Arts Dance Center, Tango on The Square, Central Park Tango,

Lafayette Grill NY, Shut Up and Dance Studios, Fond du Lac, Wisconsin and The School of Visual and Performing Arts, Stroudsburg, Pennsylvania.

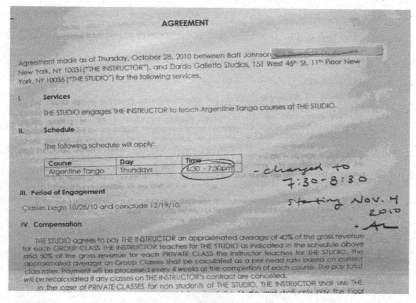

I was very happy and proud that I had a contract to teach Argentine tango in a dance school.

As you have probably noticed, there are several jokes in this book.
THIS, however, is not one of them.

It looks like a joke but I was very happy, proud, and sad to receive this check for a month of teaching something that is so dear to me. Problem? It was not that I was a bad teacher, we just could not get enough students into the school.

I wrote the short play *Tango Floor Gender Wars*, co-wrote and directed the play *Tango du Jour*, co-wrote, danced and acted in the play *Del Tingo*

Al Tango, acted and danced in the film *The Challenger* (*An Angel For Your Solitude*) with Silvina Valz which was part of the New York Tango and Film Festival, I was featured in the documentary film *New York Tango*, performed voice-overs for the stage show *Tango Connections,* Junior Cervila's *Cervila's Tango Revue* and performed voice-over segments for many professional tango teacher's instructional videos.

For several seasons I danced, hosted, acted, conceived and wrote for The Tango Zone Dance Company which performed in New York every summer for five years and at the Edmonton, Canada International Theatre Fringe Festival, the largest in all of North America.

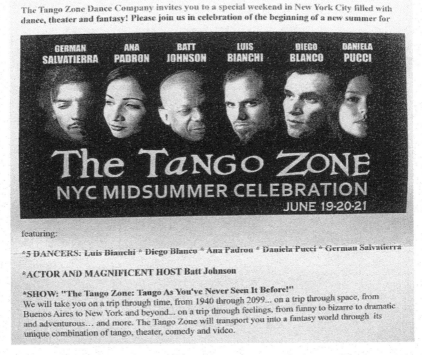

The Tango Zone Dance Company invites you to a special weekend in New York City filled with dance, theater and fantasy! Please join us in celebration of the beginning of a new summer for

GERMAN SALVATIERRA • ANA PADRON • BATT JOHNSON • LUIS BIANCHI • DIEGO BLANCO • DANIELA PUCCI

The TaNGO ZONE
NYC MIDSUMMER CELEBRATION
JUNE 19-20-21

featuring:

*5 DANCERS: Luis Bianchi * Diego Blanco * Ana Padron * Daniela Pucci * German Salvatierra

*ACTOR AND MAGNIFICENT HOST Batt Johnson

*SHOW: "The Tango Zone: Tango As You've Never Seen It Before!"
We will take you on a trip through time, from 1940 through 2099... on a trip through space, from Buenos Aires to New York and beyond... on a trip through feelings, from funny to bizarre to dramatic and adventurous... and more. The Tango Zone will transport you into a fantasy world through its unique combination of tango, theater, comedy and video.

I created, voiced and produced numerous radio specials on musicians and their instruments. I was a co-host, researcher, writer and producer on a world-wide tango radio show called *Espresso Tango Radio* (www.tangointoxication.com) with internationally acclaimed Grammy Award-Winning bandoneon player and composer, Hector Del Curto.

I also created, produced and hosted female tango fashion shows and a benefit to raise money for tango dancing children who happen to be without sight. I was chosen to be the Official Master of Ceremonies of the *7th USA Tango Championship Competition* as part of the 13th Annual New York City Tango Festival.

I wrote the CD liner notes (the information inside a CD cover) for many professional tango musicians including Argentinian musicians, Hector Del Curto, Fernando Otero, Gustavo Casenave (Uruguay) and Costa Rican bass & trumpet player Rodrigo Saenz. I also wrote a monthly column for *ReporTango* magazine, an international guide to Argentine tango. My first book on dance is called "Tango Intoxication: Wit, Wisdom, Stories & Secrets of the World's Most Intimate Dance." I worked very hard at learning tango music, culture, and history.

I am the author of three other books on subjects ranging from tango, acting and public speaking to jazz. My other books to be published are a media training manual for professional athletes, a tango poetry book and a book of quotes from African American men.

I was a writer for Japan's *Swing Journal Jazz Magazine*; a music critic for *The Kansas City Star* newspaper; a national music video host and writer for VH-1 Music Television (MTV networks), a music writer and co-host for *Only One New York*, (a weekly magazine formatted television show on PBS), a co-host and writer on *Campus America* (NCTV) and a home shopping host and writer on Q2 television (QVC Network).

I studied music and music theory at the John Theis School of Music, Kansas City, Missouri; Big Dude's Music Studio, Kansas City, Missouri; Ed Simon's (brother of Paul Simon) Guitar Study Center, New York and The Sounds of Joy Music Studios, New York.

DRUNK ON TANGO

Tango Intoxication is the feeling I crave every night even before I touch my partner's hand while entering the embrace of Argentine tango. It is a special piece of magic which stupefies me, and places me in an "intoxicant-induced" state of excitement, joy and elation well beyond the limits of sobriety: a tango high. It is as if a pulsating orb of invisible, yet blurred color surrounded and gently massaged me. This is an evasive, clandestine form of intoxication that does not readily avail itself to the uninitiated. You have to work for it and even then, there is no guarantee this sensation will ever find you.

Tango dancing has the ability to place the dancer in a trance-like state, a space where time, thirst, hunger, pain, personal and emotional problems and those of the world seem to all but completely disappear. My book *"TANGO INTOXICATION: Wit, Wisdom, Stories & Secrets of the World's Most Intimate Dance"* will help you understand and take that journey, if you choose.

For a wide variety of over 250 videos of tango entertainment, full length Argentine tango movies, documentaries, performances, lessons, tango cartoons, highly produced radio shows, short films, it even has President Obama dancing tango, and more go to
www.tangointoxication.com

I do not profess to be an authority on the culture, music, language, dance or society from which tango emerges. I am, however, a lifelong student and passionate lover of the dance and music that is Argentine tango. These are my findings based on my experiences and research of many years of studying the dance, the people and the environment. These are some excerpts from my book, "Tango Intoxication."

CHAPTER 22

Tango Negro: From Africa to Argentina

Tango Negro: From Africa to Argentina? What could THIS title possibly be about? I am sure this was the response of many of you when you first saw it. What is to follow is a series of statements based on my individual research and the knowledge of some of New York and Buenos Aires' well-known dancers and teachers.

I too, was very shocked when I first read such things as: The word "tango" is an African word meaning a certain kind of drum; or the "tanga" was where the Africans in Buenos Aires went to dance.

One of the first tangos is "El Entrerriano", written by a Black piano player by the name of Anselmo Mendizabal in 1897. Who knew? Why is this information kept from us, we lovers of all things tango? The answer is probably that few people know about these historical elements of tango.

So, I guess what I'm saying here is that tango is not a dance that started in Europe. It is a dance that started when the Argentinians used to poke fun at the Africans as the Africans danced candombe and other native dances around the year 1877 in Buenos Aires.

During this period, Buenos Aires, Argentina and Montevideo, Uruguay had a population of between 25% to more than 50% Africans. Most of them were servants of the rich families and were more integrated into the life of these families as opposed to the Africans in North America who were rarely, if ever, integrated into the families and family life of their white employers and slave owners.

In the book TANGO! published by Thames and Hudson, written and researched by Collier, Cooper, Azzi and Martin, they state:

"The contribution of the Buenos Aires black community to the invention of the tango was indirect but nevertheless fundamental, in the sense that without it there would have been no tango at all."

The Argentines danced and poked fun at the African dancers. They did it for so long that the African style of dancing caught on. Milonga dance is also rooted in African dance.

The book TANGO! continues to state:

"After the middle of the nineteenth century—according to George Reid Andrews, the historian of Buenos Aires' black communities—younger blacks in particular abandoned the candombe in favor of European imports such as the polka and the mazurka—perhaps as a means of winning greater social acceptance.

While blacks began dancing white dances, some whites reciprocated by imitating the steps and movement of African Argentine dancers..."

So, what we are dancing is something that came from Africa, basically. Most of us thought that tango was created by the people of Argentina alone, of their own devices and later refined by the Europeans.

Many believe that most things refined come from Europe. In this country, you can create an average or even inferior product, put a French name on it, and instantly the American consumer thinks that it is exotic, refined, superior in some way. Chevrolet, Le Mans, Le Baron, American cars with French names aaaaaaaaaaahhhhhhhhhhh, how exotic. Tango is *not* from Europe!

One can clearly see that music has always been a vital part of African culture.

I recently saw the documentary film, *Tango Negro: The African Roots of Tango* directed by Dom Pedro, a filmmaker from Angola. Tango musician Juan Carlos Caceres makes a very large verbal and musical contribution to this film, which was released in 2013 in French and Spanish with English subtitles. The film also contains interviews with historians and musicologists which add an additional layer of richness and academic credibility.

In it you can clearly see and hear how music was a part of the African slave's lives who were brought to Uruguay, Brazil, Argentina and other South American countries, and how their influence can be found in tango music. This is a film EVERY tango dancer should see.

If it is true that around 1877 in Buenos Aires, and Montevideo, Uruguay there was a population of between 25% to more than 50% Africans, what happened to them all, where did they go?

Many of the Africans, because of poor, unsanitary living conditions experienced a very high infant mortality rate. Of course, the black soldiers were placed on the front lines where many of them died in the Argentine War of Independence from 1810–1818. The Paraguayan War from 1864–1870 killed countless thousands more. There was a tremendous cholera epidemic between 1861 and 1864. To top it all off, there was a yellow fever epidemic in the African neighborhood in 1871.

Domingo Faustino Sarmiento was the devil who spearheaded the removal of individuals of African descent from Argentina. He was president from 1868-1874 and wanted Argentina to be more like the United States and Europe, but with NO black people. He instituted horribly oppressive racist policies, segregation, slums without sanitation and healthcare. This all sounds like the dreams of Donald J. Trump, doesn't it?

The African Argentines were sent to horrible prisons with subhuman conditions for meaningless, petty or even made-up crimes. Mass executions were not unusual occurrences.

Mass immigration of Europeans, mostly Italians, between 1861 and 1914 greatly contributed to the further whitewashing of Argentina. Countless paintings of Afro-Argentines dancing tango were re-painted with people with white skin and blue eyes. Gauchos, the Argentinian cowboy, were often indigenous or Africans. Images of these individuals were removed and repainted. The paintings of the Argentinian army were repainted to remove all black faces.

This reconstruction of a massive lie was extremely inhumane, unbelievably barbaric, and shocking. Like in America and around the world, this information is left out of school curricula.

How would you like to live in a country where the president wants to kill you simply because you don't look like him? That sounds like Trump's America.

These events, in conjunction with the fact that there was a lot of interracial marriage of African women to European men because of the shortage of African men, are all events that helped wipe out the black presence in Buenos Aires.

In addition, a large percentage of the black population moved to Brazil and Uruguay. Today, while walking down the streets of Buenos Aires, there is little if any evidence of a large black presence ever having been there. But there is one individual with a tall, slender, ever-elegant status who sticks out far from the crowd for more reasons than one, as evidence of this part of Argentina's history. That man is Facundo Posadas.

CHAPTER 23

Facundo: Born Black in Argentina, with Black Tango Blood

The following is an interview with Facundo Posadas of Buenos Aires, the world's most famous milonguero of African descent today.

Facundo started dancing candombe, the African predecessor to tango and milonga at the age of three. He has since graced stages worldwide and has spent countless hours studying the contribution of African peoples to Argentine tango.

Although his maternal grandfather was born in the United States in the 19th Century, his grandmother was a descendant of the native Indians of the region of Mendoza, Argentina. Facundo has the true blood of tango and the milonguero.

He is the grandnephew of Don Carlos Posadas who is the author of more than forty tangos. Among them are El Toto, El Jaguel, Retirao and Cordon de Oro. Many of these great compositions were recorded by such famous orchestras as those of Anibal Triolo, Carlos Di Sarli and Horacio Salgan, another Afro-Argentine. He may also be seen with his lovely ex-wife Kely (RIP) in the documentary film from Argentina called *Tango, a Strange Turn* (*Tango, Un Giro Extrano*) and other films.

And now, Maestro Facundo Posadas speaks...

Batt: What is the African contribution to Argentine tango?

Facundo: It is very, very big. The rhythm comes from Africa to Spain to Haiti. There are similarities between flamingo and candombe. When the Portuguese brought the Africans to port in South America, that port was Argentina. Although the number seems outrageous, some 150 million blacks were sent to Argentina from Africa. These numbers come from anthropology studies over many years. Out of every twelve people, two would arrive alive. No children, but they discovered the women were good mothers and acquired the customs of the area quickly. So, the white men would use the black women as a milk mother and for education.

The place where they put black people together they used to call *el tambo*. This place was used for the selling of the people or to store them. They stored them at the tambo. The black man always danced. So, this place where they danced was called the tambo. To say, "I'm going to the tambo" meant that you were going to the dance.

In the transformation of the language from the white man in South America to the people of the lands in South America, the words "I'm going to tambo" meant the dance. There was a very famous cabaret in Argentina that they called the Tambito where a lot of black people used to do their shows. They used to say, "I'm going to tambo". "I'm going to dance." or "I'm going tambito". "I'm going to the dance."

The contribution of Africa to tango is not only a name, but a rhythm as well. Milonga, which is a predecessor to tango, is an African word. Anthropologist Dr. Ferris Thompson of Yale University's Timothy Drive School's research shows that milonga is a conversation, a discussion. Later the European slave traders brought black Cuban slaves to Argentina. These slaves brought the habanera rhythm. The habanera rhythm, mixed with candombe, gives you milonga. Later on, came the milonga tango. Years later, tango emerged as its own dance. Certain anthropologists believe that the first person on earth was a black female and was born in Africa.

This first man on earth did not have a larynx and could not speak. These people had very large noses for taking in lots of air, inhaling and exhaling rapidly. They also had very large mouths that extended out to the middle of their cheeks with very large teeth and molars, especially the wisdom teeth. These teeth and strong jaws were used for cracking nuts to eat. Their language was movement. To ask for things and for communication in general was all movement. These movements had a rhythm or rhythmical sequence. They didn't just use random movement. But at that time, they had no music and without even knowing it they found the rhythm of the heart, the heartbeat, and that was the rhythm they used to move by. So again, without knowing it, using this rhythm, they were inventing music.

First, we were born, then we danced, then we spoke. Now we dance, we're born, then we speak. When the baby is in the womb they move as a method of communication. It is an embryonic form of dance. So, you see, dance is as old as life.

There is a very important movie about this that Gene Kelly narrates called *When Hollywood Danced*. In it he speaks about how old dance is from the beginning of time to Michael Jackson and beyond. One of the most fantastic things that happened to me and my ex-wife Kely (RIP) in our entire lives was the opportunity to work with Frankie Manning (RIP), the master of swing and lindy hop. Frankie used to work with the great bandleader and singer Cab Calloway.

We also worked with the Nicolas Brothers, one of whom has passed on but the other, as of this writing, is ninety-seven and is still teaching swing and tap.

We also worked with Ann Hampton, the first cousin of Lionel Hampton and the Count Basie Orchestra. All of these other movements and rhythms contributed to our understanding of dance and the human body.

Batt: What came first, tango or milonga and what did it sound like?

Facundo: Milonga came first. The first tangos we listened to were tango-milongas. Milonga has changed, times change and rhythms change. As the human landscape of Argentina changed with immigration, so did the music and the instrumentation.

The bandoneon, a German instrument that was brought to Argentina by the Austrians. The violin was introduced largely by the Italians and the piano replaced the guitar, a Spanish instrument. As these individuals became more homesick, the music started to take on a melancholy sound. Tango music is like no other music and the dance is like no other dance and I am very proud to be a member of this community.

MY FIRST TRIP TO ARGENTINA: TEN DAYS TO TANGO

Gee, I had better hurry. I only have ten days to do this. Hurry up, have fun! I want to take private lessons, group lessons, go to daytime practicas, and the milongas every night, see some of the city of Buenos Aires; see some of the countryside, learn more Spanish AND have a good time in the process... and then dance some MORE. I am starting to feel the pressure. Why do I do this to myself?

My flight, American Airlines #955 departing at 10:10 PM on a Boeing 767-300 from New York's JFK International Airport on Thursday, October 12, 2006. The date of ticket purchase? Wednesday, April 12th, 2006. Hmmm, let's see, airline ticket purchased six months ahead of actual departure date. Do you think I was excited?

I get excited about every international trip I have taken and I have taken many. But this is my first trip to the land that gave birth to tango. The last time I took an international trip with such a specific goal was when I went to Western Africa to do research my book, *What is This Thing Called Jazz?*

Buenos Aires is a town filled with poetry, poetic harmony and poetic polar opposites. It is a common thought that since Buenos Aires is the birthplace of tango that everyone loves and dances tango. Actually, a great portion of the Argentine population still believes that tango is the dance of the brothels and only the lowlifes of the society dance it.

Of course, we all know that is not true. I was once told that only about 10% of the population of the entire country of Argentina dances tango, but everyone is exposed to the music because it is truly a part of the cultural fabric of the land.

Tango music is on the radio, in radio commercials, on television shows, in television commercials, at the corner drug store, at the newspaper stand, in the coffee shop, in the restaurant, in the elevator, in the shopping mall, on the street, in the street, on the radio in the cars on the street, in the taxis, you name it. You don't hear it constantly but you hear it often. The music comes oozing from this city's every pore. Buenos Aires is to tango as Las Vegas is to gambling and Los Angeles is to film and television.

In an attempt to get musicians and dancers together to better understand one another, my partner, guitarist Adam Tully and I, created the New York Tango Social Club. It was like an open mic for musicians and the dancers danced to their live music.

I have many friends who have made the trip to Argentina before and I have noticed one profound change in them when they returned: They thought they had become instant experts on the dance simply because they had BEEN to Argentina—virtual know-it-alls. They wish! Dear God, don't let that happen to me. Actually, many of them have returned dancing worse than before they went.

I am not saying this for drama. Some actually danced worse than before they went to Argentina. I have vowed to never allow that to happen to me. Sure, I have strong opinions about certain things but I am not so naive as to think that simply crossing an international, man-made, imaginary border into Buenos Aires, Argentina is going to make me a world-class dancer or even the tango dancer I *want* to be.

I have heard people say that it takes twenty-one days to change a habit. How long does it take to learn a series of "new" habits? Habits like: good musicality, good dance posture, sternum up, shoulders back, shoulders down, shoulders relaxed, embrace comfortable, stepping on a straight leg, stepping softly on the floor, stepping on the floor and not my partner, not bumping her into other couples, not allowing other couples to bump into my partner, keeping her on her axis or on her balance, thinking about the step I am executing, thinking about the step I will execute next, listening to the music, obeying the music, interpreting the music, checking my embrace, rechecking my embrace, checking my posture, rechecking my posture, rechecking my head position, keeping my head up, not squeezing her hand, check my feet position, my waist and disassociation (meaning when my sternum is pointed in one direction and my hips are pointed in another direction), recheck the rechecked posture. That is a lot to remember and to calculate. How long will it take to change all of THOSE habits? I will tell you…years.

My plane landed at eleven in the morning on Friday, October 13, 2006. We were picked up by our tour guide, Coco Arregui (RIP) (one of the organizers of the milonga, La Nacional in New York, and he was also the husband of my private tango teacher, Maria Jose Sosa) and his son-in-law, Gustavo.

Coco Arregui (RIP), Maria Jose Sosa, Batt Johnson and Marcos Blanco.

Driving in from the outskirts of Buenos Aires to the center of town I noticed architectural changes occurring. It started to look more and more like Paris with a dash of Havana thrown in for flavor. Also, there was a lot less car, bus and industrial air pollution than I expected.

I arrived at the Hotel Castelar at twelve-fifteen and was on the dance floor a few blocks awayat three PM.I do not mess around. I have to move fast because I'm only here for a few days. Actually, I wanted Coco to have a private teacher waiting for me at the airport so I could take my first private lesson there as soon as I got off the plane. He did not have a teacher waiting for me. I guess he thought I was joking . . . I wasn't.

My first lesson, from three until five PM, was with Diego Escobar, a much sought-after dinner theater dancer and his dance partner and assistant, Iliana Molhaut. They both danced with the Miguel Angel Zotto Dance Company, which later came to New York with the show *"Tango x 2."*

At seven PM, I went to La Esquela de Tango for a milonga con traspie class with Jorge Firpo. It was a basic class but still had interesting lead elements that I had not discovered or utilized before. This school is located in the Galerias Pacifico, a fabulous high-end shopping mall, where the Julio Bocca School of Ballet is also located. Wow! What a surprise. I am right in the middle of dance heaven.

It was rapidly approaching 9:00 PM and time for dinner before going to my first milonga to dance all night long . . . as if four hours of dancing my first few hours in Buenos Aires was not enough. Guess what, it was NOT enough.

We took another of those inexpensive taxis to Los Inmortales, a legendary restaurant that has historic photographs of famous Argentine entertainers and is also known for its pizza. After dinner, we walked to my first milonga, "Plaza Bohemia." What excitement, what a surprise! After going up a long flight of stairs, a heavy velvet curtain opens and there it was in all of its splendor and brightly lit glory. I couldn't believe it was so bright, all of the lights were on. The other surprise was to see all the women on one side of the room and the men on the other. I knew about this tradition, but had never seen it. Yes, sometimes it was difficult to get the right person to acknowledge you and your cabeceo. But it worked out.

It was on this trip that I decided I wanted to dance with some large, elderly Argentinian women. I wanted to feeeel their fifty years of dancing.

I wanted to feeeel their experience, I wanted them to teach me a lesson on the dance floor and show me how it was really done.

Well, I got a chance to dance with three older ladies. Unfortunately, they had not been dancing long, but it was a nice experience for me to show my appreciation for their country, language, culture, music and dance. Every serious student of tango MUST take at least one trip to Buenos Aires, Argentina.

MY TANGO—MY STORY

The household I grew up in was located in a neighborhood that danced... constantly. If you could not dance, you were considered a freak and would be cast aside. Dancing was an important part of the culture in which I was raised, as were sports. I injured my ankle in my senior year in a high school football practice, which altered the way I walk down the street. I reinjured the ankle twice since then. Many years went by as I went into dance denial and never really thought about dancing although I knew I *could* dance (street dance).

Many, many years later, while thinking of a birthday gift for my wife at the time, I thought about a dance gift certificate. I bought one and have been dancing almost *every single day* since. I started with ballroom because I love the music of the big bands and I was a radio DJ for a station that had a listener appreciation night once a year. My listeners always wanted to dance with me, but I didn't really know how to do formal, organized lead and follow dances.

I got frustrated and finally took lessons. I learned about ten or twelve ballroom dances, then I fell in love with salsa for a few years, then I added tango in about 1998. This is about a year after I started dancing. I continued doing the other dances at the same time. One reason I think I was attracted to tango music was because whenever I heard it I would see old, grainy, classic black and white movies in my mind. I guess it is because the "Golden Age" of tango music was recorded in the 1930s and 1940s. You could hear the scratches on the old 78 rpm records. I enjoyed that. So, I decided tango was going to be my *"art"* dance. Little did I know it was going to take over my life and become my *only* dance.

I danced seven days a week for over eighteen years. Reason? Love, passion, excitement, desire, the mentally stimulating sensation of learning something new, moving my body to music, the love of music and a simple desire to became a better tango dancer.

When I decided to seriously learn tango I went to bed with headphones on *every night* for years to learn the music. Now I know "almost" every single note played by "almost" every single instrument of "almost" every single song played at most of the milongas. I feel if you want to become a good dancer, you*must*learn the music or learn to think musically. Today I am still listening, still dancing, still passionate. Now, let's go dance!

THE IDEA OF TANGO

Some common quotes you might hear about Argentine tango could be:"Argentine tango is so beautiful, but so hard to do." "How do they do that?" "It is so sexy and looks so easy to do. I thought I could just start dancing right away without lessons because I used to dance ballet."

These are comments I hear every day from my fellow dance students. Along with, "I can't do that, it is too difficult." This is usually said right after the teacher says, "Argentine tango is just a walk." But the student did not hear that because they were too busy talking and not listening to what the teacher was saying. Or they were too busy in their own heads telling themselves how difficult the dance is and convincing themselves that they can't do it.

My friend Jorge Torres, one of my favorite milongueros and teachers from Buenos Aires and the hit show *Forever Tango* always says, "Tango is just walking. One foot, then the other foot, then the other foot again. You are lucky. You are lucky that we don't have three legs and feet."

Argentine tango *is* a walk. Not only that, but it is an "improvised" walk that is done on the beat, before or after the beat of the music. Tango is unlike salsa on two, now that is difficult (Where is that damn beat?). With most dances, we step on the first beat of the music, the strongest beat. With salsa on two, you step on the second beat of the music. I can do it and do it well, but I think that it is counterintuitive. Of course, you still must dance on the beat; you just start and dance on a different beat.

In tango, you can step on the first, second, third or thirty-third beat of the music. When Fabian Peralta came to New York with Natacha Poberaj around 2004 or 2005, they performed at Il Campanello, an Italian restaurant near Madison Square Garden.

Dressed in a dark red suit with dark red suede shoes. During "Poema" he took almost half of the song just to get into the embrace. *Just getting into the embrace!* Forget about stepping. No steps were taken for what seemed like a loooong time. It was cool, very cool. I will never forget that dance because I stole a couple of steps from it. (There I go again with my big mouth telling my secrets of thievery!)

Tango is based on a walk. How did you get from the front door to the room you are in? You walked, and you have been walking for many, many years. So, the logic follows: If you can walk into this room, you can dance tango.

The common image that most Americans have of tango is a holdover from the classic 1921 black and white movie, *The Four Horsemen of the Apocalypse*. Dressed in a gaucho/flamenco type outfit, Rudolph Valentino interrupts a couple's dance, aggressively grabs the female played by Helena Domingues, like she is a sack of potatoes, and begins to walk cheek to cheek from one side of the bar to the other. This is what most American people see in their minds when you tell them that you are studying tango.

Or they immediately assume the promenade or Americana position with arms extended as they walk back and forth. The tango music they are probably most familiar with is the music to which we dance the American or ballroom tango. Of course, when I tell someone I am a tango dancer, they almost always start the "Ahhhh-rom-pom-pom-pom" of "La Cumparsita", which may well be the world's most famous tango song.

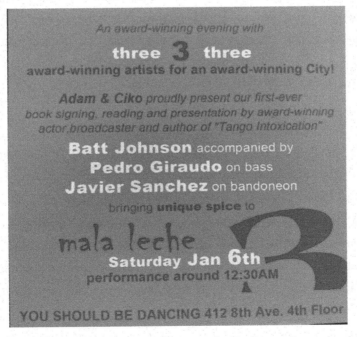

A live reading of my book "Tango Intoxication" with a live small tango band.
All of us, award-winning artists.

The music of Argentine tango is quite strange to most North American's ears. We don't really know this music, for it is not part of the North American culture. All of the other music that we dance to can be heard in many places around the radio dial. You can turn on the radio or television and hear the music of hustle, swing, west coast swing, samba, rumba, Peabody, foxtrot, American waltz, Viennese waltz, jive, jitterbug, lindy hop, merengue, cha-cha, bachata, salsa, mambo, all of it.

But, authentic Argentine tango music? Never!

You can, however find it on some internet channels these days. Until a few years ago, one could not go home after a long hard day at work and turn on the Argentine tango radio station any time, day or night or turn on the television and see the latest installment of "Tango Tonight" on BET, MTV, VH-1, National Geographic or the Discovery Channel. Today, there are a few apps that have a tango channel.

When I started writing "Tango Intoxication" around 2002 or 2003, there were over eighty (80) radio signals in New York, not one of them played Argentine tango music. There were two new satellite radio companies that broadcast one-hundred channels each. That means that on one station fifty channels would be news, sports and talk, the other fifty would be music channels, several of which are Latin but not one Argentine tango channel.

Black Entertainment Television (BET) has an afternoon Latin video show…but no tango. The cable channel, Latin Television (LTV) plays Latin music videos. You guessed it; you never see one tango video. My cable company offers something called *Music Choice*. This service has a total of forty-five (45) all music-no talk, no commercials on the channels. Of these forty-five channels, five offer Latin music. They are Mexicana, Latin Love Songs, Rock en Español, Salsa Y Merengue and Musica Latina—once again, no tango.

Unfortunately, the tango dancer or tango music enthusiast only had a few outlets to satisfy their passion. Now there is Pandora, ReporTango.net, Spotify, and a few other internet channels and apps (applications) for your smartphone that offer tango music.

Every now and then you hear tango music on a television commercial. There are two that come to mind right now. One for Bounty Quilted Napkins that has a small boy eating barbecue chicken or some other messy food, getting it all over his face and hands. He wipes his mouth and throws the towels on the floor in a huge pile. The other TV commercial is for a floor wax or cleaner. Anyway, I have a fairly extensive background in music, meaning my ear is familiar with most music of the world and I don't think that I have heard Argentine tango music more than five times in my life before I walked into a dance studio in 1997 for my first lesson.

The point is, I don't think that Argentine tango is that difficult to dance. I think that what most Americans are reacting to is *the music*. They are not familiar with the music. If you only listen to Elton John, Lady Gaga, Bruce Springsteen and Madonna, you will never understand Argentine tango.

Reading excerpts from my book, Tango Intoxication (Amazon.com)
at the 8th Annual Philadelphia Tango Festival (May 30th 2018).

We should work to reeducate our ears. To become familiar with the music, I used to lie in bed with my Walkman (now my iPod) on, before going to sleep and I would listen to tango music every night . . .*every night!* How can you not learn the music if you listen to it every night?

Now, I know it, I feel it, I understand it. Most dance students don't listen to enough music—no, let me rephrase that. Many dance students don't listen to *any* music. If you are a student, you will never learn how to interpret tango music or any music with movement of your body if you don't listen to music at times other than when it is time to dance.

In class when your teacher tells you to listen to the music, listen to the music, they mean a little more than that. Listening to music is a one-way, non-interactive activity. What they mean is respond, reply, obey, act upon, abide by, compliment, accompany, escort, reactor be in companionship*with* the music.

From one dance student to another, be smart, listen to tango music when you are not dancing. It is the only method to help you memorize the music. Music is our savior, it is what makes us want to dance.

THE SECRET SOCIETY OF ARGENTINE TANGO: THE SUB-SUB CULTURE OF A SUBCULTURE

In the year 2000, the countries of Argentina and Uruguay voted tango into UNESCO as a world national heritage. UNESCO is an acronym that stands for United Nations Educational, Scientific, and Cultural Organization, which is an agency of the United Nations. It was established in 1945 to promote and exchange information, ideas, and international culture. In 1984 the U.S. withdrew from the organization (I do not know why but it sounds like political drama to me.)

Then on September 30th, 2009, UNESCO named tango an "Intangible Cultural Heritage of Humanity". Wow! With such grand accolades, you would think tango would be much more renowned, more of a household name, and better known, but it isn't. When you compare tango music to the music of, let's say, the Rolling Stones, The Beatles or Stevie Wonder, tango is not known at all. I know what the results would be if we took a video camera out on the street and asked people at random to name just one tango song, they could not.

Tango is still an esoteric, underground secret in the United States and many other countries. Yet, you can dance tango on any given night in almost any country in the world. But, I maintain, it is still comparatively unknown.

Have you ever watched one of those old classic black and white movies on "TCM" (Turner Classic Movies) or "AMC" (American Movie Classics) that was filmed during or about the prohibition era?

These were the movies of Edward G. Robinson, Humphrey Bogart and James Cagney, true American tough guy heroes. In the late 1920s and early 1930s movie audiences wanted something more real and raw, and the films of this period reflected that. Alcohol was a part of that reality. The only problem was that alcohol was illegal.

The laws of prohibition prevented the private or commercial manufacturing, sale or consumption of alcoholic beverages. But city people were making it in their bathtubs and country people were making it in outdoor stills. As a result of these laws, the prime environment for such alcoholic consumption became the speakeasy, or back door, back alley, hidden gin joint, bar and illegal gambling establishment.

These were all secret places. When I was a very young boy, my Mom used to tell me stories of these days. The days of women bedazzled and bedecked in jewels and furs, men in top hats, fedoras, tuxedos, double-breasted pin stripped suits, some with black shirts with white ties, spats and a pinky ring.

They would walk down to a sub-street level door, knock three times, a peephole opened and someone looked out at you, and if they approved of you or if you gave the proper secret code word for that day, they would let you in. Inside, well, that's another story. You have just stepped into the world of the speakeasy. The speakeasy was so named because after you knocked on the door and the peephole opened you had to whisper (speak easy) your name, the name of the person who sent you or the secret code.

This was during the era of Prohibition in the U.S. from 1920–1933. I am sure that when you entered, there was the smell of cheap perfume, whiskey, gin, stale beer, cigar, cigarette and probably even marijuana smoke. I am sure one would hear the sounds of the roulette wheel, the clicking of the dice and the clash of the cue ball at the pool table.

I remember the first time I went to Tango La Nacional on 14th Street in New York City. I walked down under a stairway, then up a flight of stairs. I thought someone was going to open a little peephole, check me out, then "maybe" let me in.

Did I have to know the "code?" It had a very mysterious feel and aura. There was something very "speakeasy" about it. When I played a bouncer in the play *Del Tingo Al Tango* produced by Angel Clemente-Garcia and Rosa Collantes, there was a scene where men had to show the bouncer they could actually dance before they were allowed into the milonga, club or bordello. The "code" was to show their ability to dance. (I guess you have to regulate in some way.)

The world of the speakeasy was a secret world, a world that has been glorified by Hollywood and the movies they produce. The words "secret world" usually refer to some activity or organization that is dark, nefarious, clandestine, illegal or heinous. We rarely hear the word "secret" being associated with anything positive, but I think the tango world in America is a secret world and it is *very* positive. When I say the tango world in America is a secret world, I mean that very, very few people are aware of Argentine tango and the fact that one can learn it and dance it . . . in New York, every night of the week, at several venues . . . every night.

Adam & Ciko in their acting debut of a short play I wrote from a chapter in my book, "Tango Intoxication." The play may be seen on my website, www.tangointoxication.com. This played to a sold-out, over-crowded, crowd.

How many people are at La Nacional milonga in New York City on a crowdedT hursday night? Compare that to how many people would be at a Rolling Stones, Bruce Springsteen or Lady Gaga concert, even in the middle of the week when people have to go to work the next day.

Compared to most music forms, tango music is still rarely heard and the dance rarely seen by the average American person. I am waiting for the day when I see an SUV stop at a red light and the sounds of Pugliese, Varela, DiSarli or Canaro come blasting out of the windows. That will be the day tango leaps out of the dark of its comfortable, yet secret world and takes one giant step closer to the mainstream.

Do you follow the music charts? How many tango CDs appear there? Do you ever watch "Entertainment Tonight", "Access Hollywood", "E! Entertainment Television," "Extra," "TMZ," or any of those news-magazine formatted entertainment television shows? How many stories feature tango music, dancers or musicians? Not many or never. Tango is entertainment too. My point of all of this is to simply illustrate how secret our world of Argentine tango really is and how much effort we have to put forth to hear tango music and do this incredible dance. There are some of us who wish more people danced tango and there are others who don't want the milongas to be any more crowded than they already are.

Because of FaceBook and tango I have met, befriended and danced with people from Sweden, Switzerland, Norway, Iceland, Ireland, Denmark, Spain, Portugal, Germany, England, France, Italy, Poland, Ukraine, Russia, Lithuania, Morocco, Hong Kong, Korea, Japan, Taiwan, Shanghai, Brazil, Argentina, Greece, Turkey, Colombia, Bolivia, Bulgaria, Canada, Romania, Croatia, Slovenia and many other countries. There is a highly social aspect to Argentine tango. Very often you meet friends for life.

A STUDENT AWAKENING

Although it was a regular Wednesday evening, it was one I will never forget. As Carlos Quiroga, brother of the incredibly talented tango dancer, Guillermina Quiroga, and son of Coca, was creating his usual ambiance of tango intoxication as the DJ. I was standing near his DJ booth. Cecilia Saia suddenly appeared before me and asked me if I wanted to dance. It can be somewhat intimidating when an incredible world-class champion asks you to dance. But it is no secret that I am merely a student, a beginning student at the time who had only been dancing tango for a year or two. After dancing about three songs, it was abundantly clear to me that I had made the proper choice.

I have danced with professional dancers before, but dancing with Cecilia Saia, once a dancer in one of the most internationally famous tango shows of all time, *Forever Tango,* was like moving across the wooden floor with a warm stick of butter with honey and cinnamon oozing down its sides. How can someone melt into my arms, mold to my frame and react to my every musical movement without me saying a word or forcing her into the next step? Leading her is almost like leading myself.

Have you ever had those moments while practicing alone when you thought, if only I could find a partner who follows me as well as I follow *myself?* Cecilia does exactly that. She dances with two separate bodies. The upper half of her body waits for the lead, receives it, reacts by making the bottom half of her body execute the instructions of the lead a fraction of a second later, allowing ample time for the desired response. Of course, all of this is in perfect time to the music.

My friend April once referred to dancing with a good partner as "Soaking in a nice warm bath of milk." Rosa Collantes, my first serious private tango teacher would constantly say to me, "Your partner, your partner, take care of your partner first." In the book, *Paul Pellicoro on Tango*, Eleny Fotinos says, "I try to give my partner the best feeling I can."

As students, we always want to learn steps, steps and more steps. Steps alone won't make us good dancers. We need to learn more about the *feeling* we are giving our partners, and teachers need to teach more about that.

What is connection? What is lead? What is follow? How does it feel when you and your partner step softly on the floor? When your partner immediately, effortlessly, willfully and elegantly responds to your every twitch, it is like someone accurately answering your every question before it is asked and scratching every itch before you are even aware of the urge.

If, or when, you ever get the chance to dance with a professional, park your fears and accept the dance. It should be a feeling for which you will search the rest of your life.

FEELING THE TANGO TINGLE!

The "biggest" compliment for me has been, after I have danced one or two songs with a professional dancer from Argentina, to have her say, "How long have you been dancing tango?"

If they say that, I know that I have made them think, or enjoy, or experience something unusual, or regret that her national dance has spread around the globe to idiots like me, or she wishes she never accepted my offer for a dance.

This is as close as I could come to my dance dream, which I did, in fact achieve.

When I started private tango lessons with Rosa Collantes, I once said to her, "I want to be a good tango dancer. I want to be so good that the really good dancers will come all the way across the room to dance with me." Rosa said, "That's never gonna happen, tango dancer's egos are too big."

I heard what she said and I also have my thoughts, ideas and dreams that NO ONE can shatter. I worked extremely hard for several, several years with private lessons many days, sometimes five days a week, group lessons sometimes seven days a week, dancing at home alone, constantly listening to and learning tango music. I was and I am, rabid.

Then one day, after many, many years, the nice and not so nice, good and really good dancers were positioning themselves in the room to make sure I asked them to dance. If we were good friends, they would verbally ask me. Yes, this is a dream come true. The really good dancers DID, in fact, come all the way across the room to dance with me. A major portion of the Argentine culture and tango dance etiquette, is that women do not ask men to dance. But, if you are close friends, it is acceptable.

This is another project of which I am very proud. Professional bandoneon player, composer, sound engineer, and producer, Hector Del Curto and I researched, wrote, hosted, and produced these one-of-a-kind shows that may be heard on my website, www.tangointoxication.com.

I can't believe this has happened to me. But, like many things in my life, when I make up my mind to achieve something, I do it. I think I am a freak. Help me, save me.

Please do not misunderstand me. I am not being a braggadocious lout who is building himself up because he has low self-esteem. I am simply trying to recount the truths of my life as best, and as accurately as I can.

I have always been fascinated by communication:how birds chirp to one another, how the sun communicates to the sleeping plants in spring that it is time to wake up, how bats send out a sonar signal that bounces off an intruding object and communicates back that something is in their flight path. Fascinating!

Human oral communication holds the same kind of fascination for me. The human languages of Afghanistan, France, Norway, China, Alabama, all interesting. Body language possesses its own set of interesting intricacies.

The body language of ballet, the body language of boxing and the body language of Argentine tango are all very different from one another and yet, each communicates in its own way. One of the most interesting of these forms is the communication that is not SEEN by the outside observer but is FELT only by the two individuals IN the embrace of Argentine tango. This represents its own very unique, one-of-a-kind, individual and couple attribute.

Many things have been said about tango over the many years of its existence, like:

- Once you get in you'll never get out.

- You don't choose tango, tango chooses YOU!

- Tango is a vertical expression of a horizontal desire.

- Tango will change your life forever.

- The embrace of tango is like getting back to the loving arms of your mother.

- Tango is a headache!

- Tango is heartache!

- Tango is a cult.

Mariano "Chicho" Frumboli was being interviewed for a video project at the Tango Element Festival in Baltimore, Maryland in the summer of 2013. The interviewer asked, "What is tango to you?" After a long pause Chicho said, "For me, it's love. It's love. When you are dancing, when you teach, everything, it's love. Tango is love."

My ex-father-in-law is an internationally renowned legal scholar and was the oldest living Federal Judge in America. The Honorable Ruggero J. Aldisert, RIP. He would often say to me that the law is a "jealous mistress." I believe that tango is also a "jealous mistress." It will fight for your time and clamor for your attention and when it does not get it, it will punishingly make you pay.

Dance is a deep, deep passion for me. If this is what passion is and if you say you have passion for something, you do it . . . regularly. I say, *nothing gets in the way of your passion.* I am tired of hearing people say, "I have a passion for acting. I have a passion for writing. I have a passion for art and painting" But they don't DO anything about it or they do it once in a while.

I don't consider that a *passion.* That is a notion, an idea, a thought, a pastime, a hobby. The dictionary defines passion as: "noun: the trait of being intensely emotional," "an irrational but irresistible motive for a belief or action." I like those words, *irrational* and *irresistible* for they could very well define my emotional connection and passion for dancing.

I was at one of my favorite milongas, La Nacional in New York City one night, when I asked a friend to dance. We had done some practicing several times before in a private studio so I was well aware of how she danced...and she was *great.*

I used to often ask myself, "Why is she practicing with someone like ME?" She should be working with a top-notch professional tango dancer, not ME. (I later learned it was because of the out-of-proportion size egos of some of the male leaders.) Anyway, we worked extremely well together, I thought. She even asked me to teach her salsa. Which I did.

On this special night at La Nacional, we were dancing the second or third song of the tanda (a tanda is a series of songs played together before a break), and the feeling she was giving me was incredible. It was so, so, incredible. It was a combination of her rhythm and musicality, her quickness, playfulness, timing, her posture, embrace, balance, her walk.

The way she felt when she walked was excruciatingly heavenly and divine. I never felt anything like that before and I had been dancing for about eight or ten years at the time of this event.

Here is the main point of story. The feeling she was giving me was so incredible that I felt the only thing I could do to really appreciate it, to really revel in it, to really celebrate it, to really acknowledge it, to honor it, to really enjoy it, was to just stop dancing in the middle of the dance and CRY!

Just let it go, let it out...STOP and CRY! But I didn't. I held on. Can you imagine that kind of feeling, that kind of emotionality, that kind of intensity? Please, please do NOT mistake this extremely deep dance connection feeling for romance, love, lust or sex. It is none of the above. It is much deeper than any of those.

That feeling is like the kind of feeling "I imagine" a woman feels when she is in the process of giving birth. She grunts, she pushes, she screams, she cries, she is bleeding! She grunts, she pushes, she screams, she cries, she is bleeding! She curses the doctor, she curses the man who impregnated her, she even curses the person who painted the hospital delivery room walls white, and Thomas Alva Edison for inventing the light bulb that is shining in her eyes. She is in PAIN!

The pain is so excruciating she may think being hit by a truck going eighty miles an hour would feel like a pillow in comparison. She grunts, she pushes, she screams, she cries, she is bleeding!

The baby finally comes out, CATHARSIS! The doctors show the baby to the mother and it is at that point that her life is forever changed. I can only IMAGINE the feeling of the mother at that moment. I am certain the only thing she wants to do at that moment is cry AGAIN!

CATHARSIS! This is NOT the tango tingle, this is something way beyond that, and it is that very feeling that I look for every night of my life when I touch the right hand of my new or same partner before EVERY dance.

Magic, I am looking for magic and the tango tingle. I want to be taken out of the physical plane and catapulted to another dimension. I want to become tangofixified, transformed, transfixed, transcendentalized, taken out of the physical plane of existence.

If you decide to learn this dance, your life as you know it, will change forever and so will your circle of friends. You are about to fall in love with something that will never leave you, will never grow old, and will never die. It will remain forever within you, forever young, forever interesting, forever challenging and will keep you forever learning...*that* is Argentine tango. For me, dancing is trance inducing. It puts me in a transcendental meditative trance-like state.

I go to a place where time, thirst, hunger, pain, personal and emotional problems and those of the world all but completely disappear. What I get out of dancing Argentine tango is a sense of togetherness, connection (when it is right), the ultimate in lead and follow partner dancing, moving to music that is incredibly diverse with many flavors, intentions and textures. It is a tango tingle that goes up my spine and enters every pore and fiber of my existence.

I want a sense of mental and physical harmony and a feeling of oneness with myself, my partner, the music and the floor. The moment *before* my partner touches my hand to begin the embrace I am looking for magic and harmony. I am looking for the tango tingle.

An ad for my performance with Eleanora Kalganova, an internationally recognized and highly sought tango professional. Someone had the nerve to ask me how much did I pay her to perform with me? I almost slugged him. She asked ME!

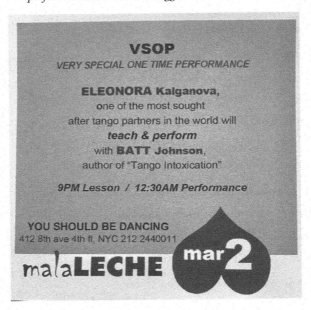

Tango is a dance that is simple but not easy to do, easy to get addicted to, but difficult to master. Perhaps anything is difficult to do well and I realize that doing things well is not the goal of all people.

Not everyone wants to get an "A" in all classes, not everyone has aspirations of performing on the Broadway stage of *Forever Tango* to wild applauds of approval. Most just want to learn enough to get by on a Saturday night, and that is ok too.

Just be kind to yourself and take it slow. Just like ANYTHING you have learned, it takes TIME, just like it took time for you to learn to walk and talk from infancy.

IT TAKES TIME! Be patient with yourself. When I interviewed Gustavo Benzecry Saba and Maria Olivera, for my book, "Tango Intoxication," her main piece of advice to all new dancers was, "Be patient with yourself."

Believe me when I say, "The tango tingle is waiting for you." But, you have to practice. It will NOT just come to you. You have to go GET IT!

Dancing well may be achieved by getting good information into your brain then into your body. It is helpful if you learn some of tango's history, well known dancers of the past, culture, rules (codes or los codigos) and language. I am speaking of both Spanish, the language of the people of Buenos Aires, as well as the language of the dance, for all dance in all cultures is body language. It is also necessary to understand the most important element of the dance, which would be in my opinion, the music. If you can find a way to fall in love with the music, I feel you'll become a much better dancer.

Skills in ANY endeavor are developed through practice and repetition. As adults, we don't think about it, but two simple things like WALKING and TALKING are not activities we were born doing. We had to LEARN how to walk and we had to LEARN how to talk. It takes time, time with concentrated efforts. That will go a long way toward helping you learn this wondrous, interesting and enchanted dance.

Reasonable skills may be obtained with a combination of group classes and private classes, but it is probably with private lessons and self-motivated practice that you will grow fastest.

This information I am giving is designed to help you overcome some of the more traditional and predictable stumbling blocks of learning tango as I know them. Some of the common problems are: understanding the music, finding the beat, dancing while touching another person and dancing (walking) with someone else immediately in front of you...facing you. Of course, the follower is walking backward...not a normal, everyday activity, right? That gets a lot of getting used to.

In the feminist influenced age of today we see more women in the role of President, COO, CEO, and now, Kamala Harris, the first female African American/Indian Vice President of the United States. Yes, there are women who are not accustomed to *being* led, they are accustomed to *leading*.

In partner dancing, someone must lead and it is the leader who performs that duty. It is usually, but not always, the man who leads. Men have to learn what leading is and how to effectively execute it and women have to learn how to prepare themselves to be led and learn how to follow. Followers don't just follow...they also DANCE! These days it is not too uncommon to see the same gender dancing together. These individuals are often simply interested in learning the other side of the dance and are not necessarily lovers. Obviously, the more you know about the dance, the better dancer you could become.

I am a lucky guy. While standing around chatting at various milongas over many years, I have received the same piece of advice independently from some of the most respected tango dancers, teachers and performers in the world: Omar Vega (RIP), Pablo Pugliese, Guillermina Quiroga, Carlos Copello, Jorge Torres and Armando Orzuza, to name a few. They all said, "The best way to become a good dancer is to first, find a good teacher."

Caution: A good or great *dancer* does not a good *teacher*, necessarily make. Just because one is a good or great dancer does not mean they are a good teacher and can pass on to YOU what they know.

Do not be fooled! I know this is hard for some to believe, but as sexy as this dance may appear, it is, more often than not, all really about the dance and not about sex. Don't get me wrong, I know there are sharks in the water. In my community in New York, there are some guys with whom I cannot have a civilized conversation about a woman's dance ability or style without them saying something about the woman's sexuality. At times, it is nauseating and I just want to slap them and wake them up.

The famous dancer who went by the name of Petroleo and claimed to have invented the turn (the giro), the contrafrente, the change of positions and the boleo once said, "I separated sex from dancing. Some men are after a leg not a female dancer, they were looking for someone to squeeze not to dance with. Not me, I was after dancing."

Juan Carlos Copes (RIP), the world's first famous stage tango dancer said: "I did in two years what normally takes six. I began knowing who danced well and who didn't, things like elegance and respect for the rhythm of every orchestra. I paid attention to every detail. It was a sick passion. I had managed to buy two suits to be paid in multiple payments: a blue one and a gray one. That is how I began discovering that my love for dance-tango had nothing to do with picking up women."

I recently met a flight attendant from France who danced well, very well. We danced several tandas together. Why? Because we enjoyed each other. Did we go home together and go to bed? Are you kidding?

We don't even know each other. Oh, by the way, she was attractive. Very attractive! But I was *not* interested in her looks or her obvious sexual accoutrement.

She was beautiful...and intelligent. Did I make a mistake? Should I have hit on her? Maybe I should have at least invited her to my brand new (at the time) condominium bachelor pad with lighting that can be dimmed at the slightest twist of a knob, for some back rubbing and a spot of heavy breathing...oops, excuse me. I digress.

WHO ARE THOSE WOMEN AND WHAT HAVE THEY DONE TO ME?

You know what happens when you start naming names. You leave someone out and feelings get hurt. I'm going to take a chance on it!

There are a few women in the New York tango community who consistently give me something *special* every time I dance with them...or even *look* at them. I am old enough, mature enough, and have danced enough tandas over the years to know the difference, instantly.

The gift they give is not tangible and is very difficult to define. It is both physical and ethereal, fog and iron, celestial, nefarious, and mental.

Maria Jose Sosa Dancer/instructor/tango DJ

It gives me a great deal of personal pride and pleasure to present this person to you. She is poised, professional and everyone who meets and or works with her, loves her . . . that is men and women. She is one of few teachers who teaches a group class like it is a private lesson, giving personalized attention to everyone in the class. This is one of many marks of a good teacher.

She is also one of few tango teachers who still studies every time she goes back to Argentina, even after over twenty-five years of dancing and teaching (as of this writing), she still studies and is an experienced leader of women and men.

I met her in 2002 in a tango play called *Del Tingo al Tango* where we were both performing as dancers and actors. I had no idea I was going to spend the next twelve or thirteen years, one to five times a week, studying tango privately with her.

I have studied with her longer than with any other teacher since my dancing started in 1997. She has single-handedly taught me the taste and feel of Buenos Aires, Argentina.

I took my first two trips to Argentina with her and her husband, Coco Arregui. Because of my work with her, I know secrets that many other tango leaders do not know. These are some secrets most men don't know because they are not women and they do not study with women. These are secrets that only a woman can teach you because she is a woman who dances with men every night. Geez, how common sense is *that*?

When I dance with her on the social dance floor, I feel like I am embracing Argentina. She is the one who took me by the hand and showed me the tastes, smells, the feel and the ins-and-outs of Buenos Aires and this dance called Argentine tango.

Ciko Tanik Dancer/instructor/tango DJ

It is very easy to see that we all bring our life and our previous life to the dance floor. Ciko was a professional architect in Turkey and New York. This gives her a very artistic eye to go with that very analytical brain. This also helps her to be a great tango teacher.

Her motivation to pursue tango has been her connection to another soul and human body, and a deeper voyage into the human spirit. During her visits to Buenos Aires she focused solely on the dance in its original habitat, exploring and studying both traditional and nuevo tango roots which developed the Argentine quality in her dance.

She embraced both open and close embrace which afforded her the ability to move more *fluidly* between the two and be more dynamic and versatile. Her technique gives her a nonrestrictive connection with various dancers. Her dance is defined by its sensuality, creative playfulness, musicality and elasticity. In addition, she is a person who has a heart as big as your head.

Another quality she possesses is, she is not afraid of, and will never run away from, a good time.

That is one of the reasons the events she organizes with her partner, Adam Hoopengardner, are so popular. Plus, she gives everyone in the room a lot of love, love like she is your first cousin.

One cold winter Wednesday night, I arrived at Adam & Ciko's "Tango Café" milonga. I had my winter boots, winter jacket and a backpack still on my back. Ciko jumped on my back like she was a champion wild bull rider... and I was the bull. When she jumped on me I still had on my backpack, and we proceeded to dance a milonga.

Yes, that was crazy, but not as *out there* as this one. It was another cold day, in fact, it was New Year's Day 2020, during the day. George was playing some good music and some great cortina's. There is a code, a rule in tango that you do not dance to the cortinas. A cortina is a non-tango song that is played between the tango music to indicate the end of that set of tango songs.

Of course, we knew that but we did it anyway. We started doing some freestyle club dancing and wild erratic movement, yet still musical. I started backing up. She came beside me and started backing up as well. Then we hit the wall. I started to go down to my knees, then to my belly, she was with me on every step. Then we started "swimming" across the wooden dance floor.

Probably one of the wildest things we've done...so far. But the night is young.

Ciko, you had better not bite me!

Uh, are you biting me?

Oh, no, she did it AGAIN! She BIT me.

Tango dancing with Ciko is so much fun because she has great technique, is very musical and really knows how to connect and listen to the leader's body. She also has a way of forcing you to listen to *her* in a very unforceful way. You won't even know you were being manipulated, manipulated with the love of dance.

Mayanne Gael Chess Dancer

If Mayanne was in the room at any given milonga, the odds of me getting some good rides were pretty high. She became one of my favorite partners. I remember when we first started dancing together, she once said, "We danced together a couple of years ago. I was a beginner and you never asked me again."

Oh, my. That makes me look pretty bad, doesn't it?

Well, I guess with time and practice, she quickly rose to the top of *my* list. One night I asked her if she wanted to practice with me. She said, "yes." We created a time and a day, rented a studio and worked. We only practiced once or twice. Then she blew me off and we never practiced again.

What happened? I *never* hit on her. I never made any advances toward her, or made her feel uncomfortable in any way (I don't think). I guess she just didn't like the way I danced.

She has that body awareness, quickness and extreme music ability that makes her so much fun to dance with. She is one of those who is totally capable of giving one that intangible "thing" that makes you feel the tango tingle.

Gayle Gibbons Madeira Dancer/instructor/choreographer/artist

Why do I love dancing with Gayle? Wow, how much time do you have?

I love dancing with Gayle because she understands humanity. She understands people, she understands movement *and*, she understands music.

Why do I love Gayle? I love her because she understands me and we laugh like hell together just doing nothing, looking at a wall, a shoe, anything, like two five-year-old children.

My feelings for her have little to do with her incredible fine artistic vision and ability, (www.gaylemadiera.com) but more to do with what she gives me when I am within her immediate sphere.

Because I can't damn stop laughing sounds like a good reason to pursue the positive. Actually, that is not the reason but it is a major contribution to that vast treasure chest of gems I receive dancing with her.

I love feeling her feet touch and press into the floor. When she presses into the floor she presses into me. I really feel her ever step, her every change of weight, her every step of her tiny size four shoes (I call them her size twos). She is light, quick on her feet, knows how to connect with the leader and follows like she is actually your skin.

Gayle claims to have been a shy child. It is obvious that she has out-grown this condition. She has always made art and danced since childhood.

When she received her Bachelor of Fine Arts degree in dance from SUNY Purchase and moved to New York City, she started making her living dancing, choreographing, teaching, and doing illustration and graphic design.

Gayle, if you read this, will you give me an extra dance because I said something nice about you?

Eleonora Kalganova Dancer/instructor/choreographer/organizer

Eleonora grew up in post-Soviet Tashkent, Uzbekistan. She was very fortunate to study extensively from an early age in many different and unique forms of dance including folk, ballroom, character, historic, ballet and modern.

After successfully completing nine years of rigorous study, she grad-uated from the State Dance Academy in Tashkent and became a principal dancer with the prestigious Alisher Navoi Theater of Opera and Ballet.

The joining of many disciplines and influences allows Eleonora to create and develop her own particular and unmistakable style of dancing tango and pedagogy. When she is on the floor, you know it.

When I dance with her, I am more myself than if I were by myself watching television at home. She is amazing. She is extremely talented, she is kind, giving, warm, extremely sensitive, and loving. When they made her,

I think they forgot the formula they used to make the mold to create her, for I haven't met anyone like her before or since.

One day, when we were preparing for our performance at milonga Mala Leche, she phoned me in the practice studio to tell me she was going to be late.

So, I started working alone. Then I went to the restroom. When I returned, she was there, at the piano, playing to the beautiful ambient, non-percussive music of Takashi Suziki that I left on before I left the room. That is when I realized that she is from another planet, gifted, talented, locked in.

I was to perform with Eleonora Kalganova again, but it was canceled because of another COVID-19 outbreak.

Eleonora does not just dance with me. She is like a cyborg, she is like a machine. She is like an alien. She gets inside of me and manipulates me as if

I were a puppet. She is like an animal with her instincts. Like the butterflies that know when it is time to fly to another continent, or the birds when they know it is time to fly south. How do they know?

She feels me. She reads me. She downloads my thoughts. She downloads my ideas. She downloads my musical DNA, which is not easy. She taps into the specifics of that particular tune. She engages immediately with songs she has never heard before and dances to it as if she had written it. Practicing with her for over a month, I witnessed this, many times.

Getting into the embrace with her is when the magic begins. I can feel her *before* we even touch .These are special moments that make this dance so inexplicably mysterious.

One day, I sent her a random message out of the blue. It said, "Every time I dance with you at the milonga, someone always tells me how much they enjoy watching us dance together. It happened again last night and you weren't even there!"

She said, "Really?" I said, "Yes, it's interesting." Her next text response was one word. "Performance?"

I thought, wait a minute. She is asking me if I want to perform with her. Waaait a minute. She is a world-class tango dancer/performer/teacher/ chorographer. I'm like a one-legged Idaho potato farmer compared to her. Then I thought, "Why not? It's *her* idea to perform together, and I do LOVE dancing with her." I said, "Sure, why not?" Well, we did and it was a BLAST!!

I don't like the way "I" danced with her that night because I tried to do too much and I lost a lot of my technique. It is on YouTube but "I" didn't put it there.

CHAPTER 24

COVID-19 The Coronavirus

The world completely stopped with the arrival of COVID-19, the Coronavirus.

The end of dancing, and almost everything else!

I was taking a walk down 5th Avenue in New York City, one of the most fashionable and expensive streets in the world with my friend Eleonora and her new baby, Bryan, and it was like a street lost in a ghost town, a disaster movie. Very few people walking around and many stores closed and boarded up.

Not being able to dance, put a cork in my overflowing bottle of love. Where is the outlet for my love and for my dance to which I am umbilically attached?

The main thing that keeps me happy in my life is simple. I only do the things that make, and keep me happy. But during the lockdown, instead of simply *being* happy, I found myself *searching* for happiness.

Living your life in a bubble of sheer joy and ecstatic happiness in an apartment alone, is not an easy thing to do. Good thing I like my apartment, and good thing I have many projects to complete, good thing I have my computer, cellphone and the internet.

I feel as though I have been deeply damaged, and sorely wronged. I can't wait to get back to the dance floor. Covid-19 has brought out an anger within me that I have never seen before. I feel so traumatized and lost.

Dancing tango was my love, my life, the bubble I lived inside of and it lived inside of me. I read about it, I wrote about it, I listened to the music, I studied the old timer's videos, and I studied the young dancers. I was in it, chest and chin deep.

Damn that virus!

Joy in the age of Covid-19 is elusively amorphous. You are always on guard, on alert, constantly looking for that thing that is going to hurt you, put you in the hospital…or kill you. Yep, it is like being in a war. Covid-19 completely changed everything around the globe.

The great jazz pianist, Thelonious Monk once said, *"Lost time is never found again."* I didn't lose two years of life. I decided to *use* these years of my life differently. I decided to write this book, finish another, and learn Spanish.

My life was altered in radical ways. I often like to feel sorry for myself, thinking that such a grave disservice has been placed upon me, but I completely understand that *my* life is not the only life trajectory placed in an alternative orbit.

If I were found guilty of a crime, I deserve to be put in prison. I feel like I *am* in prison and I didn't do *anything* wrong. I'm in a prison where I can still walk around and go to the store. I can go to bed whenever I choose. I can watch as much television as I want. But I am still in prison. I am in the prison of no hugging and no dancing.

The pandemic of the spring of 2020 took from me one of the most profound sensations I had ever experienced in my life, dance! It was about seven or eight months before I could watch a tango video without crying. I feel emotionally injured, scarred, severely punished, beaten and battered from the inside. I feel bedraggled, beat down, crestfallen, heartbroken, victimized, angry, and traumatized.

I have never felt this kind of negative, subjugating force upon my body, lifeforce and soul that I thought "I" owned. I thought "I" owned this thing I call my body, my life.

But apparently not. Apparently, the universe has alternative plans for me.

I miss dancing so much that I often get up and dance to the music in the commercials on television. I hear music, I move!

I have experienced so much pain in 2020, that now I am simply trying to protect my mind, protect my body, but most importantly, protect my *heart*, the thing I used to dance tango with every night.

I thought I was in control, then COVID-19 hit. I thought I only did the things I loved, then COVID-19 hit. I love my apartment, I love my living room but I don't want to *LIVE* in my living room.

This was the first time I understood why they call that room the "living room." That's where I have been living. At the beginning of the pandemic outbreak, I would go outside only every four days, then every three days or so.

Isolation, self-quarantine, I know I like myself, but enough is enough. At this point, I need a vacation from myself. But where do I go to get away from me?

I would go from my computer, which is in the office that I set up in my bedroom, then I would go to the bathroom. That is about twelve steps.

The trip from the bathroom to my couch in the living room is about thirteen steps.

From the couch to the kitchen is about fourteen steps, but it is a straight walk with no corners so, I always tango dance to and from the kitchen to the living room.

From my computer to the couch is about nineteen steps. From the bathroom to the kitchen is about ten steps.

From the kitchen to the computer is about seventeen steps.

Eighty-five steps to all of the major locations of my apartment. Good thing I like my apartment, but this was the life most of us were living in the beginning of the pandemic. I was afraid to go out, and the "president" was not instilling any sense of confidence within me.

For many months he refused to wear a mask, even after thousands of deaths. The Fourth of July, 2020 saw countless thousands of individuals on the beaches in Florida, California, Michigan, Arizona and many other locations with no masks and no social distancing, partying like everything was back to normal.

Four days later (7-8-2020) it was reported that there were 3,035,231 cases of infection in the U.S (50,000 new cases a day) and 132,041 deaths and 11,921,616 cases of infection worldwide with 546,318 deaths.

These are staggering figures. I believe one doesn't have to be part of an organization of white supremacists to think one is supreme, superior, and untouchable.

In the first week of October, 2020 the numbers looked a little different. There were 34,353,480 cases globally, and 1,023,983 deaths. In the United States there were 207,867 deaths, and 7,282,027 cases of infection. That is including the case of infection of the President of the United States, the individual who refused to wear a mask. He thinks he is superior and many believe that he not only thinks he is superior but is a white suprema*cist*.

This COVID-19 Coronavirus pandemic is like the Vietnam war. You know the enemy is out there but you can't see him, and you know he wants to kill you, but you can't kill him. Why? Well, because you can't *see* him!

The pandemic gave us new awareness and insight into ourselves and others. It gave us new habits, it gave us a new us. We are all learning, growing, and becoming different people. I know this situation has molded me into a slightly different person. I have always believed in the giving of love, in fact, way before flower power, Haight Ashbury, incense, and the Beatles. But now the giving of love seems to be a far more intentional pursuit, but in a different way. Now, I see it as a combatant to the horrific and vile negativity that came out of Washington, D.C. from the 45th president.

In the end, will the pandemic become realized as our friend by making us *better* people? I know we will be *different* people. These times are forcing us to get into ourselves, analyze, evaluate, re-evaluate, and go into places we never knew existed within us. I find this healthy. We are all here now, at this moment in time, to learn a lesson. I hope we do.

CHAPTER 25

Imponderables:
Things That Keep Me Up at Night

Aaaahh, I can't sleep!

Put your hands together

Why do hosts and MCs say, "Put your hands together for . . ."? If everyone put their hands together, at the same time, you would hear only one loud CLAP, or nothing at all, depending on how hard or how aggressively they put their hands together. Makes no sense to me.

Why do they say, "A person who needs no introduction?"

Yep, here is another one. Hosts and MCs introducing a well-known guest often say, "And now, a person who needs no introduction." Then they introduce them. Wait a minute, didn't you just say, they "need no introduction"? Then, why did you introduce them? Too many people often don't know what they say, and more specifically, don't know why they say it.

Tuna or Tuna fish

Why is it when the fish is swimming in the sea we call it a tuna? But when we catch it, kill it, cook it, and can it, we call it tuna FISH? Why? I don't, but many do. So, we have to catch it, kill it, cook it, and can it, before the tuna can earn the title of fish?

Salad has lettuce

If lettuce is one of the main ingredients of a salad, why is the no lettuce in macaroni salad, fruit salad, egg salad, or tuna salad.

Knives

Why don't restaurants sharpen their knives? The reason I ask is because when you go out to dinner, they bring you bread, and it is never cut all the way through. You have to pull it, tear it, get it on your hands, crumbs on the table, why? It upsets me when you go to the deli and buy a sandwich or bagel and they cut it, but they never cut it or the paper *all the way through.* It is always attached and never completely cut. Why? You order a pizza and the slices are not cut all the way through. Why?

Because

Why do people say b'cuz , or cuz instead of be*cause*?

Inches

Why do they use inches on Spanish television to indicate the amount of rain or snow instead of the metric system like they do in the countries that speak Spanish?

AM IS Morning!

Why do people say "6 AM *in the morning*?" AM and morning are the same thing. It is like saying 6 in the morning morning or 6 AM AM. If you say one, you don't need the other.

New country, new alphabet

Why do individuals who come to the U.S from other countries that don't use the same alphabet as the U.S; spell their name in a way that North Americans will never pronounce it correctly? Why? Why don't they use the alphabet the way their new country uses it so individuals can say their name correctly? Ibrahimpašić is the last name of a friend. It is pronounced Ee-bra-heem-pa-cheech. In English *pasic* is not *pa-cheech*, and an American seeing that would never say *pa-cheech*. The last name Ng is another one. It is said like Enng or like the suffix of the words writ*ing*, shoot*ing* or walk*ing*. Why do they expect us to say ING when it is written Ng? We don't know how to say that. Noog? Ne? Neg? N?

Nikola Jokić is a fantastic basketball player in the NBA in the U.S.A. He is 6' 11", 284 lbs. He came to this country from Serbia, a country that uses the Cyrillic alphabet, which looks like this:

А Б В Г Д Ђ Е Ж З И
Ј К Л Љ М Н Њ О П Р
С Т Ћ У Ф Х Ц Ч Џ Ш

The Serbian Cyrillic alphabet (Serbian: српска ћирилица/srpska ćirilica, pronounced [sȓpskaː tɕirǐlitsa]). You got it?

His name using the Cyrillic alphabet is pronounced Yo-kitch. No English-speaking person would look at *Jokić* and say *Yo-kitch*. To us it is Jo-kick, no? Why don't they spell their name so we can say it correctly the first time? Don't they get tired of correcting us?

Someone once said to me that maybe it is a matter of pride and they don't want to re-spell their name. Look at the Cyrillic alphabet. They have already re-spelled their name!

Famous American film director, actor, and writer, Peter Bogdanovich (July 30, 1939–January 6, 2022). He directed *The Last Picture Show, What's Up Doc?, Daisy Miller, Paper Moon*, and many others. He is of Serbian descent, has an "ich" at the end of his family name. I was just curious.

Why do men have nipples?

I don't get it.

Ooohhhh, it's freezing outside!

When it is twenty-five degrees outside, why do people say, "ooooohhhhh, it's freezing"? No, you're wrong it's BELOW freezing!!

When did we start speaking Standard American English?

When, how, and why did the standard American accent develop? I am certain that when the English Puritans arrived in 1620 they weren't speaking like we do today. When and how did it change?

Bedtime

Why do people refer to the time they go to bed as the time they go to sleep? How can you know what time you go to sleep? You CAN'T know, you are asleep.

A pair of pants

Why are they called "a pair of shorts" and "a pair of pants" if it is only one? A pair of scissors and a pair of glasses I kind of understand, because there are two finger holes and two lenses, but shorts and pants have three openings. A pair?

The American people

Why do ALL politicians use the term, "The American people"? NO ONE says, "The people of America," "The people of the United States," "Our U.S. residents," "The citizens of the United States," "Our family of America," "The people who have invested in our borders of North America". Ok that one was a stretch but you understand what I am saying. The American people, The American people, The American people, come on, say something else.

Active shooter

What is an active shooter? Isn't ANY shooter an *active* shooter? If you are shooting, you are shooting, right? Is that not an *action*, thereby making it *active,* thereby making him or her an *active* shooter? So, what I am saying is, anyone who shoots is an active shooter. We don't need the word *active*.

Different shade on bottom of hands and feet

Why do people of African descent have a darker shade on the hands and feet, and a lighter tone on the *bottoms* of the hands and feet? Did you ever think about that?

Reason Why?

Why do we say, "the reason why"? The "reason" IS the why. So, if you say, the reason why she went to the store was to buy a toy for her daughter," sounds redundant to me. I would say, "the reason she went to the store was to buy a toy for her daughter" or "the reason that she went to the store was to buy a toy for her daughter. Forget the word "why" it doesn't make sense to me. Yes, I know, I need more education beyond a Master's Degree.

Bathing suit

Why is it called a bathing suit? We don't bathe in it.

Yellow, orange juice

Why is the juice we call orange juice, actually yellow? Take Tropicana orange juice, for instance. You see the contents of the bottle. It is yellow but the cap on top is orange. The outside of an orange is orange. Outside the peel of the orange, is orange. But the juice from an orange is yellow. Shouldn't we call it what it is, "yellow juice"?

School teachers

Why are elementary school teachers called, school teachers? Aren't all teachers who teach in schools, school teachers? Most teachers teach in schools, right? I realize not all teachers teach in a school because I sometimes teach online. But why do we have to add the additional title of "school" to further identify the location of their place of employment. Isn't that like saying she is a hospital doctor? He is a cashier at the cash register? He is a gas station attendant at the gas station? Am I over thinking this?

Space heaters

Why are portable heaters called "space heaters?" Don't all heaters heat space? So, why is this specific type of small, portable, heat distributing device called a "space heater?" That is one of many redundancies in our language like the term "school teachers."

Blond hair & a red beard

Why do some Caucasian men have blond hair and a red beard or brown hair and a red beard? When an Asian grows a beard, it is the same color as the hair on their head. When an African American grows a beard, it is the same color as the hair on their head. When a Mexican individual grows a beard...

I am completely baffled by this biological fact that many men are walking around the planet with a two-tone head.

Straight & kinky hair on the same body

Why do Caucasian men have straight hair on their head and kinky, course beards? Why isn't the hair the same texture throughout the body? As my mother would say, "The Lord works in mysterious ways."

Why so many good-byes?

Ok, see you later. Ok, good-bye, see you, ok, bye, bye, ok, bye.

If you have friends like this, I pity you. It annoys me when I'm trying to hang up from a telephone conversation and the person on the other end says good-bye five more times. "OK, see you later. OK, good-bye, see you, I'll talk to you soon, have a nice day, enjoy, OK, good-bye, bye, bye-bye, enjoy, bye."

I know, I know, they are just being polite and not appear to hang up on you, but I got it the first time. Maybe I should just chill on that one.

Crossing the street against the traffic light in New York

It is part of New York culture to cross the street against the traffic lights, weaving our way in and out of on-coming traffic. Why? Will you be angry with *yourself* when sitting in bed #22 at Beth Israel Hospital or will you be angry with the taxi driver who put you there?

Yesterday I saw a young woman lose her shoe in the middle of the street as she raced across and in front of on-coming traffic. She stopped to get the shoe and was nearly struck by two cars. Why do we cross the street anywhere at any time? You wouldn't DARE do that in California. You would get a ticket as big as your next month's rent payment. New Yorkers are in a hurry. Why?

Baby Strollers

Why do some parents when waiting for the traffic light to change, stand in the street with a baby carriage or stroller in front of them? Don't they understand that the baby is that much farther into the street and speeding cars and cab drivers who have been driving for twelve or more hours often fall asleep as they are driving?

Cab drivers

Why do drivers, in particular taxi drivers, race up to the crosswalk intimidating and frightening pedestrians? They will usually only be able to drive an additional ten feet more before they have to stop again because there is traffic or a red light or both. Why? It is rude, it is ignorant, it completely lacks common sense.

Getting change at a store.

When I purchase something, the clerk gives me dollar bills and coins as change and they put the coins on top of the bills and hand it to me with one hand. Why do they do that? They never used to. If they don't place the coins in the center of the bills, the bills fold and give from the weight of the coins and the coins go flying all over the counter. Why don't they just put the coins in my hand and then the bills like they used to?

Why do stores always lock one door?

You go to a commercial establishment and there are two doors. You reach for one door and pull it. It doesn't move. You then push it. It doesn't move. You go to the other door and pull it. It does not open. You THEN push it and it opens. Not that I'm in that big of a hurry, but do you realize how much time was spent trying to do something as simple as opening a door? Why don't they tell us which door is locked and which way to open it? Or, they could just leave both of them unlocked. Now that sounds like the logical thing to do. Not that it is important to always look cool and in control, but I know I look like an idiot trying to do something as simple as opening a door.

Laundry

I'm a single guy who *sometimes* does his own laundry. Ok, I never do my own laundry, I take it to the corner laundromat. My question is why do they always button the top button or two when they fold my shirts? The shirt is folded. It won't come undone or anything. The dry cleaners, I understand. They don't want the shirt to fall off of the hanger. But these are not on a hanger, they are folded. It takes extra time to unbutton and it makes no sense.

The New York City Subway

I have become a New York guy. I have noticed, that when the subway trains are not going to stop in a particular station, they roar through at a high rate of speed and they blast their extremely loud air horns. Why do they blow their loud air horns as they go through?

Are they trying to tell us that they are not going to stop? I think I understand that when they do not actually come to a full and complete stop. Not stopping is a clear indication that they are not going to stop! What do they think I am going to do, try to jump on the train as it races through the station at 40 mph?

But, this I find, is the most important issue: The conductors seem to be completely unaware of the fact that there could be small children, infants or even newborns on those platforms receiving serious ear damage from those loud horns.

I know, I know, the blowing of the horn is company mandated and probably has been for over one-hundred years. But it is loud, it is frightening, it is dangerous.

Standing in the middle of the door.

Why do New Yorkers feel that it is their right to stand in front of the subway doors and not allow other passengers to enter the train? How can you stand right in the middle of the door and NOT think you are doing something wrong, something stupid?

Then there is the group of people who try to enter the train against the tide of forty or fifty people who are trying to get off the train at the same time. Don't they understand that if they would simply wait for five to seven additional *seconds*, many individuals on the train will leave the train, which will in turn immediately and automatically leave room for them? When they get on the train, they hover near the door, even when countless square feet of totally empty space exists in the middle of the train. Why do they do that?

Electronic faucets

I often find electronic faucets in the men's room that do not work the way they are designed to work. Is it me? Yes, yes, it has to be me. It has to be something with my body electricity that I inherited from my mother that prevents these devices from working with and for me. I put soap on my hands, I put them under the ill designed, "automatic," electronic water faucet and nothing happens. I remove and re-insert my hands under the faucet, I remove and re-insert, I remove and re-insert. Nothing happens, no water comes out. I do it again. All the while I am thinking "WHO THE HELL THOUGHT THIS WAS A GOOD IDEA?"

No, the REAL question is: Who approved this lame brain idea and who is making money on it? I think it came to market far too soon. I believe it came to market before it was fully developed because of the all-American greed factor. Living in America, we are the victims of so many governmental scams that is not possible to keep up with them all.

I feel the same way about electronic paper towel dispensers and electronically flushing toilets. Sometimes they work, usually they do not.

Standing where people walk.

Why do people **stand** on the side**walk**? Get outta heah, I'm tryin' na wouk heah! I have never said anything to an individual, group of individuals or tour bus operator that just unloaded thirty people onto the already crowded New York City sidewalk in the middle of Times Square. But common sense should tell you that...New York is a big, busy, bustling town. Do not clog the already crowded side "walks" with "side **standing**" by getting in the way while standing on the side**walk**.

A watch with the wrong time on purpose

Why do people put the wrong time on their watches and clocks? I realize that these days many, not all, but many watches and clocks are digitized and automatically set from a satellite. Some people set the time ahead, some set it behind. It makes no sense to me. You are the one who set the watch or clock, so you know how many minutes ahead or behind the timepiece is. So, you are not tricking or fooling yourself when you attempt something like this.

You know that is not the correct time and you know you set it five minutes ahead. You are not fooling ANYONE, including yourself.

Skin diving

When you dive, *everything* goes underwater. So, why is it called "skin diving?"

Donut holes

Why are those round balls of dough that are sugar coated, called donut holes? It's not a hole, it's a ball. If it were a hole, there wouldn't be anything in the bag, just air, holes. Actually, it is the opposite and we got it all wrong *again*. The donut should be called the donut *hole* because it has a hole in it, and the donut hole should be called the *donut*. Think about it.

Pinky ring

Why is the ring that is placed on your little finger called a pinky ring? Is it still called a pinky ring if I'm African American and my fingers are brown? A brownie ring?

Pocketbook

I'm lost. It's called a pocketbook. Yet, it can't fit in your pocket and it is not a book.

Near miss

When two airplanes almost collide in mid-air, they call it a near miss. Shouldn't it be called a near *hit*. They didn't *nearly* miss, they *did* miss. They almost *hit*.

Twins

A boy and a girl twins aren't going to like this one. We have twin beds, twin pillows, twin sheet, twin pillow cases, twin pipes, and twin carburetors. What else do we have that we call twins, excluding people? If things are called twins, they both are alike, they look alike. Twin things should look alike, right? Yes, except twin people. We call two siblings who were born at the same time, twins. Even when they do not look alike. I think siblings born at the same time, but are fraternal, should be called brother and sister. Not twins. When it is a boy and a girl, they should *definitely* be called brother and sister and not twins. Things and people should look alike to earn the title, "twins," no?

Golf ball size hail

Why does the weather person always report "golf ball size hail"? Why not marble size, grape size, walnut size, or any other size? Golf ball size hail, it is always golf ball size hail.

Egg cream

This famous New York City drink was created on the Lower East Side has no egg and it has no cream. Someone once said that it is from a Yiddish term for pure sweetness, which is "echt keem."

Head cheese

Why is it called head cheese if there is no cheese in it? I know the meat portions are from the head of a pig but where is the cheese?

Walking in the Rain

When we get caught in the rain, why do we duck our heads and lift our shoulders. We look like a turtle trying to put their heads back into their shells. Do we think that is actually going to prevent us from getting wet?

The Bullfights

Bullfighting is another misused term. Have you ever seen a bullfight? There isn't any fighting going on. It should be called bullteasing or bullstabbing.

Dog fights

In World War II, airplanes would often have aerial combat. Sometimes one plane against another plane, one on one. Why do they call them "dog fights" if there are no dogs?

Gun fights

I find this interesting. Why do they call them gun fights when the guns aren't doing the fighting? If anything, they should be called *"bullet"* fights, THAT'S what is actually doing the fighting. I can picture a guy with a barrel filled with guns throwing one after the other. "Take that, and that, and that."

Hardwood floors

Why are wood floors called hardwood floors?

PAN-demic not PEN-demic

I can forgive "regular" people for saying PEN-demic instead of PAN-demic, but not radio & television broadcasters. These individuals, at one time in America, were the representatives of how our language should be spoken. Times have changed and so have the levels of acceptance.

I cannot forgive broadcasters for mispronouncing words. We have been given the duty of being the *professional speakers of the written word.* That is what we do for a living, as actors, broadcasters, teachers, television spokespeople, and hosts...public figures in the public eye and ear. The word is pandemic, not PEN-demic.

A push *is* a shove

Why do we say, "If push comes to shove"? Wait a minute! Aren't a push and a shove the same thing?

Kicking butt

Why is it called "kicking butt" or "I'm going to kick your ass" when the butt or the ass is not involved at all? "Getting knocked on the ass" is more accurate, no?

Mugging in bad neighborhoods

Why are there muggings in "bad neighborhoods?" If I were a hoodlum, robber or a street thug, I would NOT rob in poor neighborhoods. What are they thinking? If I want to take money out of the pockets of another human being, I wouldn't do it in a neighborhood where they don't have any money.

Walking fast

My mom was born in 1912. Whenever some old black & white film footage of days gone by would come on television, I would always wonder if my mom walked fast when she was young. So, one day I asked her, she thought I was nuts.

ATM machines

When banks close at night they usually have ATM machines available. Why are they so open with giant windows so every crook within a mile radius can see you taking cash out?

Big building, no address

In the City of New York's midtown area there are many office buildings with no addresses on them. How would you like to be the new mailman on the beat there?

Toothpaste

Why is it called "tooth" paste, when you brush more than one tooth? It should be called TEETH PASTE, no?

Dogs on a leash

You're walking down the street and someone is approaching with a dog on a leash. Why do dog owners allow their dog to come into your path causing you to either trip over the dog or get tripped by the leash?

No. 7

The word number is spelled, n-u-m-b-e-r. Why do we use No. as the abbreviation? We should use *nbr* or *num*. The letter "o" doesn't even appear in the word *number*.

Air condition the outdoors

Why do some large buildings in New York open their doors during hot summer days to let the air conditioning out? Are they trying to condition the outdoor air? If it is too cold inside, why don't they simply turn down the thermostat? I'm confused.

Why salty water tears?

Why does salty water come out of our eyes when we cry? Why is water even expelled period when we cry?

Aborigines

Why do they call the native people of Australia aborigines or aboriginals? If they were the first people there, they should be called originals, no?

Bikinis

On hot days, why do people in Western countries take off their clothes, put on bikinis and expose their skin to even more direct sun and heat? In Middle Eastern desert countries, they put on clothes, cover their whole body with a robe-like garment, head included. We both can't be right...or can we?

Cursive handwriting

With autocorrect, children are losing the ability to spell, computer games, cellphones, and computers are ruining their eyesight, and they are no longer being taught how to write in cursive in school. Wait a minute! Cursive? Why do we need to know THAT? When was the last time you read a book, newspaper, magazine, or FaceBook post in cursive, 1467?

Happy birthday to you

Why is it called your birthday? It is NOT your birthday. You were only born ONCE, so you have only ONE birthday, that is the day you were born, your day of birth, your birthday. You are not born again every year on the same day. It should be called the anniversary of your birth, or your anniversary day, or your birthiversary, or something else.

The bathroom

Why do we call the place we go to eliminate our waste, the bathroom? Public "bathrooms" don't have bath tubs at all. Some of these "bathrooms" are NOT a place I would want to take a bath.

Chicken fingers?

What? The first time I heard someone order chicken fingers, I thought, "why would someone want to eat chicken toes?" There is no meat on them and they're ugly as hell. Two years later I saw frozen chicken feet in the grocery store.

First floor-Second floor

The second floor of a building is NOT the first floor, it is the SECOND floor. Calling the second floor the first floor is like counting 0, 1, 2, 3. Who does that? When you walk into a building, what is the first thing you step on? The floor! That is the FIRST floor. I have had this discussion with many international friends. They INSIST that the second floor is the first floor. They say that the first floor is the ground floor. Wait a minute, is it the ground or is it the floor? The ground floor is what they have been taught, their culture dictates that, and they never bothered to question it. I question everything that doesn't make sense. The first floor is the first floor. The ground is outside where there is dirt, not cement, not asphalt.

Fresh as a daisy

Why is the daisy the freshest flower of them all? Is it? Why do we say fresh as a daisy, why not fresh as a rose, or fresh as a tulip, or fresh as freesia?

A walk, in baseball

In the game of baseball when a batter receives four pitches that the umpire calls balls, the batter gets to go to first base free. They call this a walk, but the batter does not walk to first base, he jogs there. They should call it a "jog" instead of a "walk," no?

He died, he was a good man

"Why is it that you never hear anything bad about a person when they die?" "Oh, he was a good soul." He was a wonderful father and husband." "He always had a kind word for everyone." You NEVER hear things like, "He was a rotten SOB." He was a lying thief who stole from my store." "I used to hear him beating his wife late at night on the weekends. I think he drank." It sounds like only good people die.

Serial Killers

The guy next door just shot and killed 10 people. "Oh, my, he was such a quiet guy." "He always said hello, I would never think that he could do something like that." "He was a quiet guy, always stuck to himself." I'm beginning to think that those are the ones we have to watch out for.

Middle-aged

I have heard this term all of my life. I never knew what it really meant. I think middle age should be your age when you die divided by two. Since we don't know when we're going to die, we don't know when we were middle age.

Good money

Why do people call a certain amount of money, *good money*? Isn't *all* money *good* money?

I think I'm being too picky. I think I'll stop now.

The best place anyone could ever be . . . in your mother's arms.

The End…for now.

More About the Author

Batt Johnson is a trailblazer. He rose to the top of the music radio broadcasting industry in major market Rock 'n Roll, Pop, Jazz, R&B (Urban),and Country music formats in New York City, and across the United States.

Very few broadcaster/actors have performed to this extent on such diverse platforms, in one of the most complicated industries in the world, in the most competitive communication marketplace in the world, New York City.

There are approximately 13,769 radio stations with about 51,558 on-air broadcasters in the United States. *Radio & Records Magazine* once ranked Batt Johnson at number nine, and the only African American on that top-ten list.

Mr. Johnson has appeared in *New York Newsday, The New York Times, Black Achievers Magazine, New York Daily News, Fred Magazine, New York Post, Billboard Magazine, Radio & Records Magazine, The Pittsburgh Press,* and others.

He has successfully performed as an actor in television commercials, home shopping host on "Q2 Television," corporate films, plays, feature films, cartoon voices, newscasting, print modeling, hand modeling, radio commercials, videos ,media trainer for doctors, lawyers, politicians, the NBA, U.S. Air Force, and the U.S. Tennis Association.

His acting awards include *The New York Film and Video Festival's Bronze Medal* for an Eastern Airlines commercial; a *Mic Award* for creative excellence for cowriting, voicing, and producing a radio commercial for Tactel Cellular Phones, a nominee for a *Clio Award* for a New York, Maryland, and Arizona State Lottery TV commercial, and two *International Film and Television Festival Awards* for American Express and Gulfstream Aeronautical Corp.

Mr. Johnson earned a Bachelor of Arts Degree in Social Theory (sociology) and Media Studies from Empire State College. His Master of Arts Degree is in Communication Arts & Sciences with a focus in television from the New York Institute of Technology and New York University.

Batt Johnson was an adjunct college professor at New York University; the New York Institute of Technology; Mercy College; the Weist-Barron School of Television; Cornell University, and Mercy College. He also taught Argentine tango at the Dardo Galletto Studios; Piel Canela Latin Arts Dance Center; Tango on the Square; Central Park Tango; Lafayette Grill NY; Shut Up and Dance Studios, Fond du Lac, Wisconsin; and The School of Visual and Performing Arts, Stroudsburg, Pennsylvania.

He wrote the short play *Tango Floor Gender Wars*, cowrote and directed the play *Tango du Jour*, cowrote, danced, and acted in the play *Del Tingo Al Tango*, acted and danced in the film *The Challenger* (An Angel for Your Solitude) with Silvina Valz, which was part of the New York Tango and Film Festival. He was featured in the documentary film *New York Tango*, performed voice-overs for the stage show *Tango Connections*, Junior Cervila's *Cervila's Tango Revue* for cruise ships, and performed voice-over segments for many professional tango teacher's instructional videos.

For several seasons he danced, hosted, acted, conceived and wrote for The Tango Zone Dance Company which performed in New York every summer for five years and at the Edmonton, Canada International Theatre Fringe Festival, the largest in all of North America.

Batt Johnson created, voiced, and produced numerous radio specials on musicians and their instruments. He was a cohost, researcher, writer and producer on a world-wide tango radio show called *Espresso Tango Radio* with internationally acclaimed Grammy Award-Winning bandoneon player and composer, Hector Del Curto. They may all be heard on www.tangointoxication.com.

Batt also created, produced and hosted female tango fashion shows and a benefit to raise money for tango dancing children who happen to be without sight. He was chosen to be the Official Master of Ceremonies of the *7th USA Tango Championship Competition* as part of the 13th Annual New York City Tango Festival.

Batt wrote the CD liner notes (the information inside a CD cover) for many professional tango musicians including Argentinian musicians, Hector Del Curto, Fernando Otero, Gustavo Casenave (Uruguay) and Costa Rican bass player Rodrigo Saenz. He also wrote a monthly column for *ReporTango* magazine, an international guide to Argentine tango.

He was a writer for Japan's *Swing Journal Jazz Magazine*; music critic for *The Kansas City Star* newspaper; national music video host and writer for VH-1 Music Television (MTV networks), music writer and cohost for *Only One New York*, a weekly magazine formatted television show on PBS, co-host and writer on *Campus America* (NCTV) and a home shopping host and writer on Q2 Television (QVC Network).

Batt also studied music and music theory at the John Theis School of Music, Kansas City, Missouri; Big Dude's Music Studio, Kansas City, Missouri; Ed Simon's (brother of Paul Simon) Guitar Study Center, New York; and The Sounds of Joy Music Studios, New York.

He has had many adventures in his travels to over twenty countries.

But the truth is, he simply wants to dance tango.

ADDITIONAL BOOKS BY BATT JOHNSON

Powerful Principles for Presenters

Tips for Public Speakers Using Proven Communication Techniques from Commercials, Television, and Film Professionals

Rich & Famous in Thirty Seconds

Inside Secrets to Achieving Financial Success in Television and Radio Commercials

Foreword by Richard Lewis

What Is This Thing Called Jazz?

Insights and Opinions from the Players

Foreword by Wynton Marsalis

Tango Intoxication

Wit, Wisdom, Stories & Secrets of the World's Most Intimate Dance

BOOKS TO BE PUBLISHED

Score with the Media

Proven Media Training Techniques for Professional Athletes

My Tango Diary Secrets

A Whimsical Collection of Original Quotes, Notes & Anecdotes

The Wit & Wisdom of African American Men

In Search of the Perfect Quote

Acknowledgements

Thank you, William McKinley Johnson, my father, who gave me wisdom beyond words.

Pearlie Johnson, my mother, who taught me to listen to and respect women.

Connie Rae Johnson, my sister, who gave me the idea to write this book and to my sister, Gloria for always supporting me.

Buzz Bennett, for starting my professional broadcasting career. You're a God!

The Weist-Barron School of Television, for starting my acting, television, modeling, and acting teaching career.

New York City, for teaching me that all things are truly possible and for helping to create a new Batt.

Craig Hutchison, Borough of Manhattan Community College, for your keen eye and editing expertise.

Merriam-Webster's Collegiate Dictionary, Wikipedia, Google, and YouTube for your massive archival contributions.

Daniela Bertone, for reigniting my love of language with your stimulating Spanish lessons. You have changed my life.

Quincy McCoy for including me in your book, *No Static: A Guide to Creative Radio Programming*.

Jane Elliott for your insight, candor, and willingness to point out standard American social wrongs as norms.

Thank you to all of my salsa teachers at DanceSport Dance Studio who taught me polyrhythms and how to move to them. My body still uses that information daily.

Gayle Gibbons Madeira for giving me years of fantastic dances and outrageous behavior and laughter on the dance floor. Thank you for your knowledge and assistance in the creation of my website, tangointoxication.com.

Tioma Maloratsky for Milonga Ensueño and for keeping Gayle calm.

Adam Hoopengardener and Ciko for Tango Café, Mala Leche and for your love and trust in me.

A separate thank you to Ciko for her intrusive, wizardly, sassy, yet magical inspiration for this book's cover photo.

Maria José Sosa, Coco Arregui (RIP), and Juan Pablo Vicente for Milonga La Nacional where I have been a member since 2002.

Thank you, Chuck Lasheid for constantly telling me, over many years, to write this book.

Thank you, to all 173 of my tango teachers for giving me that very special part of you that changed the course of my life.

Photo Credits

Mathias P.R. Reding-Black Lives Matter

Samantha Sophia-Young boy reading Bible in bed

Nathan Bumlau-Dirty hands praying

Tubarones-Black mom kissing child

Victor Candiari-Baby breastfeeding

Ivan Samkov-Priest in bedroom

Lukas-Control board

Ekrulila-45 rpm records by window

Anastasiya Vragova-White paint on hands

Kristina Nor-Hand scratching back

Eduard Delputte-Soldier in the field

Filip Andrejecic-Marching soldiers

Dre Newsome-Man walking down stairs

Harrison Haines-Abandoned Building

Eloi Omella-Lower Manhattan aerial shot

Bruno Figueiredo-Trump poster

Ketut Subiyanto-Blonde Asian girl in kitchen

J. Kotter-Retro typewriter

Viktor Forgacs-Crowded subway

Pexaby-Army drill sergeant yelling

Nsey Benajah-Man yelling in anger

Sandra Salmans-NY Times, Kick-FM

J. Amill Santiago-Dr. Martin Luther King, Jr. statue

Bret Sayles-Stop White Supremacy

Denniz Futalan-People sleeping on sidewalk

Spencer Davis-Eiffel Tower side street

Marri Shyam-Elephant in front of Mt. Kilimanjaro

Lukas Hartmann-Bars at Night

K. Mitch Hodge-Giant Cowboy Boot

Lan Yao-Beautiful Vietnamese Children Playing

Adeyemi Emmanuel Adebayo-African American Woman Singing in Church

Ferdy Jayadi-African Children Diving for Coins

Cottonbro-African American Child Boxer

Pixaby-Army Sergeant Yelling

Mattia Ascenzo-Hand in Front of Face saying "NO!"

Carlos Andrés Dueñas-Cover Photo, Back Photo, Author Pointing to Man in the Sky, Author Being Fired, Author Being Bitten (3 photos)

Pixaby-Combat Soldiers Running

Jakayla Toney-A "NO" Sign in a Tree Trunk

Pema Lama-The Ginza, Tokyo, Japan

Redd-Back of Kimono & Store, Japan

Vince Gx-Woman Walking w/Baby on Back in Senegal

Dapo Abideen-Super Tall Basketball Player

Wendy Wei-Woodstock

Unseen Histories-Young Boy at Drinking Fountain with "Colored" Sign

Simon Fital-Two Biplanes Flying

Maria Oswalt-Breonna Taylor Sign at Protest Rally